CHRIST *and* TIME

OSCAR CULLMANN, DR. THEOL., D.D.

*Professor of New Testament and Early Christianity
at the University of Basel
Director of Studies in the Origins of Christianity
at the École des Hautes-Études, Sorbonne, Paris*

CHRIST *and* TIME

THE PRIMITIVE CHRISTIAN CONCEPTION
OF TIME AND HISTORY

Translated from the German by

FLOYD V. FILSON

Philadelphia
THE WESTMINSTER PRESS

The original edition of this book was published in Germany under the title *Christus
und die Zeit* by Evangelischer Verlag A.G.,
Zollikon-Zürich, Switzerland.

BT
78
.C83

PRINTED IN THE UNITED STATES OF AMERICA

To the University of Lausanne
and Especially to Its Theological Faculty
in Gratitude
for the Conferring of an Honorary Doctorate

" Jesus Christ the same yesterday
and today, and forever."
— HEB. 13:8.

TRANSLATOR'S PREFACE

PROFESSOR CULLMANN's book on CHRIST AND TIME is undoubtedly one of the most significant theological works that Europe has produced within the last decade. The vigorous discussion which its publication has evoked makes it clear that the author has dealt in a scholarly and vital way with a central issue of Biblical study and Christian theology. It is not surprising that a second German edition has been needed. The book has also appeared in French, and translations into other European languages are in process.

This volume is significant not only for its challenging presentation of Professor Cullmann's own position, but also because it carries on a spirited and informative debate with several leading European scholars whose works are not available to the English-speaking reader. The author sharpens the issues between himself and such noted scholars as Rudolf Bultmann, Karl Barth, Emil Brunner, and Martin Werner, who is now the leading advocate of the " consistent eschatology " position to which Albert Schweitzer gave such prominence. The reader of CHRIST AND TIME thus gains an insight into trends that have marked the last ten years of Biblical study and theological discussion in Europe.

The author has kindly read the translation and made a number of discerning suggestions. He assures me that I have rendered his thought faithfully; upon me, however, rests the responsibility for any limitations in English style. I am grateful to him for his personal courtesy as well as for the vigor and originality of his book.

FLOYD V. FILSON.

McCormick Theological Seminary,
Chicago, January 10, 1949

CONTENTS

FOREWORD

THE OBJECT of the present work is to determine what is central in the Christian proclamation. We are tempted to represent as the "kernel" or "essence" of this proclamation that which appeals to us personally, and to consider as external and dispensable "framework" that which is strange to us. It is due to the richness of the Christian message that the question as to the central element from which all the other features are to be explained arises at all, and the endeavor to determine this central element must be designated the one great task of New Testament scholarship, and perhaps of all Christian theology.

Primarily this is a problem of historical theology, but the answer to it is of the greatest importance for the theologian. It is quite clear that the above-mentioned subjective attitude, even when it is ever so unconscious, must be rejected as entirely unfitted to solve the problem. For on no account can the criterion by which to determine the essential Christian kernel be any previously established position, for example, a philosophical standpoint. It is amazing to see with what naïve unconcern this or that feature of the original Christian message is all too often arbitrarily selected and regarded as central, in accordance with a standard which obviously is brought to the New Testament *from the outside,* whereas for the Primitive Church this feature is indeed present, but instead of really standing in the center is itself to be explained by reference to another feature which is the true center. If the representatives of the various Christian groups, and perhaps even the opponents of the Christian faith, would for once agree that in determining the essential Christian kernel they would make an honest effort to renounce all standards derived from any other source than the most ancient Christian writings themselves, they would already by this conscious effort have made a great advance toward a fruitful discussion.

To this task, which is so urgent for the understanding of the Christian faith, the present work seeks to make a contribution. At the outset, therefore, I should like to request all its readers that in reading they first of all put aside completely the question which, understandably enough, lies close at hand, whether a New Testament statement can be an important part of the Christian message if it contradicts this or that philosophical conception of whose correctness we are convinced. The entire interest should rather be concentrated upon another question: In what does the *specifically Christian element* of the New Testament revelation consist? That is to say, precisely what is there which it does not have in common with philosophical or religious systems?

Three very different publications of recent years have helped me to sharpen my understanding of the central New Testament teaching. Each of them represents a clear point of view: Martin Werner's *Die Entstehung des christlichen Dogmas* (The Origin of Christian Doctrine), 1941; Rudolf Bultmann's *Offenbarung und Heilsgeschehen* (Revelation and Redemptive Event), 1941; and finally Karl Barth's *Kirchliche Dogmatik* (The Theology of the Church), 1939 ff. From my critical debate with them the reader will confirm the fact that I have learned from all three, though to be sure in quite different ways. To Martin Werner's conception of the place of eschatology in the Primitive Christian proclamation I stand in direct contradiction, in spite of all my recognition of the elements of truth contained in the fundamental position which he and Albert Schweitzer hold. With Rudolf Bultmann I am in agreement, from the standpoint of form criticism, in recognizing the necessity of grasping the theological meaning of the redemptive history from its presentation as a whole; but I consider it impossible to regard the fact of a development in time as only a *framework*, of which we must strip the account in order to get at the kernel (" de-mythologizing " or " myth-removal "). My criticism of Karl Barth rests upon a more positive basis. I see that I am united with him in recognizing that strictly Christocentric character of New Testament theology to which he in his *Dogmatik* gives so powerful an expression. When I here demonstrate that his conception of time, in which I see the last but quite momentous remnant of the influence of philosophy upon his exposition of the Bible, is incompatible with that of Primitive Christianity, I believe that thereby I am carrying out his Christocentric program on the field of New Testament exposition and by means of exegetical methods.

There is need of a word of explanation for the fact that I have followed to an unusual degree the scholar's vice of self-citation. This is due to the fact that all my works for the past ten years, although each time from a different angle, have treated the problem that is here under discussion. Thus these works are in a very real sense to be regarded as studies preliminary to this book, which now attempts to fashion the results obtained into a systematic presentation. Since, with one exception, I did not wish to reprint those works here, I could not avoid referring to them in all cases where proper understanding of my meaning demanded it. Almost every chapter of this book will make it clear that I attach to my investigation of *Die ersten christlichen Glaubensbekenntnisse*, 1943 (Eng. tr., *The Earliest Christian Confessions*, 1949), special significance both in determining what is central in the earliest Christian proclamation and in establishing the criterion by which to determine this central element.

I wish to express my hearty thanks to Rev. Mr. Werner Kohler, now of Nesslau, and to Mr. Ernst Hanselmann, student of theology, for their valuable secretarial work, and to Mr. W. Kohler in addition for the preparation of the index. Without their help the book could not have appeared.

Basel,
   December, 1945.

FOREWORD TO THE SECOND EDITION

SINCE THIS second edition has become necessary sooner than I had expected, it will show no essential change. To be sure, the book has been the subject of numerous reviews from the most varied positions, and above all from the Catholic side; and these reviews, both by their extensive agreement, which quite surprised me, and by their critical and dissenting statements, might have caused me to recast the entire volume. But the reception that my work has enjoyed seems nevertheless to give a positive justification to the necessity, dictated by circumstances, of issuing it in essentially unchanged form.

The criticism that has been directed against my position concerns chiefly two points. First of all, the question as to the relation between time and eternity. Perhaps at a later time I shall have an opportunity to take up the objections that have been raised in connection with this subject. At the moment I wish only to remark that perhaps my critics have not given sufficient attention to the chapter on " God's Lordship Over Time." From this chapter it becomes clear that I have by no means overlooked the fundamental difference between the infinity of God's time and the finiteness of the limited time that is comprehensible to man. Moreover, I admit that my book does not solve many questions that the systematic theologian must ask. Is it not the most valuable service that the New Testament scholar can render to the systematic theologian that he permits the questions that are not solved in the New Testament itself to stand as questions? And does not the real responsibility of the exegete in relation to systematic theology lie precisely in this limitation, so that his duty is to hand on these questions in the very form in which they are presented by the objective New Testament data?

The other point concerns the problem of " Scripture and Tradition." On the Catholic side it has been welcomed that I, in contrast to the conception that ofttimes dominates in Protestantism, have shown how the period of the Church is built into the redemptive history. Nevertheless, I hold fast to the distinction between the *Apostolic* period, which I include in the central event itself, and the period of the *Church*, which is to be subjected to control from that center (Part II, Chapter 4). This distinction carries with it the subordination of tradition to Scripture. I hope that I may have an opportunity to discuss this point further with the Catholic theologians.

In conclusion, I wish to clear away the misconception that I have written this book out of interest in the speculative question concerning time, or that I have taken as my preconceived starting point a " geometric figure." Regardless of the title of my book, my primary concern is not with the question of time but with the presentation of the Biblical redemptive history. To clarify it I have sought to reproduce from the New Testament the Biblical conception of time and the division of time.

Basel,
    July 1, 1948.

INTRODUCTION

THE PROBLEM

OUR SYSTEM of reckoning time does not number the years in a continuous forward-moving series that begins at a fixed initial point. That method is followed, for example, in the calendar which Sextus Julius Africanus created at the opening of the third century A.D., and in the Jewish calendar, which thinks it possible to fix the date of the creation of the world, and hence designates that event by the year 1 and simply numbers forward from that point. Our system, however, does not proceed from an initial point, but from a *center;* it takes as the mid-point an event which is open to historical investigation and can be chronologically fixed, if not with complete accuracy, at least within a space of a few years. This event is the birth of Jesus Christ of Nazareth.[1] Thence proceed in opposite directions two enumerations, one forward, the other backward: " after Christ," " before Christ."

The practice of numbering back from the birth of Christ, to be sure, did not prevail until the eighteenth century.[2]

[1] On the question of the chronology of Jesus' life, see Maurice Goguel, *Vie de Jésus*, 1932, pp. 205 ff. (Eng. tr., *The Life of Jesus*, 1933, pp. 223 ff.) , and Ch. Guignebert, *Jésus*, 1933, pp. 101 ff. (Eng. tr., *Jesus*, 1935, pp. 96 ff.) , where also further bibliography is given. Since in any case the *birth* of Jesus is fixed with only approximate accuracy by our year 1, he who aims at strict accuracy would have to say " before and after Christ " instead of " before and after Christ's birth."

[2] To whom this usage goes back has not yet been determined. Bossuet, to be sure, in the first edition (1681) of his *Discours sur l'histoire univer-selle,* already numbered the pre-Christian period on the margin as the

Prior to that, and indeed from the Middle Ages, it had long been the practice to reckon the years following the birth of Christ as "years of the Lord"; this method had been introduced in A.D. 525 by the Roman abbot Dionysius Exiguus. Down to the eighteenth century, however, the numbering of the pre-Christian period was not oriented with reference to the date of the birth of Christ; rather, the pre-Christian years continued to be dated, in accordance with older calendar systems, from the Creation.

Hence the theologically decisive and interesting point is not the fact that goes back to Dionysius Exiguus, that the birth of Christ was taken as the starting point of subsequent enumeration; a similar practice had been adopted previously in Babylon, where the enumeration was carried forward from the conquest of the country by Seleucus Nicator, and in Rome, where it was carried forward from the year the city was founded or, in a later system, from the year of Diocletian's accession.[3] The decisive thing is rather the practice, which has been in vogue only for the last two centuries, of numbering *both forward and backward* from the birth of Christ. Only when this is done is the Christ-event regarded as the temporal *mid-point* of the entire historical process. The point of departure here, therefore, is not the beginning of the series of happenings. This beginning, according to this enumeration, lies rather at an undetermined point on the line that runs back from the mid-point, just as the end lies at an undetermined point on the line that stretches forward; on both sides the possibility remains open of unlimited further enumeration. When we consider the entire line in its chronological course, the result is that the large numbers of the pre-Christian period move in a decreasing series toward the number one, while the years after

---

"years before Jesus Christ"; in addition, however, he preserved as a designation of these years the customary enumeration of world periods starting from the Creation.

[3] This enumeration with reference to Diocletian was long in vogue even among the Christians, who, to be sure, designated the *anni Diocletiani* as *anni martyrum*.

Christ, on the contrary, move forward from the year one into ever larger numbers.

We shall see how this scheme of conceiving time and history corresponds to the Primitive Christian conception of time and history which is to be analyzed in this study. If our task were to present in graphic form the result of our investigation, this Christian system by which we reckon time could serve as pattern.

We say "Christian system of reckoning time." But it is the common system in the Western world. For the attempt to abolish it, undertaken by the French Revolution in the year 1792, was only a brief episode. Yet today scarcely anyone thinks of the fact that this division is not merely a convention resting upon Christian tradition, but actually presupposes fundamental assertions of *New Testament theology* concerning time and history. These presuppositions are just as foreign to present-day thought as the Christian calendar is familiar to it. To this strangeness we desire to point in the following introductory remarks; they simply present in a preliminary way, but in all their bluntness, the consequences that result from the conception which Primitive Christianity had of time and history. The analysis of the problems that are thereby raised is reserved for the main portion of the book.

1. "BIBLICAL HISTORY" AND HISTORY

In dealing with the historical import of the political and cultural transformations that Christianity has produced, the modern historian may when pressed find a historically confirmed meaning in the fact that the appearance of Jesus of Nazareth is regarded as a decisive turning point of history. But the *theological* affirmation which lies at the basis of the Christian chronology goes far beyond the confirmation that Christianity brought with it weighty historical changes. It asserts rather that from this mid-point all history is to be understood and judged; it asserts that this fact, given the number one, is the final meaning and the criterion of all history before

and after it, and that in *both* directions the content represented by the unlimited series of numbers is to be placed in
relation to and explained by that which is meant by the number one. This historical claim, made for a Galilean prophet's
brief activity, ending with execution under a Roman governor
who ruled Judea under Tiberius, contradicts the modern historian's principle of historical writing.

Now it is to be granted that Primitive Christianity does not
set *every* historical occurrence in *direct* historical connection
with the work of Jesus, and, further, that for general history it
shows only a very little interest. Only in the margin do references to so-called secular history appear in the New Testament. The Primitive Christian consideration of history con-
centrates primarily upon a definite number of events of a quite
particular sort, of which some happened before while others
will happen after Christ; and its chief aim is to set these quite
definite occurrences in relation to the central event which took
place in Palestine about the year one. Its concern is thus chiefly
with " Biblical history," which, to be sure, is presented as a
connected history, not as a sum of separate stories. Jesus Christ
is first of all the mid-point and meaning only for this thus delimited history; compared with general history, it forms a line
which, though not shorter, is yet infinitely smaller. Thus even
from this viewpoint there remains wide room for the historian
to carry on his particular task of organizing and investigating
general history, as he is accustomed to do, in quite other
" secular " connections, and he can do this without coming
into conflict with Primitive Christianity's Christocentric view
of history.

This latter view, however, makes the claim that upon the
basis of the slender Christ-line of the Biblical history it is entitled to render a *final judgment* even on the facts of general
history and on the contemporary course of events at any
period.

If, then, we had previously defined the Primitive Christian
conception of time and history in such terms that according

to it all that happens is judged on the basis of the work of
Jesus Christ, this is now to be made more explicit in the following way: The work of Christ is *primarily* the mid-point of
a special happening or process which extends the length of the
time line; this process, in the sense that early Christianity gives
to it, is to be designated as the Christ-process. In a *secondary*
way, however, this process, for the Christian, is also the measuring standard of general, so-called " secular," history, which
when seen in this light ceases to be secular to him.

In this work we are concerned to make clear also this *final*
claim of Biblical history in relation to general history.[4] For
the problem here treated must not be rendered inoffensive in
the way in which this so readily happens among non-Christians
and Christians alike: both groups often surround the Biblical
history by high walls, so that all access to general history is
made impossible.

What does the historian, who seeks to be only a historian,
have to say to this New Testament judgment on the history
that he investigates? He rightly considers that such a final
judgment, on the basis of a norm regarded as absolute, is not
his own task. To be sure, he should maintain toward such an
undertaking the same neutral attitude that he would take toward any given " philosophy of history," which also passes a
final judgment on the historical events studied by the historian
but does so from a philosophical or religious-philosophical
standpoint. In reality, however, matters so stand today that
the historian will more readily permit a supplementary philosophical view of history than he will a Christian one in the
sense already characterized. This comes from the fact that the
Christian absolute norm *is itself also history* and is not, as is
the philosophical norm, a transcendent datum that lies beyond
all history. The Primitive Christian norm, as we have seen,
consists not only in a single historical fact, but in a temporally
connected historical series of a special kind, namely, the Bibli-

[4] See Part III.

cal history. Thus in this case the norm belongs to the very field of the historian. Precisely for this reason it is difficult for him to recognize it as an absolute criterion.[5]

History is here judged by history, but by such a one as must appear quite problematic from the " purely " historical standpoint. To be sure, the facts of which the normative Biblical history is composed — not all, but a great number — are capable of being established by the historian, and thanks to his study they are thrown into a clearer historical light. Nevertheless, this " normative " Biblical history, in the form that we shall analyze according to the New Testament sources, must as a whole appear to the historian a quite queer construction. The stress on the history of a small people; the combining of its external history with facts that, historically regarded, are at best to be called " faits divers " (sundry odd facts) ; the continual connection of these facts with historically unverifiable facts of the remotest past as well as of the present and future; and especially the explanation of the whole from that mid-point, the work of Jesus of Nazareth, which taken by itself only belongs to the " faits divers " of the history of the Roman Empire — all these things must make this history appear to the " pure historian " as a completely arbitrary compilation, which he will reject as being no valid norm to use in passing judgment on the entire sweep of history.

The problem of Biblical history here emerges as a theological problem. For although individual basic facts of this Biblical history are subject to historical investigation, yet as a whole, in its grouping, interpretation, and joining of events with the historical action of Jesus, it takes on meaning only when this central historical action of Jesus of Nazareth is rec-

---

[5] E. Troeltsch (see especially *Der Historismus und seine Probleme,* 1922) seeks to " overcome " all such dogmatic treatment of history in theology, on the ground that this treatment is irreconcilable with the relativity of all history. He, on the contrary, seeks to find the norm in an undogmatic consideration of the whole of history. In reality, however, he has derived the norm from an area that lies beyond all history, that is, from a philosophy of value.

ognized as *absolute divine revelation* to men. Without this faith, not only is it impossible to ascribe any normative value to that entire Biblical history, but that history must actually seem to be without meaning. Where on the contrary this faith is present, no other norm can exist outside of this Biblical history, which is then designated as the history of revelation and redemption.[6] Here the *close connection between Christian revelation and history* comes to light, and here in the final analysis lies the " offense " of the Primitive Christian view of time and history, not only for the historian, but for all " modern " thinking, including theological thinking; the offense is that God reveals himself in a special way and effects " salvation " in a final way within a narrowly limited but continuing process.

2. BIBLICAL HISTORY AND THEOLOGY

We shall establish the fact that Primitive Christianity places both the divine creation " in the beginning " and the divine goal of all becoming " at the end of the days " in precisely the same Christocentric perspective of Biblical history, that is, in precisely the same temporal Christ-line which it uses to view the historical events in which figure the people of Israel and the activity of Jesus and the apostles and the Primitive Church. In this cosmic extension of the historical line, that which is so offensive for modern thought in the claim of Christian revelation becomes particularly clear, namely, the fact that *all Christian theology in its innermost essence is Biblical history;* on a straight line of an ordinary process in time God here reveals himself, and from that line he controls not only the whole of history, but also that which happens in nature! There is here no room for speculations concerning God that ignore time and history.[7]

Here the full and final consequences are drawn from the

---

[6] See footnote 10 of this chapter.

[7] In this sense we are to understand Pascal's famous words: " The God of Abraham, the God of Isaac, the God of Jacob, not of the philosophers and the scholars."

fact that it is God's very nature to reveal himself, and that this his revelation, his " Word," is an action: " Without this Word nothing was *done*" (John 1:3). The Word, the Logos, is God in his revelatory action. Nowhere, however, is God's action more concretely revealed than in the history which, to speak theologically, presents in its innermost nature the revelation of God to men. Primitive Christian theology treats this fact with unreserved earnestness; it makes the offensive assertion that the climax and central point of all revelation is the fact that the self-revealing God, that is, his Word, his Logos, *once* entered so completely into history that this unique entrance can be designated by dates just as can every other historical event: under the emperor Augustus (Luke 2:1); under the emperor Tiberius (Luke 3:1). The same Word of God who proclaims himself as creative action and will proclaim himself at the end in the new creation " became flesh " in Jesus Christ (John 1:14); that is, he has become history in all his fullness. Nowhere has the unity of the entire revelatory process as a Christ-process — a unity which in the New Testament is everywhere more or less presupposed — found more powerful expression than in the prologue of the Gospel of John, where creation and redemption appear as a single process in which Christ and revelation are active.

As soon as the historical work of Jesus of Nazareth is regarded as the *full* expression of the divine revelatory action, the necessity inevitably results of combining all remaining divine revelatory action with it on one unified Christ-line to present a single " Biblical history." It follows that wherever God has revealed himself and will yet reveal himself, from the Creation on to the new creation at the end of time, this " Word," which back then at that definite time became flesh, must be at work. If in addition to this one " Word," in addition to this one agent of the divine revelation which unfolds in time, we were to assume yet another, the Christian faith would thereby be given up, the faith that the work of Jesus of

Nazareth presents the absolute revelation, that — to speak in the language of the prologue to John — the person of Jesus Christ, the Incarnate One, is identical with the divine Logos, the revealing Word (John 1:14; cf. also ch. 5:17 ff.) .

To the making clear of this unified Christ-line all the efforts of Primitive Christian theology are dedicated. They lead to the demonstration that all theology is in this sense Biblical history. The earliest Christian confessions also fit this view. As we shall see,[8] they do not, in the manner of the later Church creeds, rend asunder the divine revelatory action, as though in creation only God the Father and in the historical redemptive work only the Son were the actor in the revelatory proceeding; they are not framed as though in the article of faith concerning God one should speak in speculative, philosophical, metaphysical language and only in the article concerning Christ speak of revelation in history, and even then do so without reference to creation. Rather, in the earliest two-part confession, it is said: "*One* God the Father, from whom are all things and we unto him, and *one* Lord, Jesus Christ, *through whom are all things and we through him*" (I Cor. 8:6) . Christ is thus the mediator of the entire process, the cosmic as well as the historical. Wherever the subject of discussion is God's revelatory action — and to it belongs creation in a special degree — there, in the Primitive Christian view, the subject of discussion is Christ, the same person whose incarnation can be dated in an ordinary chronological manner.

Upon this basis the New Testament, without further ado, can refer to Christ passages in which the Old Testament speaks of God, the Lord, the *Kyrios*. Of this the most striking example, which must actually arouse to opposition everyone who is not familiar with this New Testament thinking, is Heb. 1:10, where all that is said in Ps. 102:26 ff. concerning the making of the world by God is explicitly ascribed to " the Son ": " Thou, Lord, in the beginning hast laid the founda-

8 See pp. 112 ff.

tions of the earth, and the heavens are the work of thine hands! "

It here becomes quite clear that everything that the first Christians proclaim in their writings is revelation of God's action in Christ, and accordingly constitutes a continuous Christ-process. So it corresponds fully to the basic purpose of the New Testament writers when the presentation of so-called " New Testament theology " takes as its principle of division the redemptive history.[9] With every other division, even the trinitarian, one runs the risk of introducing into the New Testament a later speculative formulation of questions which is foreign to Primitive Christianity; one runs the risk of obliterating or at least weakening Primitive Christianity's thorough orientation to revelatory and redemptive history. This latter development happened quite early; the theological debates of the ancient Church, under the influence of Greek speculative thought, permit Primitive Christianity's central conception of time and history to fall into the background.

It is not our task to give in the following chapters an exhaustive presentation of " New Testament theology." We shall rather investigate in all their complication and range the *basic presuppositions of all New Testament theology,* that is, the New Testament conception of time and history.

The " Biblical history," which we, in accordance with all that has preceded, can also designate as " revelatory history "

---

[9] In this principle of arrangement seems to me to lie the lasting merit of its most recent presentation by Ethelbert Stauffer (*Die Theologie des Neuen Testaments,* 1941), much as I would have to oppose many details of this work. Would it not suit the subject matter better if the modern systematic theologian were to choose this principle of arrangement instead of the trinitarian one? I direct this question to Karl Barth, who, as is well known, arranges his broadly planned work along trinitarian lines. Would not the outline constructed on the basis of redemptive history and dominated by Christology have corresponded better to the consistently Christo-centric treatment of the material, which for the first time is carried through precisely by Barth in so powerful a way?

or — since indeed all revelation is God's love — as "redemptive history," [10] is the heart of all New Testament theology. This has been more correctly and more sharply seen by those who reject Christianity than by many Christians, more sharply even than by many Christian theologians. For it simply is not true that one can give up this entire redemptive history of the New Testament with a perfectly free conscience and yet hold fast to the Christian faith. This attitude, held by many, proceeds from the false presupposition that the redemptive history is only an external framework which the Christian faith can unhesitatingly discard. In reality that which then remains as alleged "kernel" is not at all a particularly characteristic feature of the Christian revelation. Thus, for example, the command of love, which as such is of course found also in non-Christian religions, only receives its specifically Christian significance and its deeper meaning by its anchorage in that history of revelation and redemption.[11] Moreover, in this connection, the love of enemies only receives its Christian theological foundation in this same context, in the fact that Christ died for even our enemy, that in Christ God loves even our greatest enemy.

In a separate section [12] we shall seek to show that by this emphasis on the central significance of the Biblical redemptive history, the command which in Christ is directed to the individual man is not at all pushed into the background, but rather is placed in its truly Christian light. The frequently rather cheap playing off of "life" against "doctrine," of ethics against theology, is thus not in keeping with the situation here, for in Primitive Christianity they are inseparably connected.

[10] Although the expression "redemptive history" (*Heilsgeschichte*), which has established itself in theology chiefly through the influence of v. Hofmann, has become far too much a battle cry with which the theological position of the "Erlangen School" is customarily designated, we shall nevertheless use it in this book, since it comes very close to expressing the thing with which we are dealing. Perhaps "revelational history" (*Offenbarungsgeschichte*) is still more comprehensive.

[11] I Cor. 8:11: "The brother for whom Christ died."

[12] See Part IV.

The rejection of the Christian faith, in so far as it takes place on account of the conception of salvation as effected by revelation in history, rests upon a more correct grasp of what is essential and central than does the preaching of a Christianity that is deprived of its life nerve, that is, of the "offense" of the redemptive history.

Here we must name Celsus, the great adversary of the Christians in ancient times. In this point he recognizes something quite central in Christianity, even if, in order to combat Christianity, he actually treats as ridiculous that which we designate as redemptive history, namely, the idea of the election of a people, the idea of the divinely willed concentration upon this one small line. Thus he caricatures the faith that discerns salvation in history: "Jews and Christians appear to me like a host of bats or ants who come out of their hiding places, or like frogs who sit in a swamp, or worms who hold a meeting in the corner of a manure pile and say to one another: 'To us God reveals and proclaims everything. He does not trouble himself with the rest of the world; we are the only beings with whom he has dealings. . . . To us is subjected everything: the earth, the water, the air, the stars. Because it has happened that some among us have sinned, God himself will come or will send his own Son in order to destroy the wicked with fire and to give us a share in eternal life'" (quoted in Origen, *Against Celsus,* IV, 23). In the form of a caricature the redemptive history is here sketched in its close connection with the cosmic process.

The present volume simply seeks to show on the basis of the Primitive Christian sources that this history is not, to use a word of Rudolf Bultmann, a "myth" of which the New Testament revelation can be unclothed; [13] nor does it present a secondary adaptation of the Christians to Jewish conceptions, which affect the kernel of the Primitive Christian proclamation to such a limited extent that this "kernel" can be re-

[13] See R. Bultmann, *Offenbarung und Heilsgeschehen,* 1941. In regard to eschatology R. Bultmann championed this standpoint at an even earlier time. See especially his book concerning *Jesus,* 1926 (Eng. tr., *Jesus and the Word,* 1934).

moved from the shell of those conceptions. We here seek to
show by pure historical study that the specifically " *Christian*
kernel," as we derive it from all the Primitive Christian
sources, really stands or falls with the redemptive history.

Albert Schweitzer as a historian has already shown this in a
problem dealing with one part of our more comprehensive
question, that is, in the problem of the *completion* of the redemptive history in Primitive Christian eschatology. His historical conclusion is clear: All presentations of the preaching
of Jesus that seek the kernel elsewhere than in this eschatology
are reinterpretations which do violence to the historical truth.
For the teaching of Paul, Albert Schweitzer has furnished the
proof of the same position.[14] We shall here undertake to show
that this judgment holds good generally for the Primitive
Christian view of redemptive history, and that in Primitive
Christianity eschatology cannot be detached from this entire
redemptive line, which is related not only to the future but
also to the past and present.[15]

He who refuses to be satisfied with the historical proof that
the redemptive history is the heart of the Primitive Christian
New Testament preaching, and is determined to go on to take
his own chosen attitude to it, should know that he thereby
makes his personal decision for or against the Christian message itself. In saying this we do not intend to support a rigid
Biblicism; for it is characteristic of such a false Biblicistic attitude that it treats *all* statements in the Bible as of equal
worth, while we here are raising the question of what is *cen-*

[14] See Albert Schweitzer, *Die Mystik des Apostels Paulus*, 1930 (Eng.
tr., *The Mysticism of Paul the Apostle*, 1931). In this book, which theologically is his most significant work, Schweitzer shows in a particularly
clear and truly classical way how for the apostle the significance of the
present for redemptive history is bound up with the future.

[15] We shall show, however, that in Primitive Christianity the center
is the resurrection of Christ, and that the expectation concerning the future depends on faith in the bearing that the present, as determined by
Christ's resurrection, has upon redemptive history; the dependence is not
vice versa. For criticism of " consistent eschatology," see especially pp.
58 ff., 81 ff., 140 f.

tral. The total view of redemptive history does not belong to those necessarily outmoded framework elements, such as the Primitive " world view " of the Bible, which do not touch the kernel of the matter.

Therefore it is hard to understand the attitude of Albert Schweitzer and especially of his pupils, the representatives of the so-called consistent eschatology: they reject in their theological position that which they have recognized in historical study to be the center of the New Testament faith, and yet, in what seems to me a very inconsistent manner, they affirm this faith.[16] They hold fast to some element which, along with other elements, is *also* found in this Christian faith, but they actually detach this element from those basic presuppositions of the New Testament which in their historical study they have recognized as the kernel. This arbitrarily chosen element (such as " reverence for life ") they designate as essential only because it appears to be something decisive when viewed from the standpoint of some philosophical judgment concerning our " existence," that is, from a position which in itself has nothing to do with the Christian message. This attitude, paradoxically enough, has in common with the harshly Biblicistic view the fact that, as far as systematic theology is concerned, the question concerning what is central is not put *from the standpoint of the Bible.*

Less arbitrary is the positive solution of Rudolf Bultmann. In his previously mentioned writing, *Offenbarung und Heilsgeschehen* (Revelation and Redemptive Event), 1941, he undertakes the " de-mythologizing " of the New Testament; that is, he strips the Christian proclamation of its time setting in redemptive history. Bultmann thus endeavors, in opposition to " consistent eschatology," to lay bare the " central " kernel in connection with the New Testament; he does this at least to the extent that he inquires concerning the meaning — nontemporal and nonhistorical — of the redemptive-historical " myth " itself. Yet when he thus from the outset regards the temporal and historical element as a mythological covering

16 See especially Martin Werner, *Die Entstehung des christlichen Dogmas,* 1941, and for a criticism of this view, Oscar Cullmann, " Das wahre durch die ausgebliebene Parusie gestellte neutestamentliche Problem " (*Theologische Zeitschrift,* 1947, pp. 177 ff.) .

that can be separated from a kernel, *this* a priori is not derived
from a historical investigation of the Primitive Christian attitude; it must then be asked whether in reality the existence
philosophy of Heidegger, with which the enduring kernel is
found to agree (Bultmann, *op. cit.*, p. 49) , is not the starting
point of the entire undertaking. Fritz Buri, in his article on
" Das Problem der Prädestination " (The Problem of Predestination, in *Schweizerische Theologische Umschau,* 1943,
pp. 41 ff.) , undertakes to connect this act of Bultmann in
stripping off the mythology with that of M. Werner in stripping away the eschatology. In opposition thereto it must at
least be said that Bultmann's demand for removing the entire
mythology is much more consistent than is the demand for removal of the eschatology. For the New Testament statements
about salvation that refer to the future are quite closely connected with the faith in the redemptive process of the past and
the present.

R. Bultmann's standpoint is connected with his form-critical
way of considering the Gospels, as he has set it forth in the
foreword to the second edition of *Geschichte der Synoptischen
Tradition* (The History of the Synoptic Tradition) , 1931. It
is certainly the great merit of the advocates of form criticism
that they have emphatically brought it to the attention of his-
torians as well as theologians that the Gospels are not biographies, but are rather witnesses of faith. In my article on " Les
récentes études sur la formation de la tradition évangélique "
(Recent Studies of the Formation of the Gospel Tradition,
in *Revue d'Histoire et de Philosophie religieuses,* 1925, pp.
574 ff.) , I myself showed explicitly the theologically significant consequences of the form-critical attitude of Bultmann,
and pointed to the fact that the biographical-historical presentation of the Gospel tradition is only the garment for the
Primitive Church's witness to its faith in Christ. But the final
step, which Bultmann has taken in his above-cited book
(*Offenbarung und Heilsgeschehen,* 1941) , in which the entire
Biblical history of the New Testament is characterized as being only a myth that does not suit the kernel, shows me that
the rightly affirmative evaluation of form criticism should have
had from the outset a limiting addition, which was also lacking in the article I then wrote. This addition is to the effect
that the history must in any case maintain its right to this
extent, that this very witness of faith which comes to expression in the Gospel tradition has history itself as its object,

since indeed it declares that Jesus of Nazareth is the Christ of Israel.

To affirm or reject the Christian proclamation does not mean to affirm or reject some feature or other which may *also* be found in it; it means rather to affirm or reject the actual center of this proclamation.

That this center is the Christian conception of time and history will be shown in what follows. Since we here content ourselves with establishing this historical conclusion, this work is historical in character and belongs in the realm of New Testament theology; in this connection, however, the lines are to be extended into the later history of doctrine where this proves advisable. The significance of this study for one's attitude to the Christian faith, in case the result is correct, follows of course from what has already been said.

The unique element in the Christian conception of time as the scene of redemptive history is of a twofold character, and we desire to distinguish the two sides by treating them separately in the first two chapters of this book. In the first place, salvation is bound to a *continuous time process* which embraces past, present, and future. Revelation and salvation take place along the course of an ascending time line. Here the strictly straight-line conception of time in the New Testament must be defined as over against the Greek cyclical conception and over against all metaphysics in which salvation is always available in the " beyond," and we must show how according to the Primitive Christian view revelation and salvation actually " occur " in a connected manner during the continuous time process.

In the second place, it is characteristic of this estimate of time as the scene of redemptive history that all points of this redemptive line are related to the *one historical fact* at the mid-point, a fact which precisely in its unrepeatable character,

which marks all historical events, is decisive for salvation.
This fact is the death and resurrection of Jesus Christ. Here
we intend to show how the different individual sections of the
whole line are constantly determined from this mid-point, but
yet have their own significance in time. Whereas the first chapter deals with that which the New Testament designates as
οἰκονομία (dispensation),[17] whereby the divine plan of salvation is viewed in its entirety, the second chapter deals rather
with the ἐφάπαξ (once only, once for all),[18] the unrepeatable
and once-only character of the redemptive process.[19]

[17] Eph. 1:10; 3:2; 3:9; Col. 1:25.
[18] Rom. 6:10; Heb. 7:27; 9:12; 10:10.
[19] We employ this New Testament term in spite of the misuse it has
suffered in political speeches of the most recent period, in which it means
practically the opposite of what we here intend. There it points to the
transient significance of alleged human exploits rather than to their decisive importance for all times.

PART I

THE CONTINUOUS REDEMPTIVE LINE

οἰκονομία

1

THE SIGNIFICANCE OF THE NEW TESTAMENT TERMINOLOGY FOR TIME

PRIMITIVE CHRISTIAN FAITH and thinking do not start from the spatial contrast between the Here and the Beyond, but from the time distinction between Formerly and Now and Then. In saying this we do not mean that the mainly spatial contrast between visible and invisible does not here exist. There is in the New Testament an invisible heaven and a visible earth; invisible powers and authorities are at work, while man observes only the visible deeds executed by the earthly agents of those powers.[1] But this invisible course of events is itself completely subjected to the progress of time. The essential thing is not the spatial contrast, but the distinction which faith makes between the times. Thus the author of The Epistle to the Hebrews, in his famous definition of faith (ch. 11:1), names first of all the " assurance of things *hoped for,*" that is, things which are future. Thereby he also gives to the further definition, the " conviction of things not seen," a reference to the time process.

The emphatically temporal character of all expressions of faith is connected in the New Testament with the Jewish

---

[1] Thus the executive power of the State is the administrative organ for the " rulers of this age " (I Cor. 2:8). In the light of this fact we should also understand that the " authorities " of Rom. 13:1, in keeping with the meaning which this plural always has for Paul, are the powers that stand behind the actual executive power of the State. On this subject, see Part III, Chapter 3.

valuation of time,[2] and this in turn shows close contacts with Parsiism.[3] Nevertheless, it will be shown in this and the following chapters that the New Testament writings for the first time give to all revelation an essential anchorage in time; here for the first time the time line is consistently carried through in its central significance for salvation and faith. Thus it is not as if we had to do with a Jewish survival; rather, that which is intimated in Judaism is here completely carried out.

In this respect the terminology of the New Testament is characteristic. Here, in decisive passages, all the expressions for time that were available in the Greek language occur with special frequency; prominent are the words for " day " ($\dot{\eta}\mu\dot{\epsilon}\rho\alpha$) , " hour " ($\ddot{\omega}\rho\alpha$) , " season " ($\kappa\alpha\iota\rho\dot{o}s$) , " time " ($\chi\rho\dot{o}\nu os$) , " age " ($\alpha\dot{\iota}\dot{\omega}\nu$) , and " ages " ($\alpha\dot{\iota}\ddot{\omega}\nu\epsilon s$) . It is no accident that we constantly encounter these and similar expressions,[4] among which the emphatic " now " ($\nu\hat{v}\nu$) and the emphatic " today " ($\sigma\dot{\eta}\mu\epsilon\rho o\nu$) must also be mentioned; indeed, we find all the terms so used as to throw this very time aspect into a notably theological light.

For all statistical and lexicographical material which relates to these words we may refer to the older and the more recent New Testament lexicons, especially that of G. Kittel, which seeks to bring out the theological significance of the words in question. To be sure, theological understanding necessarily encounters limits in the separate treatment of a single word. Therefore we here desire to show in a connected survey how

[2] Gerhard Delling, in *Das Zeitverständnis des Neuen Testaments,* 1940, wrongly seeks to show that in the problem of time there is a gulf between Judaism and Christianity. In any case, the difference does not lie where he seeks it. See footnote 25 of this chapter.

[3] This is to be fully conceded in spite of the scientific nonsense which has been put forth concerning Parsiism in New Testament publications of the past decade, in order to give to Christianity the appearance of an " Aryan " home.

[4] Such vague time formulas of transition as " after these things," " straightway," etc., which in the Synoptic Gospels connect the various fragments of tradition, do not come into consideration here, since they were introduced by the authors only to create a literary framework. See Karl Ludwig Schmidt, *Der Rahmen der Geschichte Jesu,* 1919.

even this terminology expresses the distinctive quality of the Primitive Christian thinking concerning time.

The two ideas that most clearly elucidate the New Testament conception of time are those usually expressed by *kairos* (καιρός, " a point of time ") , and *aiōn* (αἰών, " age ") . It is not easy to find an adequate translation for the various expressions that refer to time. The translation at times must be determined by the theological content which results from the context. That these terms can also be used in the New Testament without special theological reference becomes clear as one uses the lexicons.

The characteristic thing about *kairos* is that it has to do with a definite *point of time* which has a fixed content, while *aiōn* designates a *duration* of time, a defined or undefined *extent of time*. In the New Testament both terms serve, in a manner that corresponds remarkably well to the matter in hand, to characterize that time in which the redemptive history occurs.

Kairos in secular usage is the moment in time which is especially favorable for an undertaking; it is the point of time of which one has long before spoken without knowing its actual date; it is the fixed day, which in modern jargon, for example, is called D day. It is human considerations that cause a point of time to appear especially adapted for the execution of this or that plan, and thus make it a *kairos*. In this secular sense Felix says to Paul: " When I have a convenient season, I will call for thee " (Acts 24:25) .

The New Testament usage with reference to redemptive history is the same. Here, however, it is not human deliberations but a divine decision that makes this or that date a *kairos,* a point of time that has a special place in the execution of God's plan of salvation. Because the realization of the divine plan of salvation is bound to such time points or *kairoi* chosen by God, therefore it is a redemptive *history*. Not all fragments of ongoing time constitute redemptive history in the narrower sense, but rather these specific points, these *kairoi*, singled out from time as a whole.

What we said in the Introduction concerning the relation of the redemptive history to general history finds its confirmation in this central New Testament time concept of the *kairos*. Regarded from the historical standpoint as man sees it, the choice of the *kairoi* that constitute the redemptive history is arbitrary. The New Testament, therefore, gives as the principle of this divine "selection" of the *kairoi* only the "sovereign divine power": "the *kairoi* which the Father in his sovereign power has fixed" (Acts 1:7). To men, even to the disciples, it is not granted to know the date of the still future *kairoi*. The apostle Paul reminds the Thessalonians of the sudden inbreaking of these *kairoi* (I Thess. 5:1 f.).

The Apocalypse of John (chs. 1:3; 11:18) also designates the decisive moment of the eschatological drama as a *kairos* and says of it that it is "near," in the same sense in which the nearness of the Kingdom of God is announced in the Synoptic Gospels. *Kairos* appears likewise in the Synoptic Gospels with this eschatological application (Luke 19:44; 21:8), and the same usage occurs in I Peter 1:5. As in the passage just named, so also in the Pastoral Epistles the *kairoi* refer to the still future stages of the redemptive history.[5] In these Epistles, especially by the addition of the adjective ἴδιος, "appropriate,"[6] it is emphasized that the sovereign power of God fixes these *kairoi* in the context of his entire plan of salvation: "the appearance of our Lord Jesus Christ, which the blessed and only Sovereign will show at the appropriate *kairoi*" (I Tim. 6:14, 15).

In the same Epistle to Timothy we are shown the relation of these still future *kairoi* to an already past *kairos* of this same

[5] See also II Thess. 2:6, where we hear that even for the revelation of the Antichrist the *kairos* is fixed.

[6] The word ἴδιος is also understood by W. Bauer, in his *Griechisch-Deutsches Wörterbuch zu den Schriften des N.T.*, 1928, as an expression that lays particular emphasis upon the "appropriate time."

divine line of salvation: " Jesus Christ has given himself as a ransom for all, as a witness to appropriate *kairoi* " still to come (I Tim. 2:6) .

Quite in agreement with this, however, the Epistle to Titus designates the time of the "revelation" of the proclamation of Christ, a time that already lies in the *past*, by precisely the same term "appropriate *kairoi*" (Titus 1:3) . So also The First Epistle of Peter describes as a *kairos* the time of the Christ-event, which from the standpoint of the author had already been completed. The Old Testament "prophets searched to learn what or what manner of *kairos* was meant by the Spirit dwelling in them, when it testified to the sufferings destined for Christ and to the subsequent glory" (I Peter 1:11) .

It is not merely in the faith of the Church after the death of Christ that this role of a central *kairos* in the divine plan of salvation is ascribed to the work that the incarnate Christ performed. Rather, Jesus himself, according to the Synoptic witness, characterizes his Passion as his *kairos;* by this Greek word the Evangelist, no doubt accurately, translates the Aramaic word which Jesus used. At the time of the preparation for the Last Supper Jesus sends forth his disciples with the message: " The Master sends word: My *kairos* is near " (Matt. 26:18) . We are reminded of the first preaching of Jesus: " The kingdom of God has come near." To the *kairos* to which Jesus points as the completion of his own work is thus ascribed a quite decisive significance in the course of events which lead to the Kingdom of God. We know this from other sayings of Jesus, altogether apart from the occurrence of the word *kairos*. We hear that even in the very fact of Jesus' appearance, above all in his healings, the Kingdom of God has broken in. That the decisive *kairos* of Christ's death and resurrection, and of the victory thereby achieved over the world of demons, is already announced in preceding *kairoi* of his earthly career, becomes clear to us in another passage of the Gospel of Matthew when the demon-possessed speak thus: " Hast thou come hither to torment us *before* the *kairos?* " (Matt. 8:29) .

Nowhere does that which the New Testament understands by *kairos* come to clearer expression than in John 7:3 ff., a passage which in this regard is truly classic. In it Jesus says to his unbelieving brothers: "*My kairos* [to go up to Jerusalem] has not yet come; *your kairos* is always ready" (v. 6). This means: For you there is no *kairos* in the meaning found in the New Testament redemptive history, no times that God in his sovereign power has fixed and that therefore have a special significance in relation to his plan of salvation.[7] For the others there applies only the secular use of the word *kairos*, where everything depends solely on the human decision as to whether a *kairos* is favorable or not. They can go up to Jerusalem at any time; Christ cannot, for he stands in the midst of the divine plan of salvation, whose *kairoi* are definitely fixed by God.[8]

Upon the basis of the deed of Christ, however, there also exists in the present period of the Primitive Christian Church a divine *kairos* for the believer: "The *kairos* has come for the judgment to begin at the house of God" (I Peter 4:17). Hence the demand in Colossians and Ephesians (Col. 4:5; Eph. 5:16) to "redeem" the *kairos;* and if the "Western" reading in Rom. 12:11 is correct, Paul there summons his readers to place themselves at the service of the *kairos*. In these passages is meant the present *kairos*, whose significance in the entire plan of salvation is known to the believer upon the basis of the past *kairos*, that is, the death and resurrection of Christ.

[7] Without the use of the word *kairos*, precisely the same idea is present in the Cana story in John 2:4, which as a whole forms an exact parallel to the section John 7:1–13; cf. O. Cullmann, *Urchristentum und Gottesdienst (Abhandlungen zur Theologie des Alten und Neuen Testaments,* No. 3), 1944, pp. 42 ff. When Jesus here says to his mother: "Madam, why do you interfere in my affairs; my hour has not yet come," his words have the same meaning as does the answer given in John 7:6. The words τί ἐμοὶ καὶ σοί correspond to ὁ δὲ καιρὸς ὁ ὑμέτερος πάντοτέ ἐστιν ἕτοιμος.

[8] R. Bultmann, in *Das Evangelium des Johannes,* 1941, p. 220, is here again interested only in the question of decision, not in that of the genuine time quality of the *kairos* concept in its relation to the entire redemptive line.

Thus we see that in the past, the present, and the future there are special divine *kairoi*, by the joining of which the redemptive line arises.[9] The necessity of connecting the *kairoi* with one another has become clear to us especially in I Tim. 2:6, in connection with the two other passages cited from the Pastoral Epistles.[10]

This conception of special points of time at which the self-revealing God, in the execution of his plan, effects salvation is by no means bound to the one expression *kairos*. On the contrary, the specifically New Testament usage of other words for time serves to express the same idea, and does so once again in reference to the past, the present, and the future. As first in importance we must here mention the expressions " day " and " hour."

To designate the beginning of the eschatological drama which still lies in the future, Primitive Christianity took over from Judaism the concept of the " day of the Lord " (*yōm Yahweh*).[11] In Mark 13:32 Jesus speaks of " that day and hour," concerning the time of which no one knows.

Here again those decisive events connected with the work of Jesus, who appeared in the flesh, are called in a special sense " day " or, as the Gospel of John prefers to say, " hour." The above-mentioned utterance of Jesus in the Gospel of John, in which he explains that he himself is bound to fixed *kairoi*, is inevitably brought to mind when Jesus says in the Gospel of Luke (ch. 13:32) : " I cast out demons and perform healings today and tomorrow, and on the third day I am perfected."

Above all, however, we must here recall the numerous Johannine passages in which Jesus speaks of his " hour " and

---

[9] That the entire " secular " process is determined by divine *kairoi* we hear in the Areopagus speech (Acts 17:26). God has " determined in advance the *kairoi* of all peoples on the face of the earth." Here emerges the problem of the relation between the redemptive history and general history; to this we shall devote a separate section (Part III).

[10] See pp. 40 f.

[11] See Acts 2:20 (from Joel 2:31) ; II Tim. 1:12; 1:18; 4:8; Acts 17:31.

where in every case the hour of his death is meant.[12] It is the
central point, the central hour in the Christ-event. But from
it a light falls on the other instances in the Johannine narrative concerning the life of Jesus where the hour is fixed. Indeed, it is in itself noteworthy that precisely the Gospel of
John, which otherwise shows much less interest than the Syn-
optics for the chronological and geographical framework of
the history of Jesus, presents an amazingly precise chronological placing of certain narratives: " it was about such and such
an hour." This probably can be explained only by concluding
that the Fourth Evangelist thereby intends to show that this
life is really a redemptive event and so is bound to the time
fixed for it by God. The time of Christ is not " always ready "
as it is for the unbelieving brothers (John 7:6).

In this connection we must likewise place the emphatic
" now " (νῦν), which we often find used in the New Testament to stress the fact that the present period of the Apostolic
Age belongs in an outstanding way to the redemptive history
and is thus distinguished from all other times. For example,
it is said in Col. 1:26 that " the mystery which has been hidden
for ages and generations has *now* been revealed to the saints,
to whom God has willed to make it known." [13] It is in a similar sense that the author of The Epistle to the Hebrews speaks
of his own time as "today " (σήμερον, ch. 3:7, 13, 15).

Thus here also we reach the result that all these expressions
refer to moments or at least to sharply defined periods of time
in the past as well as in the present and future. God chooses
these moments or periods of time for the realization of his
plan of salvation, and does so in such a way that the joining
of them in the light of this plan forms a meaningful time line.

The terms treated thus far cluster around the central concept of *kairos* and characterize the decisive stages of time in-

[12] O. Cullmann, *Urchristentum und Gottesdienst* (*Abhandlungen zur
Theologie des Alten und Neuen Testaments*, No. 3), 1944, pp. 41 ff.
[13] Cf. Eph. 3:5; Rom. 16:25 f.

dividually in their separate significance. The other word, αἰών ("period of time," "age"), that is so frequent in the New Testament, is to be so defined that it focuses upon the extension of time and expresses duration.

This word, like the Hebrew ōlām, takes on at times a spatial meaning and so comes to mean "world"; it thus becomes a synonym of "world," "universe" (κόσμος).[14] In the overwhelming majority of passages, however, we find the original use of the word, that is, as an expression of time.

The quite varied use of αἰών in the New Testament writings is extremely instructive for the understanding of the Primitive Christian conception of time. It can be shown that this one word serves here to designate both an exactly defined period of time and an undefined and incalculable duration, which we then translate by the word "eternity." Thus it comes about that the same expression that refers to the present "evil" age (Gal. 1:4) can be a characteristic of God, the "King of the ages" (I Tim. 1:17).[15] This ambiguous usage of the same word, which has its counterpart in the usage of the Hebrew ōlām and the Persian zrvan, will help us, in a separate later chapter, to determine correctly the relation between time and eternity in the New Testament.

Even here, however, the conclusion should be laid down that eternity, as meant in this linguistic usage, is not to be interpreted in the Platonic and modern philosophical sense, where it stands in contrast to time; it must rather be taken as

14 See, for example, Heb. 1:2. Further material excellent for orientation is given in the article on αἰών by H. Sasse in the *Theologisches Wörterbuch zum Neuen Testament*, Vol. I, pp. 203 f.

15 We probably should agree with H. Sasse, *op. cit.*, p. 201, when he, in connection with the late Jewish usage in which these same words are linked, understands the genitive here in the sense of the Hebrew construct state, and accepts as the *original* meaning only that of "eternal king." To be sure, he leaves open the possibility that the meaning "Lord over the Ages" is also subsequently introduced into the expression. This is what E. Stauffer, in his *Theologie des Neuen Testaments*, 1941, p. 59, assumes has happened in our passage.

endless time.[16] This is clear, indeed, from the fact that the
use of the plural " ages " is particularly preferred when eternity is mentioned. Although the rhetorical tendency to liturgical pathos is certainly a contributing factor here, yet the fact
that one can speak of eternity in the plural proves that it does
not signify cessation of time or timelessness. It means rather
endless time and therefore an ongoing of time which is incomprehensible to men; or, as it may be still better expressed,
it means the linking of an unlimited series of limited world
periods, whose succession only God is able to survey.

Thus in the New Testament field it is not time and eternity
that stand opposed, but limited time and unlimited, endless
time. Moreover, the thoroughly temporal manner of thinking
is not surrendered even when the New Testament speaks of
this limitless time. This latter time is not different from the
former. The difference consists only in the fact that it is not
limited. When the Christian writers, in their statements concerning calculable time, look backward, they write ἐκ τοῦ αἰῶνος (" out of the age "), ἀπ' αἰῶνος (" from the age "), or even
ἀπὸ τῶν αἰώνων (" from the ages ") ; [17] when they look forward,
they write εἰς αἰῶνα (" into the age ") or εἰς τοὺς αἰῶνας (" into
the ages "). Both usages agree completely with those of the
Old Testament. Eternity, accordingly, is designated by the

---

[16] This has been quite correctly recognized by H. Sasse, *op. cit.*, pp. 201 f.
Even the Jewish conception of eternity (with the exception of Slavonic
Enoch 65) is not that of timelessness, but that of endless time, and for the
New Testament also it holds true that " statements concerning the eternal
existence and action of God are made in the form of *prae* (before) and
post (after) ." Unfortunately Sasse, in his further discussion in the same
article, obscures this insight when he writes on p. 202 that the eternity of
God and the time of the world " stand in deepest contrast to one another,"
and when on p. 205, in the section concerning the present and the future
age, he speaks of the dualistic teaching of the Bible concerning time and
eternity.

[17] The expression " before the ages " (I Cor. 2:7) does not prove that
eternity would be timeless because lying " before time." Either " ages " is
used here in the sense of limited time (between the Creation and the end)
or, as is also possible, we have here the spatial use of " ages " (see above) .
In this latter case " before the ages " would be exactly parallel to " before
the foundation of the world " (Eph. 1:4; John 17:24; I Peter 1:20) .

term αἰών, which carries a time meaning.[18]

By remembering this fact we can understand the familiar New Testament usage, which likewise roots in Judaism, in which the word " age " is used to express the divine division of time into this present age (αἰὼν οὗτος or ἐνεστώς) and the coming age (αἰὼν μέλλων).[19] Here too it is not the case that by this distinction time and eternity are set in contrast as opposites; nor is it true that " this age " means time while " the coming age " means timelessness. Rather, the coming age's future character, expressed in the added participle,[20] is to be taken seriously. The coming age is not, for example, already present as eternity. To be sure, there exists a radical contrast between the two ages, of which the one is characterized as " evil " (Gal. 1:4); but this is not meant in the sense that the one is temporal while the other is timeless — in both cases, indeed, the thing meant is called " age." The contrast and the evil character of the one age are not connected with the time quality as such, but with the event that stands with determinative role at the beginning of this period of time. That event is the Fall. The fall into sin did not create the time category itself, but it involved in the power of evil the course of events that fills this age, while the course of events that fills the coming age is marked by the conquest of the evil powers.

There also exists, to be sure, a distinction in time between the two ages, the present and the future. But here too the question involved is only that of the limits. The present age is limited in *both* directions: in the backward direction by creation, in the forward direction by the eschatological drama. The coming age is limited on *one* side but unlimited on the other; its beginning is limited, inasmuch as it begins with the events that are pictorially described in the apocalypses, but

---

[18] Concerning the Old Testament terminology for time, see C. v. Orelli, *Die hebräischen Synonyma der Zeit und Ewigkeit*, 1871.

[19] The numerous supporting passages are cited by H. Sasse, *op. cit.*, pp. 205 f.

[20] This future idea is expressed not only by μέλλων, but also by ἐρχόμενος or ἐπερχόμενος.

no limit is set for its end. In other words, it is without end but not without beginning, and only in this sense is it " eternal." Precisely from the fact that the coming age of the Bible has a beginning in time we perceive that its eternity is not that, for example, of the Platonic view.

If we wish to understand the Primitive Christian use of αἰών (" age "), we thus must free ourselves completely from all philosophical concepts of time and eternity. In summary, it may be said that the temporal sense of the word in the singular and in the plural has in view a longer duration of time, and specifically:

1. Time in its entire unending extension, which is unlimited in both the backward and the forward direction, and thus is " eternity." [21]

2. Limited time, which lies between Creation and the eschatological drama, and thus is identical with the " present " age, " this " age.[22]

3. Periods of time that are limited in one direction but unlimited in the other, and specifically:

a. The period to which the phrase ἐκ τοῦ αἰῶνος, " out of the age," points back,[23] i.e., the time that lies before the Creation. On the side of Creation it has an end and so a limit; but in the backward direction it is unlimited, unending, and only in this sense is it eternal.

b. The time that extends beyond the end of the present age (αἰών μέλλων, the " coming age "). It thus has in the so-called eschatological drama its beginning and so a limit; but in the forward direction it is unlimited, unending, and only in this sense is it eternal.

---

[21] To this use of αἰών corresponds the adjective αἰώνιος, " agelong," " eternal." Since eternity in this sense comes into consideration only as an attribute of God, the adjective αἰώνιος has the tendency to lose its time sense and is used in the qualitative sense of divine-immortal.

[22] In this sense of limited " ages," I Cor. 10:11 speaks of " the ends of the ages." With Christ the final phase of the limited world period has dawned.

[23] See p. 46.

This schematic survey shows that only this simple rectilinear conception of unending time can be considered as the framework for the New Testament history of redemption. Along this consistently rectilinear line of the ages lie the *kairoi* determined by God. Thus just as God fixed the individual providential points or seasons of the redemptive history, so also he determined the just named divisions of the ages in which this history occurs.

None of the New Testament expressions for time has as its object time as an abstraction. This is not even the meaning of χρόνος, " time." This word is not used as it is in Greek philosophy, where it serves to designate time as such, in its problematic character. In the New Testament we find this word for " time " used in concrete reference to the redemptive history; it may have the meaning of " season " or of " age," or it may signify simply some space of time that is to elapse. Thus even the well-known passage in Rev. 10:6, where it is said that there will be no more *chronos,* is not to be understood as if the era of timelessness were meant; rather, on the analogy of Hab. 2:3 and Heb. 10:37, we must translate: " There will be no more *delay.*" [24]

The terminology of the New Testament teaches us that, according to the Primitive Christian conception, time in its unending extension as well as in its individual periods and moments is given by God and ruled by him. Therefore *all* his acting is so inevitably bound up with time that time is not felt to be a problem.[25] It is rather the natural presupposition

[24] So also, in agreement with almost all expositors, E. Lohmeyer, *Die Offenbarung des Johannes,* in the *Handbuch zum Neuen Testament,* edited by H. Lietzmann, 1926, *ad. loc.,* although he also cites Bede's interpretation, which leans toward a philosophical understanding: " *mutabilis saecularium temporum varietas cessabit,*" " the changeful variety of this world's periods of time shall cease."

[25] G. Delling, in *Das Zeitverständnis des Neuen Testaments,* 1940, thinks that in Judaism time was not felt to be a problem, but that for Hellenism, on the contrary, it was a difficult problem never solved. Chris-

of all that God causes to occur. This explains the fact that in a great majority of cases the terminology of the Primitive Christian writings has a time reference. Each individual item of the redemptive history has its fixed place in time. Of the law it is said quite concretely, in a section which is thoroughly theological and doctrinal, that it came 430 years after the promise (Gal. 3:17) ; on the other hand, it is said that in the redemptive process this law " entered in along the way " (Rom. 5:20) ; moreover, the preceding survey in Rom. 5:12–14 is in its theological import completely anchored in chronology.

Christ, however, who is the divine revelatory Word himself, the mediator of all divine action, is so fully and closely connected with endless divine time that the author of The Epistle to the Hebrews can actually set forth his nature in time terminology: *" Jesus Christ, the same yesterday and today and into the ages"* (Heb. 13:8) .

Similarly, The Revelation of John ascribes to him participation in God's eternity, when it designates him as the one who is " the first and the last, the beginning and the end " (chs. 1:17; 2:8; 22:13) .

---

tianity, he thinks, is distinguished from both in so far as it overcame time by the knowledge of the inbreaking of eternity. This would presuppose that for Primitive Christianity time as such was after all a problem to be overcome. This, however, is not the case. Rather, Primitive Christianity stands in this point much closer to Judaism than Delling supposes. Time is not something hostile to God that must be overcome. Certainly not by eternity, as though this meant a contrast to time. That which Delling calls the inbreaking of eternity is in reality something quite different; it has to do with the new time division effected by the work of Christ. See Part I, Chapters 4 and 5.

2

THE LINEAR CONCEPTION OF TIME IN THE REVELATORY HISTORY OF THE BIBLE AS CONTRASTED WITH THE CYCLICAL CONCEPTION OF HELLENISM

OUR STUDY of terminology has shown that in the Primitive Christian conception time is not a thing opposed to God, but is rather the means of which God makes use in order to reveal his gracious working. On the one side, time does not stand in contrast to God's eternity; on the other side, it is thought of as a straight line, not as a circle. Mention is made of a "beginning" (ἀρχή) and an "end" (τέλος). As soon as "beginning" and "end" are distinguished, the straight line is the suitable illustration to use.

All philosophical speculation concerning the nature of time, such as is carried on throughout the whole course of Greek philosophy without ever coming to a solution of the question,[1] is quite foreign to Primitive Christianity. Indeed, we can clearly define the conception of the course of time which the New Testament presupposes by stating it in opposition to the typically Greek idea, and we must start from this fundamental perception, that the symbol of time for Primitive Christianity as well as for Biblical Judaism[2] and the Iranian religion is the *upward sloping line,* while in Hellenism it is the *circle.*[3]

---

[1] G. Delling offers a summary in *Das Zeitverständnis des Neuen Testaments,* 1940, Chapter 1, pp. 5 ff.

[2] The situation is different in Philo of Alexandria, who also in this respect is strongly influenced by Platonism.

[3] G. Hölscher, *Die Ursprünge der jüdischen Eschatologie,* 1925, p. 6, has pointed out this radical contrast which exists between the eschatologi-

Because in Greek thought time is not conceived as an upward sloping line with beginning and end, but rather as a
circle, the fact that man is bound to time must here be experienced as an enslavement, as a curse. Time moves about in
the eternal circular course in which everything keeps recur-
ring. That is why the philosophical thinking of the Greek
world labors with the problem of time. But that is also why
all Greek striving for redemption seeks as its goal to be freed
from this eternal circular course and thus to be freed from
time itself.

For the Greeks, the idea that redemption is to take place
through divine action in the course of events in time is impossible. Redemption in Hellenism can consist only in the fact
that we are transferred from existence in this world, an existence bound to the circular course of time, into that Beyond
which is removed from time and is already and always available. The Greek conception of blessedness is thus spatial; it is
determined by the contrast between this world and the timeless Beyond; it is not a time conception determined by the opposition between Now and Then.[4] On the basis of the cyclical
conception of time, it cannot be determined by the time factor.

---

cal thinking of Judaism and the cyclical conception of Hellenism. For the
New Testament, Gottlob Schrenk, in " Die Geschichtsanschauung des
Paulus " (Jahrbuch der theologischen Schule Bethel, 1932, pp. 59 ff.) , a
work which is noteworthy for our problem in still another respect, has
distinguished the Pauline conception of time from the cyclical conception
of Hellenism (Posidonius) . In addition, M. Doerne, in " Annus Domini "
(Luthertum, 1936, pp. 17 ff.) , has strongly emphasized, in opposition to
Th. Knoelle and W. Stählin, the conception of time as a straight line. So
has G. Delling in Das Zeitverständnis des Neuen Testaments, 1940, p. 148,
where he refers to Aristotle's statement in the Physics, 4:14: " For indeed
time itself seems to be a sort of circle." See also J. Guitton, Le temps et
l'éternité chez Plotin et Saint-Augustin, 1933. Note further my article, " La
pensée eschatologique d'après un livre récent," in Revue d'Histoire et de
Philosophie religieuses, 1938, pp. 347 ff. On the other hand, it is confusing
when J. Jeremias, Jesus als Weltvollender, 1930, pp. 8 ff., accepts for the
New Testament the conception that world history proceeds in circular
movements.

[4] See on this point, E. v. Dobschütz, " Zeit und Raum im Denken des
Urchristentums " (Journal of Biblical Literature, 1922, pp. 212 ff.) .

In the Primitive Christian preaching, on the contrary, salvation, in keeping with the Bible's linear understanding of time, is conceived strictly in terms of a time process. The expectation of the coming Kingdom of God is not to be so dissolved that it means " always standing in the situation of decision." [5] Were that done, the event of the coming of God's reign would not be " an event in the course of time." The coming consummation is a real future, just as the past redemptive deed of Jesus Christ, in spite of the fact that it is the interpreting mid-point of all times, is from the standpoint of the Church a real past, and just as the present of the Church, stamped as it is with a thoroughly time-conditioned character, is bound back to this past and forward to that future.[6] The New Testament knows only the linear time concept of Today, Yesterday, and Tomorrow; all philosophical reinterpretation and dissolution into timeless metaphysics is foreign to it. It is precisely upon the basis of this rectilinear conception of time that time in Primitive Christianity can yield the framework for the divine process of revelation and redemption, for those *kairoi* which God in his omnipotence fixes, for those ages into which he divides the whole process. Because time is thought of as an upward sloping line, it is possible here for something to be " fulfilled "; a divine plan can move forward to complete execution; the goal which beckons at the upper end of the line can give to the entire process which is taking place

[5] So R. Bultmann, *Jesus*, 1926; see especially pp. 49–54 (Eng. tr., *Jesus and the Word*, 1934, pp. 51–56). When nevertheless Bultmann holds fast to the view that the divine Lordship is " pure future," this is after all only a concession to the Biblical *terminology*. For a future that is stripped of its time character is no future. The " expectation of an end of the world which is to come in time " belongs, according to Bultmann, to " mythology " (*ibid.*, p. 53; Eng. tr., p. 56). It is really strange that there has been so much excitement over the appearance of Bultmann's work *Offenbarung und Heilsgeschehen*, 1941; this conception of " myth " is already essentially present in his 1926 book on *Jesus*.

[6] Moreover, the emphasis on our being " contemporaneous " with that event of the past, a position so dear to the heart of Kierkegaard, must not lead us to use this position to abolish the time character of the redemptive process. See pp. 146, 168 f.

all along the line the impulse to strive thither; finally, the decisive mid-point, the Christ-deed, can be the firm hold that serves as guidepost for all the process that lies behind and for all that lies ahead.

In Biblical thinking there exists, we may say, congenial harmony between the redemptive process thus understood and time thus understood. Indeed, we have seen that in the New Testament time is never spoken of in an abstract manner, but is always mentioned in connection with the redemptive process. The New Testament's favorite expression of "fulfillment," of the "completion" of time (πλήρωμα, πληροῦσθαι), also points to this connection and faithfully represents the rectilinear conception of time and history.

Because time in Hellenism is not conceived in a rectilinear manner, the scene of the working of providence (πρόνοια) can never be history as such but only the fate of the individual. History is not under the control of a *telos* or end goal. From this standpoint, in so far as the need of man for revelation and redemption is to be satisfied, it can take place only in the direction of timeless mysticism, which thinks in spatial concepts.

If today, in the prevailing attitude, the radical contrast between Hellenistic metaphysics and Christian revelation is often completely lost, this is due to the fact that very early the Greek conception of time supplanted the Biblical one, so that down through the history of doctrine to the present day there can be traced a great misunderstanding, upon the basis of which that is claimed as "Christian" which in reality is Greek. The root of the heresy, if we are to designate as heresy what is really apostasy from Primitive Christianity, is the dissolving into metaphysics of the Primitive Christian conception that redemptive history is bound to the upward sloping time line.

If Platonic Greek influence on The Epistle to the Hebrews were actually so profound and decisive as it is often asserted to be, it should show itself precisely in this central point. But, as a matter of fact, here also the invisible is thought of primarily in terms, not of space, but of time. The Epistle speaks not only of the Beyond but also of the *future* Jerusalem, of the future city (Heb. 11:10, 16; 13:14). Therefore it is said that we " wait " for it. To be sure, even now in the present an invisible process is going on, but it is a process that takes place in time; it therefore stands in connection with that unique process of the past and the future.

The first apostasy from the Primitive Christian understanding of time is not found in The Epistle to the Hebrews, nor in the Johannine writings. In this central question, as we have already seen in the discussion of the *kairos* concept and shall see again later,[7] these writings are not controlled by a Hellenistic slant. The first apostasy comes rather in *Gnosticism*.

The marks of ancient Christian Gnosticism are manifold, and can be classified in various ways. In the last analysis, they may all be traced back to the Greek, and so to an un-Biblical, concept of time. From that point of view the redemptive history can only be rejected as barbarism, or else it must be given a radically new meaning.

Thus it happens that in all Gnostic systems the following features go hand in hand:

1. Rejection of the Old Testament, both in its explanation of history as the creative action of God and in its claim that the history of Israel constitutes a redemptive history.

2. Docetism, which is not exhaustively presented in the theory that has given the name to this heresy, the theory according to which Jesus possessed only the semblance of a body but had no actual human body; its chief distinguishing mark is rather to be seen in its rejection of the judgment that redemptive history passes on the quite ordinary particular historical event that occurred in the incarnate Christ, and that includes the offensively ordinary fact of the death on the cross. Thus here also we have to do with the denial of the redemptive significance of an event that occurred in time.[8]

[7] See p. 89.

[8] We shall show (Part II, Chapter 1) that ancient Christian Docetism assumes two different forms. It is common to both that the redemptive worth of Christ's death is rejected, and in connection therewith the fact

3. Rejection of the Primitive Christian eschatological expectation, whose characteristic distinction in terms of time between the present and the future age is replaced by the Greek metaphysical distinction between this world and the timeless Beyond.

Whoever takes his start from Greek thought must put aside the entire revelatory and redemptive history. Hence it is not accidental that in the older Gnosticism, as in modern philosophical reinterpretations of the New Testament witness, all of the three Biblical positions named above are given up in one complete surrender.

It is also no accident, however, that among the theologians of the second century none fought Gnosticism with such acuteness as did Irenaeus, who with unyielding consistency carried through the time line of redemptive history from the Creation to the eschatological new creation. Down to the theologians of the "redemptive history" school in the nineteenth century, Joh. Tobias Beck, Joh. Chr. K. von Hofmann, Carl Aug. Auberlen, and Martin Kähler,[9] there has scarcely been another theologian who has recognized so clearly as did Irenaeus that

---

itself is denied. Especially favored is the theory according to which, in the instant at which the suffering of Jesus began, a substitution took place; Simon of Cyrene was crucified while Christ ascended to heaven (Irenaeus, *Against Heresies*, I, 24, 4; see also I, 27, 1). According to the Gnostic view, so complete an entrance into history as the suffering on the cross under Pontius Pilate presents is not compatible with the redemptive activity of Christ. We return to the question of Docetism in Part II. It is a real problem today; for it can be shown that Docetism is also present in all the modern Christological discussions in which a choice is made as to what is and is not central for salvation on the basis of this or that idealistic position, rather than on the basis of what the Gospels themselves present in the history that they transmit.

[9] In a certain sense the federal theology of Joh. Cocceius can already be regarded as the forerunner of theology presented as redemptive history (see Gottlob Schrenk, *Gottesreich und Bund im älteren Protestantismus, vornehmlich bei Johannes Cocceius*, 1923). Concerning the nineteenth century representatives of the theology which centers in redemptive history, see Gustav Weth, *Die Heilsgeschichte, Ihr universeller und ihr individueller Sinn in der offenbarungsgeschichtlichen Theologie des 19. Jahrhunderts*, 1931, and Folke Holmström, *Das eschatologische Denken der Gegenwart*, 1936.

the Christian proclamation stands or falls with the redemptive history, that the historical work of Jesus Christ as Redeemer forms the mid-point of a line which leads from the Old Testament to the return of Christ. Therefore also no theologian of antiquity grasped so clearly as did Irenaeus the radical opposition which emerges between Greek and Biblical thinking as to this point, namely, the question of the conception of time. Irenaeus is the theologian of antiquity who understood the Greek world in its innermost nature, and yet undertook no such violent reductions and reinterpretations of the New Testament message as were practiced, not only by the Gnostics, but also by the Alexandrian scholars Clement and Origen.[10]

It is by this contrast between the Greek and the Biblical conceptions of time that the unusually severe clash between Hellenism and Biblical Christianity is explained; in the same way is also explained the initial process of the Hellenizing transformation of Christianity.[11] These two things, the hostile clash and the Hellenizing of Christianity, constituted together

[10] In Irenaeus, to be sure, we may say that this rectilinear character of the redemptive history actually overreaches itself and collapses. Hence it comes about that Irenaeus does not understand the sinful fall of Adam as the positive act of revolt and disobedience, but rather ascribes it to the natural immaturity of Adam, as somewhat counted on from the outset; thereby, of course, its significance is minimized. For Irenaeus the line runs on in so straight a course that the break which resulted from the fall into sin is not sufficiently taken into account. Everything is merely fulfillment. With this is connected the fact that for Irenaeus the redemptive line strains so intently to its goal that on its course the intermediate period between the resurrection and return of Christ is not sufficiently taken into account. This becomes clear when Irenaeus, in interpreting the ancient Christian confession, transfers into the future the subjection of the "lordships and powers" which according to Phil. 2:6 ff. and the other earliest confessions has already taken place from the time of Christ's death. See my work, *Die ersten christlichen Glaubensbekenntnisse*, 1943, p. 56 (Eng. tr., *The Earliest Christian Confessions*, 1949, pp. 61 f.). Having taken this position, Irenaeus must then reject also the reference of the "authorities" of Rom. 13:1 to the invisible lordships who stand behind the State (*Against Heresies*, V, 24, 1), since no time is left to them for a temporary activity connected with Christ. On this subject see pp. 196 f.

[11] The contrast between Hellenism and Christianity is well presented by L. Laberthonnière, *Le réalisme chrétien et l'idéalisme grec*, 1904; and also in the already mentioned work by Jean Guitton, *Le temps et l'éternité chez Plotin et Saint-Augustin*, 1933.

the chief theme of doctrinal debate in antiquity, and fundamentally they have remained so to this day, in so far as modern
philosophical thinking roots in Hellenism.

There can be no real reconciliation when the fundamental
positions are so radically different. Peaceful companionship is
possible only when either Hellenism is Christianized on the
basis of the fundamental Biblical position or Christianity is
Hellenized on the basis of the fundamental Greek position.
The first-named possibility, the Christianizing of Hellenism,
has never really been achieved. Tendencies in this direction,
however, are found in the New Testament itself, especially in
the Johannine literature, which has its orientation in the redemptive history and whose time concept, as we have already
said, is thoroughly Christian and Biblical, but which, on the
other hand, takes up and Christianizes such Hellenistic concepts as that of the Logos.

Wherever in the course of doctrinal development there has
occurred a debate between Hellenism and Christianity, it has
almost always had its fundamental outcome in the realization
of the second-named possibility, the Hellenizing of Christianity. This has meant that the New Testament's time-shaped pattern of salvation has been subjected to the spatial metaphysical
scheme of Hellenism.

This is shown most tangibly — but not only there — in the
collapse of the Primitive Christian eschatological expectation.
In the confirmation of this fact we must agree completely with
M. Werner, who intensively studies this problem in his explanation of the origin of the Christian doctrine.[12] But against
Werner's *explanation* of this fact it must be strongly emphasized that this question as to how, under Hellenistic influence,
the collapse of the Primitive Christian eschatological expectation occurred must not be considered in an isolated way; it
must rather be given its place in the larger problem as to how
the entire Biblical scheme of redemptive history, in which eschatology is only one member, came to be Hellenized. In this
process of Hellenization we have to do with the question not

[12] Martin Werner, *Die Entstehung des christlichen Dogmas*, 1941.

only of the future but of *time in general*. For this reason alone it is misleading when Werner makes the nonoccurrence of the Parousia responsible for the process of Hellenization. This process affected not only Christianity but all ancient religions, even those in which there was no eschatology in the Biblical sense, and so no expectation of the Parousia. If, however, the debate with Christianity ran its course in a much more sharpened form than did the debate with any other religion, this is due precisely to the radically un-Greek conception of time which the Christian redemptive history presupposes.

Although Christianity shares this conception of time with Judaism and to a certain degree with Parsiism, our investigation will show that in Primitive Christianity the line of redemptive history is carried through as a connected and upward sloping line in a much more consistent way than was possible in the Old Testament. This is connected with the fact that in the New Testament the present also can be drawn into the redemptive process in a special way, as the "time between Resurrection and Parousia." An event of the past, the death and resurrection of Christ, is regarded as the decisive mid-point of the entire line of revelation, and in this way the connection of the future with what has previously happened is no longer left vague and undefined; rather now for the first time, on the basis of the fixed orientation to *that mid-point in time,* the line can be clearly drawn from the beginning on, in its unbroken continuity. The point of view that redemptive history presents is indeed found in the Old Testament, but nevertheless only in a preparatory way; it can be constructed into a straight and complete line only in the light of the fulfillment which has already taken place in time, in the death and resurrection of Christ. To this there is no analogy in any other religion, not even in Parsiism. That is the reason why the debate with Hellenism presents from the beginning the great problem of Christian theology.[13]

[13] In saying this I have also given an implicit answer to the objection which M. Werner, in the *Schweizerische theologische Umschau* for September, 1942, made in reply to my criticism of his thesis. In the *Kirchen-*

If we did not desire as a matter of principle to avoid all theological slogans, we would be tempted to oppose to the slogan of the " consistently eschatological " way of looking at the New Testament that of the viewpoint marked by the " consistently historical method of revelation." He who speaks only of eschatology sees the entire question in a cramped perspective.[14]

---

blatt für die Reformierte Schweiz, June, 1942, I had sought to refute Werner's assertion that the Hellenization of Christianity is explained only by the delay in the Parousia. My argument was that the process of Hellenization was a universal phenomenon in the religious history of antiquity; this process laid hold not only of Christianity but also of other ancient religions in which the delay of the Parousia plays no role. To this M. Werner, in the above-named article, objected that in no other religion did the conflict with Hellenism have such far-reaching consequences as in the Christian religion, and that this fact is explained only by the delay in the Parousia. The observation that the collision is here seen in a particularly accentuated form is correct, but it is explained, as we have seen, by Hellenism's radically different understanding of time, which excludes any and all revelation in history.

[14] In Karl Barth's discussions of the situation before time, above time, and after time *(Kirchliche Dogmatik,* II, Part 1, 1940, pp. 698 ff.) , we believe that we find (see pp. 62 f., 66) the last traces of a philosophical and non-Biblical statement of the relation between time and eternity. Yet it seems to us that in this section he has well shown the necessity of treating the problem of time *as a whole;* hence we are not to give a one-sided emphasis which treats the situation before time along the lines of the Reformers' theology, the state above time along the lines of the theology of the eighteenth and nineteenth centuries, and the situation after time ceases along the lines of " consistent eschatology."

3

TIME AND ETERNITY

THE CONTRAST which we have shown to exist between the Greek and the Biblical conception of time appears in a particularly clear way in the determination, so important for our problem, of the relationship between time and eternity. We must here refer back to Chapter 1, concerning the New Testament terminology dealing with time, and we must now go on to define more closely the conclusions there reached. We do this in order to show how these conclusions differ from the Greek conception, present above all in Platonism, of the way in which time and eternity are related.[1]

For Greek thinking in its Platonic formulation there exists between time and eternity a qualitative difference, which is not completely expressed by speaking of a distinction between limited and unlimited duration of time. For Plato, eternity is not endlessly extended time, but something quite different; it is timelessness. Time in Plato's view is only the *copy* of eternity thus understood. How much the thinking of our days roots in Hellenism, and how little in Biblical Christianity, becomes clear to us when we confirm the fact that far and wide the Christian Church and Christian theology distinguish time and eternity in the Platonic-Greek manner. This then has important consequences, and when the New Testament perspec-

[1] From another point of view, namely, that of a debate with the " dialectic theology," the problem is treated in a more philosophical manner by Hans Wilhelm Schmidt, *Zeit und Ewigkeit, die letzten Voraussetzungen der dialektischen Theologie*, 1927.

tive of redemptive history is thereby affected, it leads to a radical transformation of the Primitive Christian preaching.[2]

To Primitive Christianity, as to Judaism, the Greek manner of distinguishing between time and eternity is quite foreign. The reason is that here the relation between time and eternity is never the object of a speculation; if the relation comes to discussion at all, this results from faith in a divine revelation which is anchored in time. We have seen that Primitive Christianity knows nothing of timelessness, and that even the passage Rev. 10:6 is not to be understood in this sense.[3] From all that has been said in the two preceding chapters it results rather that eternity, which is possible only as an attribute of God, is time, or, to put it better, what we call " time " is nothing but a part, defined and delimited by God, of this same unending duration of God's time. Nowhere does this come so clearly to expression as in the already established fact that the word used to express eternity, $\alpha i \acute{\omega} \nu$ ("age"), is *the same word* that is also applied to a limited division of time; otherwise expressed, between what we call eternity and what we call time, that is, between everlastingly continuing time and limited time, the New Testament makes absolutely no difference in terminology. Eternity is the endless succession of the ages ($\alpha i \acute{\omega} \nu \epsilon s$). In order, therefore, to do justice to the Primitive Christian conception, we should possess a terminology that would take account of this fact.[4] Since such does not exist, we in what follows will preserve the usual terminology, but constantly remind ourselves that above the distinction between " time " and " eternity " stands the one time concept of the age ($\alpha i \acute{\omega} \nu$), which includes both.

Karl Barth also, in contrast to his earlier publications, lays very strong emphasis in his *Dogmatik* (Vol. II, Part 1, 1940,

[2] As in Martin Dibelius, *Geschichtliche und übergeschichtliche Religion im Christentum*, 1925.

[3] See p. 49.

[4] The demand for the introduction of a special terminology is also raised by H. W. Schmidt, *Zeit und Ewigkeit*, 1927.

pp. 685 ff.) on the temporal quality of eternity. But the philo-sophical influence which controls the conception of time in his earlier writings, especially in the Commentary on Romans,[5] is still operative in the *Dogmatik* of 1940; here still, in spite of everything, he takes as his starting point a fundamental dis-tinction between time and eternity, and refuses to regard eter-nity as " time stretching endlessly forward and backward " (p. 686). The time-marked character of eternity, which Karl Barth strives so urgently to bring out in this section of his book, is understood in the Biblical sense only when the symbol of the straight line is applied to both, to time and to eternity, so that this very time during which the creation exists appears as a limited portion of the same line, and not as something essentially different. Of this fact Karl Barth's figurative man-ner of expression fails to take account when he says that eter-nity " surrounds " time on all sides (p. 698), or " accom-panies " it (p. 702). Here emerges the danger that, after all, eternity may again be conceived as qualitatively different from time, and so as a result there may again intrude that Platonic conception of timeless eternity which Karl Barth in the *Dog-matik* is nevertheless plainly striving to discard.

Thus time and eternity share this time quality. Primitive Christianity knows nothing of a timeless God. The " eternal " God is he who was in the beginning, is now, and will be in all the future, " who is, who was, and who will be " (Rev. 1:4). Accordingly, his eternity can and must be expressed in this " naïve " way, in terms of endless time.[6] This time quality is not in its essence something human, which first emerged in the fallen creation.[7] It is, moreover, not bound to the creation.

[5] For the presentation and criticism of his earlier conception of time see Folke Holmström, *Das eschatologische Denken der Gegenwart*, 1936, pp. 212 ff., 325 ff., and especially Karl Barth's self-correction in *Kirchliche Dogmatik*, Vol. II, Part 1, 1940, pp. 714 ff.

[6] This holds true also against Folke Holmström, *Das eschatologische Denken der Gegenwart*, 1936, pp. 204 ff., who demands on p. 209 that the " naïve" concept of time (" chronologically limited duration ") be ac-cepted in Christian theology, but that the " naïve " concept of eternity (" endless duration of time ") be as decisively rejected.

[7] So Karl Heim, *Glauben und Denken*, 1934, pp. 376 ff. Also Walter Künneth, *Theologie der Auferstehung*, 1933, in which time is understood as a "creation" and as the "world form of the fall," and therefore as " identical in form and content with the existence of man " (p. 170). In

When it is said in Heb. 1:2 that God has " created the ages,"
the meaning here is not that "time" has been created; we
have rather the spatial use of the word αἰών, a usage which is
also attested elsewhere (see H. Sasse, in Kittel's *Theologisches
Wörterbuch zum Neuen Testament,* article on αἰών, p. 204).
The word is here identical in meaning with "world" (κόσμος).

If we wish to grasp the Primitive Christian idea of eternity,
we must strive above all to think in as unphilosophical a manner as possible. To be sure, there appears on the margin in
the New Testament a primitive beginning; the prologue to
the Gospel of John, in the opening verses, speaks not in the
historical tense of the aorist, but in the imperfect tense: " in
the beginning *was* [ἦν] . . . ," that is, before the Creation
(John 1:1). But the imperfect indicates only that at that time
no revelatory event in the real sense had as yet taken place.
Nevertheless, this series of events is already being prepared,
in the foreordination of God (John 17:24; I Cor. 2:7; Col.
1:26; Eph. 3:11). Similarly, on the outermost limit of that
which is reported in the New Testament, we hear concerning
a " Sabbath rest of God " (Heb. 4:9), where God will be " all
in all " (I Cor. 15:28). But by this too it is meant only that
the Biblical process of revelation then comes to its conclusion.
Only on the very margin of the New Testament is there mention of that original condition in which this process has not
yet occurred and of this final condition, following the eschatological drama, where this process is no longer going on. The
time of " rest " is never the really independent object of attention in the New Testament, not even — especially not — in
the Apocalypse of John. For it regularly belongs to the essential nature of the Bible that it speaks only of God's revelatory

---

this linking of time and sin the Greek time concept most clearly continues
to work; this is true, indeed, of by far the most of the theologians who
have dealt with the problem, including still Karl Barth in his *Dogmatik*
of 1940. In the next chapter it will be shown how sin in fact does have
something — indeed, a great deal — to do with the division of time, but
not with time itself. See Part I, Chapter 5.

action.[8] Accordingly, where the Biblical statements go beyond the beginning and the end of this action, this always happens only in order to show how God's revelatory action connects with that existence of his which lies before the Creation and after the end of the world. Hence, in the last analysis, that condition of rest which appears on the margin is after all fitted into the series of revelatory events, in that during the rest this process is first prepared and then becomes operative in its effects. The Primitive Christian preaching views that condition of rest only in the light of that process. The very consideration that all Biblical statements deal with God's revelation, with God's action, should keep us from proceeding to an understanding of the Biblical thought about time — the Old Testament thought as well as that of the New Testament — by taking as starting point a speculative concept of eternity; we must not start from an eternity concept which is separated from this revelatory happening; we must not start, for example, from a speculation concerning the "rest" of God. For this reason eternity can be conceived in Primitive Christianity only as endlessly extended time.

It should be added that the erroneous importation into Primitive Christian thinking of the Platonic contrast between time and timeless eternity has no connection with the few "marginal passages" that mention the existence of God before the Creation and after the end of the world. It connects rather with the Biblical distinction between the two ages, the "present" and the "future" ages. It is a favorite practice to identify the "present" age with "time" and the "future" one with "eternity." To this, however, it must at once be replied that the future age in the New Testament is an actual future, that is, a future *in time*. All talk about the coming age

[8] To the question as to the rest of God before the Creation, Calvin, as is well known, gave the answer which had already been given before him: "God was not idle, but was creating hell for curious questioners." Luther too rejected all questioning as to God's activity before the Creation with the answer: "He went into the woods and cut rods with which to punish good-for-nothing questioners!"

that does not take this time quality in full earnest is philosophical reinterpretation.

When Karl Barth, in his *Kirchliche Dogmatik* (Vol. II, Part 1, 1940, pp. 709 f.; cf. also Vol. I, Part 1, 1932, pp. 486 f.), makes eschatology into the "state subsequent to time," where "there will be time no longer," when he gives future character to this "state subsequent to time" only with the qualification that this holds good merely "from our point of view," and when he goes on to declare that the final state (τὸ ἔσχατον) is "still future" only from our point of view, there evidently lies at the basis of these statements a philosophical standpoint which is foreign to the New Testament. The Bible knows no other point of view about time than that of the revelation that has come to us; it regards a particular event as the mid-point of time, and so for this point of view future simply means future, and not a timeless eternity that is future only "for us." We believe that we are fair to the ultimate *intention* of Karl Barth when we stress the fact that upon the ground of the Biblical revelation everything divine, including God's eternity, can be seen only "from our point of view," that is, from the revelation that came to us in Jesus Christ in the years 1–30. Whatever ideas one may form concerning God's eternity "in itself," they must not destroy the characteristic perspective in which Primitive Christianity sees all revelation. This perspective is that of a point of time.

The time character of the future becomes especially clear from the fact that the eschatological drama, as it is pictured in the Apocalypses, including the New Testament ones, takes place in a thoroughly chronological progression; this is true in the more detailed Johannine and Synoptic apocalypses as well as in the Pauline eschatological passages. In this connection we must bear in mind not only the millennial Kingdom of the book of Revelation and the numerical data which point to the limited duration of certain events, but also the entire structure, which characterizes this process not as timeless but rather as occurring in time.[9] In these writings we hear of

[9] This should be emphasized also in opposition to the "timeless" exposition of the Apocalypse of John by E. Lohmeyer, *Die Offenbarung des Johannes,* 1926 (*Handbuch zum Neuen Testament,* edited by H. Lietzmann).

" afterward " and " then," and this occurs not merely in the book of Revelation, but particularly in Paul. Read, for example, the short passage I Cor. 15:23–28, and note the heaping up of expressions for time: " thereafter " ($ἔπειτα$), " then," " next " ($εἶτα$), " whenever " ($ὅταν$), " then " ($τότε$). Moreover, we dare not weaken the time character of the coming age by pointing out that after all, at the end of this whole process which takes place within that phase, God is " all in all " (I Cor. 15:28). The new age does not begin only then; rather, all that the preceding passage has announced concerning the eschatological drama already falls in the coming age. *Within* the new age the Lordship of Christ, which has been established ever since the ascension, *continues on in time,* until the Son himself at a definite time is " subjected to the Father who subjected all things to him." But independently of that fact, this conclusion that God is " all in all " signifies, as already said, only the end of the Biblical revelatory process.

Another reason why the future age cannot be taken as timeless eternity and contrasted with the present age is that the coming age is *not a mere return to the primitive beginning.*[10] In this fact also is shown its time character. In reality the New Testament, as we have seen, recognizes not only two but at least three ages:

1. The age before the Creation, in which the revelatory process is already being prepared in the divine predestination and in the Logos, who is already with God.

2. The " present " age, which lies between the Creation and the end.

3. The " coming " age, in which the eschatological drama falls. The first and third by no means coincide. In the first, the Creation is not yet present; it is only being prepared. In the third, the first Creation is replaced by the new creation. All this can take place only in a time framework that continuously moves straight forward; it cannot occur in the framework of a dualism between time and timeless eternity.

[10] The difference between the time of the beginning and the end must not be obscured by the foggy concept of " primal history." See p. 101.

In the next chapter we shall show how the two-part division is superimposed upon the three-part scheme. A decisive event is regarded as the mid-point of the entire time line. From this point, then, the entire section that lies before this center appears as preparation for this one point where time is fulfilled. The decisive red line in a thermometer of endless extension is there reached, but the thermometer itself extends still farther above the red line. The red line introduces a two-part division. This does not do away with the previously mentioned three-part scheme: before the Creation, Creation, new creation; but it is superimposed upon that scheme.

This, however, means that the worth of an epoch of time does not consist in its reference to a timeless eternity; each epoch has its own full meaning precisely as a portion of time. This meaning is recognized, however, only from the mid-point which itself is time. We shall show this for the entire line of salvation in Part II. Thus the reason that the present phase of time, which began with the resurrection of Christ and still continues, is of interest for redemptive history is not that it stands in relation to a timeless eternity which surrounds it; rather, it has its own worth precisely in its time character and in its connection with the fact of Christ's resurrection at a specific point of time.

The so frequently cited [11] and famous word of L. v. Ranke, that "every age is immediately related to God," is emphatically not meant in this New Testament sense. Instead, it carries the idea of relation to a timeless God, as becomes clear from the subsequent part of that sentence.[12] According to the Primitive Christian conception, on the contrary, the inherent worth of every epoch is determined by its relation to a central event in time.

[11] Here we should mention, among others, E. Hirsch, Karl Barth, Paul Althaus, Emil Brunner, and Heinrich Barth.

[12] L. v. Ranke, *Ueber die Epoche der neuern Geschichte*, 1917, p. 217. On this point see F. Holmström, *Das eschatologische Denken der Gegenwart*, 1936, p. 203.

4

GOD'S LORDSHIP OVER TIME

IT WOULD BE a fateful error to draw from the foregoing the false conclusion that in the New Testament the incomprehensibility of the endless extension of eternal duration in both directions was not felt. To be sure, we have emphasized that eternity is conceived as different from time only with respect to its unlimited character, and that as a result eternity is understood as an endless time line; by this, however, we do not intend to say that Primitive Christianity lacked the perception that this eternity, which is endless time, is only possible as a divine attribute, and by men can only be stated but not understood. This feeling of man's incapacity to conceive or even to survey the "ages of the ages" is constantly present. Nevertheless, even where it appears with particular intensity, eternity is conceived as a thing measurable in time, although it is endless and therefore known only to God.[1] "One day is with the Lord as a thousand years and a thousand years are as one day." With this saying, whose second part comes from Ps. 90:4, the author of Second Peter (ch. 3:8) gives a reminder to the impatient mockers. Here again the purpose is to assert, not the timelessness of God, but rather the endless character of the time of God, which he alone can grasp and which can be expressed only by saying that for God the standards for measuring time are different. He alone, indeed, can conceive,

[1] Hence the distinction which has such fundamental significance for H. Bergson has no relevance for Biblical thought about time.

survey, and control this endless line, since in its unlimited form it is only his own line. Only to him does eternity belong. He is the Lord over the ages (I Tim. 1:17). This his Lordship is shown in the fact that he alone knows the *kairoi* or seasons of his redemptive action, that he alone knows *the* day and *the* hour, which are unknown to " the angels in heaven " and even to " the Son " (Mark 13:32).

This Lordship is also shown in the fact that with God there are, on the one hand, pre-existence and predestination, and that with him, on the other hand, an event of the future can, in accordance with his mind, already be anticipated. Our own election, predestination, is a manifestation of the divine Lordship over time, and here already it is shown how the viewpoint of redemptive history affects the individual life of the believer in Christ.[2] The election goes back to a decision made long ago by God (Rom. 8:28 f.); indeed, the believer is chosen " from the beginning " (II Thess. 2:13). The salvation to which the believer is called, which for him will be decided only in the midstream of the course of the divine working and will be fulfilled only at the end, is already present from the beginning in God's foreordination; but it is present precisely as *fore*-ordination. It would be contrary to the meaning that is contained in this word if from it one were to conclude that there is a timelessness or superiority to time in the realization of our salvation. It is not the attainment of our salvation that is elevated above time; on the contrary, this attainment is completely bound to stages in time: divine foreordination — Christ's atoning death — the final glorification. But God is superior to time. He rules over time. From the beginning he is in control of these stages.

Thus I Cor. 2:7 speaks of " God's wisdom, the hidden wisdom which God has *fore*ordained from eternity to our glory." Thus the Son, who carries out this redeeming work for men, is with God from the beginning. " Before the foundation of the world " God loved him (John 17:24). Christ is already " fore-

---

[2] This question is to be treated in Part IV of this book.

known," before the foundation of the world (I Peter 1:20), as a sacrificial lamb, and in the creation of the world its Redeemer already takes part.

Although, as we have heard, Christ in his incarnation does not share in God's knowledge concerning the day and the hour, yet through his revealing and redeeming work he is the bearer of God's Lordship over time. In him the entire redemptive time can be surveyed. Hence it results that where Christ acts the future process is already determined. Thus already in his lifetime Jesus sees " Satan fall like lightning from heaven " (Luke 10:18), although manifestly the final victory over Satan is still future. Moreover, all Jesus' healings of the sick and raisings of the dead signify that he is victor already over Satan's kingdom: " If I by the Spirit of God [Luke 11:20: by the finger of God] drive out demons, then the Kingdom of God has already come to you " (Matt. 12:28). Those raised from the dead, the young man at Nain and Lazarus, must indeed die again, for they have not yet been raised to a " spiritual body." And yet in the presence of Jesus death has already lost its sovereign power over them. Particularly characteristic for this anticipation by Christ of the results of future events is the word of the Gadarene demoniac to Christ: " Have you come here to torment us *before the time?* " (Matt. 8:29). The demoniacs themselves thus note that here, even before the time, a decision is made whose effect for the kingdom of Satan still lies in the future.

It is the great merit of W. G. Kümmel to have shown that the temporal tension between present and future exists for Jesus even in the Synoptic Gospels, in so far as the future is there regarded as already fulfilled in his person, and yet is still awaited.[3] Hence the tense relation between this and the

---

3 W. G. Kümmel, *Verheissung und Erfüllung, Untersuchungen zur eschatologischen Verkündigung Jesu (Abhandlungen zur Theologie des Alten und Neuen Testaments,* No. 6), 1945. In addition to this unusually important work, see also his article, " Kirchenbegriff und Geschichtsbewusstsein in der Urgemeinde und bei Jesus " (*Symbolae Biblicae Upsalienses,* Vol. I), 1943. He here shows in a splendid way how an analogous

coming age, in the form in which Primitive Christianity later presents it for the time between the resurrection and the return of Christ, cannot be regarded as a mere " escape from embarrassment," intended only to cover up the disillusionment that resulted from the delay of the Parousia. It rests rather upon faith in the divine Lordship over time, which can be demonstrated in this same way, and independently of all delay in the Parousia, to be present in the Synoptic portrayal of the life of Jesus.

The Lordship of God over time, as it becomes manifest on the one hand in predestination and pre-existence and on the other hand in the Christ-event, signifies nothing else but that he, the Eternal One, is in control of the entire time line in its endless extension. It means therefore that in the action of Christ the entire line is influenced in a decisive manner, and that in the central event of Christ the Incarnate One, an event that constitutes the mid-point of that line, not only is all that goes before fulfilled but also all that is future is decided.

But also in the further development of the redemptive history, which sets in from this mid-point and thence moves forward, it is manifest that the Christ-event signifies a revelation of the divine Lordship over time as a whole. Thus the Holy Spirit is nothing else than the anticipation of the end in the present. This is clearly indicated by the Pauline designations " firstfruits " (ἀπαρχή; Rom. 8:23) and " earnest " (ἀρραβών; II Cor. 1:22; 5:5), but also by the speech of Peter (Acts 2:16 ff.) after the Pentecost event. In this speech the apostle, making use of Joel 2:28–32, interprets the outpouring of the

---

conviction exists in the Primitive Church, except that there the future is anticipated, not in Jesus, but in his Church. In dealing with this point I should prefer to emphasize especially the analogy, which seems to me to be more important than the difference. Kümmel seeks, by establishing the difference, to demonstrate the spuriousness of the logion in Matt. 16:18 concerning the Church. His discussion, on the contrary, seems to me actually to support the genuineness of this saying, especially since he is further of the opinion that Jesus expected an interval of time to elapse between his death and the Parousia (see the discussion in *Verheissung und Erfüllung*, pp. 38 ff.) .

Holy Spirit upon the Church as a sign of the fact that the "last days" have dawned, in other words, that a new time phase has begun, with which the redemptive history has come nearer to its conclusion. This eschatological connection of the Holy Spirit also comes to expression in the very introduction to the book of The Acts (ch. 1:6 ff.). There the disciples ask the Risen One concerning the date of the coming of the Kingdom of God, and in his answer Christ refuses this information, since the fixing of this date belongs solely to the omnipotence of God. However, he does point to that which for them in the present is alone important with reference to the end, namely, that they shall receive the Holy Spirit.[4] In the Spirit the end is even now anticipated.

Inasmuch as according to the Primitive Christian faith the Church now becomes the place where the Holy Spirit is active (Acts, ch. 2), the Church itself is included in the divine Lordship over time, and, so to say, takes part in it. For it now lives in this unique relation of tension between present and future, and it does so by reason of the Holy Spirit, who is powerful in it and who signifies the anticipation of the end.

In the Primitive Christian worship this anticipation becomes visibly apparent. For the essence of the Primitive Christian worship by no means consists only in preaching and reading of the Scripture in accordance with the synagogue pattern; rather, the specifically Christian feature in the Primitive Christian assemblies manifests itself in its clear goal, the building up of the body of Christ. Christ's resurrection body is to gain a definite form in the congregation. Therefore the high point of every Primitive Christian service of worship is the solemn meal in which Christ is present with his people.[5] On the

[4] The reference to the missionary activity to which the Holy Spirit impels the Church also has eschatological character. It is indeed the universal conviction of Primitive Christianity that the end will come only after the Gospel has been offered to all peoples. On this subject see pp. 157 ff.

[5] For the detailed demonstration of this, see O. Cullmann, *Urchristentum und Gottesdienst* (*Abhandlungen zur Theologie des Alten und Neuen Testaments*, No. 3), 1944. I there seek to prove that in the earliest

other hand, this solemn meal looks both backward to the Last
Supper of the historical Jesus and to the Easter meals of the
Risen One with his disciples, and forward to the end, which
already in Judaism had been represented by the picture of
the Messianic meal. Thus in every Primitive Christian service
of worship there occurs the thing significant for our problem,
that here in Christ the *entire* redemptive line becomes clear.
It is not as though the unique character of its development in
time were done away; but Christ grants to his congregation
assembled at table a survey of the interconnection of the entire redemptive process, and lets the Church share in its
fruits.[6]

To the same conclusion points also what is probably the
most ancient liturgical prayer, "*Maranatha*" ("Our Lord,
come!"), which was certainly understood in its double meaning as a prayer for the coming of the Risen One into his assembled congregation and at the same time for his coming
at the end, which is prefigured in the present coming to the
service of worship. Particularly characteristic in this regard is
Rev. 3:20. Here the Risen One says: "Behold, I stand at the
door and knock; if any man hear my voice, and open the door,
I will come in to him, and will sup with him, and he with
me." The thought here is certainly of the Eucharistic celebration, and yet in the framework of the book of Revelation what
is in mind is also the Messianic meal at the end of the times.
It may be shown as a general conclusion that the Apocalypse
is full of allusions to the Primitive Christian worship. Hence
this writing may definitely be regarded as one of our most important sources for the study of that worship; for example, the
entire vision on Patmos takes place on a "Lord's day," and
accordingly on the day when the believing congregation as-
sembles to worship God. In the worship of God there now

---

times an assembly of the congregation without celebration of the Lord's
Supper was unthinkable.

[6] We return later to this question of the worship service. See pp. 155 f.,
169.

takes place each time that which only at the end of the times forms the conclusion of the redemptive history. Thus also the Christian day of worship, the day of the resurrection of Christ, is called the " Lord's day," and here also the thought may be not only of the day of resurrection but likewise of *the* day of the Lord, *yōm Yahweh,* which is expected in the future.[7]

That which is true of the service of worship is also to be said concerning the sanctification of the individual believer. We shall show in a separate section of this book how the redemptive history works out for the individual. But even here we wish to emphasize that with regard to his sanctification the believer in Christ shares in the anticipation of the future. It is the fundamental motif of all New Testament ethics that upon the basis of the Holy Spirit, and by faith in the work performed by Christ, man *is* that which he *will become* only in the future, that he is already sinless, already holy, although this becomes reality only in the future.

Thus faith in the Christ-event already permits the disciple of Christ to " taste the powers of the future world " (Heb. 6:5) . He experiences in this way the Lordship of God over time. *This, to be sure, does not mean that the development of the redemptive process in time has become unimportant in its time quality for him who believes.*

When Karl Barth *(Dogmatik,* Vol. I, Part 1, pp. 62 ff.) speaks of the fact that the person redeemed in Christ already lives as such in the future or becomes " a contemporary of the prophets and apostles," while the sinner, on the contrary, lives in the past even when he commits the sin only in the future, he thereby points to the above-indicated New Testament situation; nevertheless, with this terminology he hardly does justice to the Biblical conception. For he here confuses with time itself the new division of time which has actually been made in Christ (see the next chapter) . Time itself, even in its further course, preserves its significance for redemptive history. The

---

[7] This latter point I owe to the work of Markus Barth, *Der Augenzeuge,* which was available to me in manuscript. (Translator's note: this work was published in 1946.)

new fact is only that the center of time has been fixed at another place.

For the believer it is of importance that he lives precisely
in the present with its quite particular relation to the redemptive history; he no longer lives in the past, not even that of the
apostles and prophets, and he does not yet live in the future.
To be sure, faith allows him to share at the present time in the
saving gifts of the entire time line, even in those of the future;
according to The Acts, the Spirit even now at times invades
the area of physical life, in healings of the sick and raisings
of the dead, a redemptive action which comes to its full expression only in the future. Thus the thing in question is not a
sharing by the believer in the Lordship of God over time; it
is not as though he were competent to leap over the periods of
time.[8] Even the believer remains in the present; this is shown
by the fact that his participation in specific future gifts of
grace is always provisional; the sick who are healed and the
dead who are raised, in The Acts as well as in the Gospels,
must indeed all die again, in order to be finally raised only at
the end. Thus the man of whom the Holy Spirit takes possession is not freed from his human inability to master time in
its endless extension; that is, the Spirit does not enable him to
escape from the period of time in which he is placed; He is
only the " earnest," only the " firstfruits " (accordingly an element of linear time, not of a timeless eternity) ; but the Holy
Spirit does permit the man to share in the gifts of the *entire*
redemptive line.

In yet another way, however, the Holy Spirit permits the
divine Lordship over time to become a reality for the believer.
He permits him to survey what takes place along the entire
redemptive line. Here again we do not mean that the believer
by his knowledge is master of all the time schedule of the redemptive process. This idea is everywhere expressly rejected

[8] This is also to be said concerning Kierkegaard's previously mentioned
concept of " contemporaneousness." See pp. 146, 168 f.

in the New Testament, and this knowledge is in a particularly emphatic way preserved for God alone, who in his omnipotence determines the *kairoi* (Acts 1:7). Even the knowledge of the incarnate Christ finds here its limits (Mark 13:32). The limitation of the knowledge of the Son is asserted only with reference to this question of chronology. The reckoning of hours and days is regarded as a completely blasphemous undertaking, which even the possession of the Spirit cannot justify. Yet the possession of the Spirit gives a survey of what occurs along the entire redemptive line. This is the result of the revelation which "now" is made to those who believe in Christ, in order that they may learn from the Christ-event to understand the successive stages of the entire redemptive history. Upon the basis of this revelation they learn to grasp the connection between what happens in the past, the present, and the future. They do not, indeed, survey the individual *kairoi* of the future, but they do know how the process proceeds and comes to its fulfillment. They also recognize the division of time on the basis of the fixed point at which Christ appeared in history. This is what it means when in various places in the New Testament it is explained that "the redemptive plan (οἰκονομία) of the mystery which before times eternal was hidden in God" "is *now revealed* to his saints, to whom he willed to make it known" (Eph. 3:9; Col. 1:26; Rom. 16:25 f.; Titus 1:2 f.; I Peter 1:20).

When Paul speaks of the "mystery," he means thereby the stages of the redemptive history. This expression, which is connected with the "redemptive plan," indicates that a special revelation was needed in order to gain this insight into God's plan.

This knowledge of the divine economy fills the apostle with wonder and causes him to cry, "O the depth of the riches, the wisdom, and the knowledge of God!" The "incomprehensibility of his judgments" and the "unsearchable character of his ways" for human understanding come to his mind precisely through his insight into the divine economy, an insight granted him by the Holy Spirit (Rom. 11:33). Just prior to this joyous cry of wonder he announces in this passage of Romans the "mystery" of the redemptive process, according to which the hardening of Israel promotes the "entrance" of the full number of the Gentiles, but lasts only until this function is fulfilled, whereupon at the end Israel also will be converted (Rom. 11:25 ff.).

This knowledge, which is "now" available in the Church to all members of the congregation by reason of the Holy Spirit who is at work in it, was already proclaimed in fragmentary form to the ancient prophets by the Spirit; they searched "what or what manner of time the Spirit of Christ which was in them did signify, when it testified beforehand the sufferings of Christ, and the glory that should follow." Thus writes the author of First Peter (ch. 1:11), and in the next verse he states specifically that in this way the Spirit gave the prophets an accurate survey of the succession of events in time; he did this by teaching them that the decisive action would not occur in their time but rather when "the Spirit from heaven" would be sent to the earth and into Christ's congregation, in whom the preachers of this plan of salvation then appear.[9] Indeed, the fact of this preaching itself belongs in this plan as an integral part of it. It is a decisive point of the redemptive history, at which this knowledge is made available to all believers in the Church of Christ. The author of the same First Epistle of Peter does full justice to the immeasurable greatness of the grace which this knowledge signifies, when at precisely this place he writes that "the angels desired to look into [those mysteries]" (v. 12). By this revelation all believers become prophets in this wider sense.

In addition, to be sure, there are also prophets in the narrower sense. To their number belongs the seer of The Revela-

---

[9] This knowledge, too, extends only to the general division of time into stages, not to definite dates.

tion of John. By this prophetic survey of time we may perhaps explain the difficult passage in Rev. 12:1 ff., where the seer speaks of the birth of the Messiah in the future.[10]

In summary, then, it may be said that God alone rules over time, for he alone can survey it in its entire extension, and measure it with measures which are as different from ours as the duration of a day is different from the duration of a thousand years. He as Lord over time can "compress" it (I Cor. 7:29: "the *kairos* is shortened"), inasmuch as he determines the duration of the different periods of time, the "ages." He, accordingly, in the exercise of this Lordship over time, can "shorten" the days, as it is said in Matt. 24:22. He alone fixes the terminal points of his *kairoi*. Although he mediates to believers in Christ the revelation of the decisive occurrence which has already taken place on the cross and in the resurrection, he does not permit them to overleap the stages of that process in the same way in which he himself controls time in its endless and immeasurable character; he does not permit them to do this either by their action or by their knowledge of the dates. He does, however, permit them, on the one hand, even now to "taste the powers of the future world" (Heb. 6:5), and so even now to experience as something working in themselves that which happens in the future but is now by God's act anticipated; he permits them, on the other hand, to grasp the redemptive process in its large stages and in its entire direction, and above all to recognize that through Jesus Christ, his cross and his resurrection, something decisive has

---

10 Eberhard Vischer, in *Die Offenbarung Johannis, eine jüdische Apokalypse in christlicher Bearbeitung,* second edition, 1895, builds particularly on this chapter to defend his thesis, according to which the entire writing is a Jewish book which only later was revised by a Christian. Even in this case the Christian reviser, who permitted this chapter, with its future reference, to stand in his now Christian book, must have given some thought to the matter, unless we are to assume that he made his revision in a thoughtless manner. E. Lohmeyer, in *Die Offenbarung des Johannes,* 1926, p. 106, believes that he finds in this chapter a support for his thesis of the "timelessness" of the Apocalypse of John.

happened with reference to the division of time, although time, even redemptive time, still proceeds in its normal calendar course. It will be shown in the following chapter wherein consists this division of time which is " now " announced to us, and how it influences our knowledge of the entire redemptive line.

5

THE NEW DIVISION OF TIME FROM THE CENTRAL POINT OF THE REDEMPTIVE HISTORY

WE HAVE SEEN that the Biblical time line divides into three sections: time before the Creation; time from the Creation to the Parousia; time after the Parousia. Even in Judaism we find interwoven with this threefold division, which is never discarded, the twofold division into this age and the coming one — a division that goes back to Parsiism. In this Jewish twofold division everything is viewed from the point of view of the future. The decisive mid-point of the two-part time line appears here as the future coming of the Messiah, the coming of the Messianic time of salvation, with all its miracles. At that point we find in Judaism the great dividing point that separates the entire course of events into the two halves. This accordingly means that for Judaism the mid-point of the line which signifies salvation lies in the future.

The chronologically new thing which Christ brought for the faith of Primitive Christianity consists in the fact that *for the believing Christian the mid-point, since Easter, no longer lies in the future.* This recognition is of immense importance, and all further considerations concerning the lapse of time lose their fundamental significance for the Primitive Church in view of the completely revolutionary assertion, which is shared by the entire Primitive Christian Church, that the mid-point of the process has already been reached.

We must constantly keep in view this difference between Judaism and Primitive Christianity, because it is decisive for our understanding of the Christian division of time. The mid-point of time is no longer the future coming of the Messiah, but rather the historical life and work of Jesus Christ, already concluded in the past. We now see that the new feature in the Christian conception of time, as compared with Jewish conception, is to be sought in the *division of time*. The conception of time as such is not different, for in both cases we have to do with the linear concept of time, in which the divine redemptive history takes place upon an upward sloping line. Common to both is also the threefold division mentioned at the opening of the chapter. Furthermore, in both cases that threefold division is cut across by a twofold division into this and the coming age.

The radical, momentous contrast has to do with this twofold division. It may be illustrated by the following drawing:

JUDAISM:

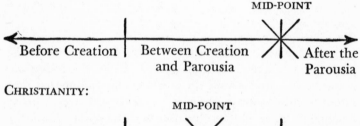

CHRISTIANITY:

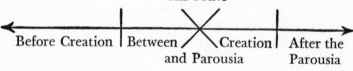

In Judaism, it is clear, the twofold division fits harmoniously into the threefold division, for here the mid-point between this age and the coming one coincides exactly with a division point that already exists in the threefold division, namely, with that point which separates the second section from the third. In Primitive Christianity, on the contrary, the threefold division and the twofold division literally "cut across" one another. Here, that is to say, the mid-point be-

tween "this" and the "coming" age does not coincide with
a division point of the three-part line, but falls in the middle
of the second section, where it creates a new division point.

The threefold division still continues to exist for Primitive
Christian thought. In it the Christ-deed has made no change.
But the twofold division has been changed by Christ. The second section ("between Creation and Parousia") is now split
in two. As far as the twofold division is concerned, the part
that follows the mid-point already belongs to the new age, although according to the still existing threefold division the
third section, that is, the final period beginning with the Parousia, has not yet come.

Hence the entire attitude of the Primitive Christian writings toward the problem that concerns us in this book is radically different from that of Judaism. The entire New Testament, including the Synoptic Gospels, holds the view that the
mid-point of time no longer lies in the future but in the past,
or in the present for Jesus and the apostles. This is true not
only in the sense that all New Testament writings were written after Easter — this also, to be sure, should be noticed, for
even the Synoptic Gospels were written in the light of the
Easter event, which had already occurred; [1] it also holds true,
as we have already seen, for Jesus himself. For him too, his
coming signifies that the mid-point of the process has already
been reached in his lifetime. Therefore he sees Satan already
fallen from heaven, he already expels demons "by the finger
of God," he heals the sick, he checks the power of death, he
forgives sins and explains that the Kingdom of God has already come, although he holds fast on the other hand to the
future character of this Kingdom.

It is for this reason that the proof which W. G. Kümmel has
provided in his above-mentioned writing, *Verheissung und
Erfüllung (Abhandlungen zur Theologie des Alten und Neuen
Testaments,* No. 6), 1945, is so very important; he shows how

[1] This method of considering the Gospels on the basis of form criticism
is to be used also in the study of our problem.

even for Jesus the preaching that the Kingdom of God is present stands with all emphasis alongside the preaching that the Kingdom of God is still to come.

How both things are possible at the same time, and whence the indicated tension comes, I believe must be explained by the fact that precisely in Christ time is *divided anew*, inasmuch as it has received a new center; and hence a new twofold division is imposed upon the still continuing threefold division. This signifies, as we have seen, that the center no longer coincides, as it does in Judaism, with the beginning of the last section of the threefold division; it falls rather in the middle of the section that lies between the Creation and the Parousia, while according to the still valid threefold division the final section only begins at a later time.

The expectation thus continues to exist just as in Judaism. What the Jews expected of the future is still expected of the future; but the future event is no longer the center of the redemptive history; rather, that center lies now in a historical event. The center has been reached but the end is still to come. I may illustrate this idea by an example: *The decisive battle in a war may already have occurred in a relatively early stage of the war, and yet the war still continues.* Although the decisive effect of that battle is perhaps not recognized by all, it nevertheless already means victory. But the war must still be carried on for an undefined time, until "Victory Day." Precisely this is the situation of which the New Testament is conscious, as a result of the recognition of the new division of time; the revelation consists precisely in the fact of the proclamation that *that event on the cross, together with the resurrection which followed, was the already concluded decisive battle.* In this faith-given knowledge, which likewise has as a result a harvesting of the fruits of that battle, consists that participation of faith in God's Lordship over time of which we spoke in the preceding chapter.

Upon the basis of this position, however, we must now say against Martin Werner, as well as against Albert Schweitzer, that the entire perspective in which they place the New Testament is not correct. They regard as the mid-point of the process the future coming of the Messianic Age, whereas the mid-point of time in the entire New Testament and *already for Jesus* is rather the historical work of Jesus himself. Accordingly, everything is to be explained from the point of view, not of the future, but of this event. It simply is not true that Primitive Christianity has the same eschatological orientation as does Judaism. To be sure, it has *also* an eschatological orientation. The Jewish expectation concerning the future retains its validity for Jesus and throughout the entire New Testament, but it is no longer the center. That center is the victorious event which the historical Jesus sees is being fulfilled in the exercise of his calling: " The blind see, the lame walk, lepers are cleansed, the deaf hear, the dead are raised, and to the poor the gospel is preached " (Matt. 11:5) . For the Primitive Church after the death of Jesus, the crowning act of this work is the mighty fact of the resurrection of Christ. No other point of time in the entire process, either in the past or in the future, can have so central a significance as this one does for men who are convinced that Jesus Christ has risen in bodily form as the first-born of the dead!

This cannot be sufficiently emphasized in opposition to the so-called " consistent eschatology." The primary thing is not the eschatological expectation, but this conviction concerning the resurrection. The expectation concerning the future remains such, to be sure, in its full time sense; but its fulfillment is no longer the central division point between this age and the coming one. The twofold division no longer fits neatly into the threefold division, but rather imposes a new scheme upon it. As a result, the New Testament solution, which proceeds from the assumption of a decisive battle already victoriously concluded, but which yet does not set an end to military actions as long as the armistice has not been signed, is not a solution resulting from an embarrassment that we would have to trace back to the " nonoccurrence of the Parousia " (M. Werner). It rather roots primarily in the thoroughly *positive* conviction that the mighty Christ-event has given a new center to time, and so it roots in the faith that the fulfillment has already taken place, that it is no longer the Parousia but rather the cross and resurrection of Christ that constitute the middle point and meaning of all that occurs.[2] The entire process that develops in time finds in these events its middle point, first of all in a pure time sense, but then also for purpose of orientation, that is, of giving meaning to the whole. Since the juxtaposition of " already fulfilled " and " not yet fulfilled " is already present with Jesus, it is clearly impossible 'to represent the Primitive Christian solution, in contrast to the eschatological attitude of Jesus himself, as a " solution inspired by embarrassment."

This conclusion seems to me to refute the entire New Testament basis of " consistent eschatology."

He who does not see that the radically new thing in the New Testament is the Primitive Christian shifting of the center of time can understand Christianity only as a Jewish sect. In reality, the Christian hope is not the Jewish one. To be sure, hope is also present in Primitive Christianity in its full intensity, indeed in increased intensity, although the event hoped for is no longer the center of time. The fact that the Primitive Christian hope is still more intense than the Jewish one might give rise to the erroneous opinion that, according to the New Testament, eschatology stands in a particularly explicit way in the center of what happens. Intensity and central position, however, are not to be confused. In reality, the increased intensity of hope in Primitive Christianity is to be explained by the very fact that the center of time is not in the object of hope but rather in an already occurred historical fact. This then means that the hope for the future can now be supported by faith in the past, faith in the already concluded decisive

---

[2] This is quite well seen by G. Delling also; see *op. cit.*, pp. 102 f. But when, on p. 106, Delling once more speaks of the overcoming of time, he again introduces un-Biblical categories into the New Testament.

battle. That which has already happened offers the solid guarantee for that which will take place. *The hope of the final victory is so much the more vivid because of the unshakably firm conviction that the battle that decides the victory has already taken place.*

With this decisive battle is connected the New Testament "expectation of the imminent end." This expectation, which is so much discussed by Martin Werner, really roots in the faith that the redemptive event has already occurred and been completed. It must be strongly emphasized that this faith is the prior ground of the expectation that the end is imminent. Therefore it is not true that this faith in a fulfillment that has already taken place in Jesus Christ is a "substitute" for the unfulfilled expectation of the immediate coming of the Kingdom of God; on the contrary, this faith produced the expectation. The essential point in the proclamation that "the Kingdom has come near" does indeed concern chronology, but in the closest connection with the knowledge concerning the already reached decision. The chief point in question, therefore, is not the limitation that the imminent end will come within a generation, although this limitation is actually present in the New Testament. The theologically important point in the preaching of the nearness of the Kingdom of God is not this fact, but rather the implicit assertion that since the coming of Christ we already stand in a new period of time, and that therefore the end has drawn nearer. To be sure, Primitive Christianity conceived this nearness to be at most a matter of decades and not of centuries or indeed millenniums. But this error in perspective, which in isolated passages is corrected in the New Testament itself (II Peter 3:8), does not constitute the theological content of the statement that "the Kingdom has come near." This statement has to do primarily, not with the determination or limitation of a date, but with the division of time of which we are speaking in this chapter. *The error is explained on a psychological basis in the same way that we explain the hasty determinations of the date of the end of*

*the war when once the conviction is present that the decisive
battle has already taken place.*

Thus also the three much discussed Synoptic passages, Mark
9:1; Matt. 10:23; and Mark 13:30, whose meaning, moreover,
is not clear,[3] do not deserve the outstanding significance that is
usually ascribed to them. Even if they have in view, not the
death of Jesus, but a date occurring some years or decades
after the death of Jesus, it still remains true that this erroneous
indication of date is not the decisive thing. The interpretation
of the Evangelists, who in any case referred the words to the
death of Jesus, is even then correct in a higher sense.

It is emphatically not true that the Primitive Christian hope
stands or falls with this expectation of the imminent end, although this would be the case if in fact the limitation of date
were the main point. We see this indirectly in the apostle Paul
as an example. He himself in his later letters altered his original opinion, expressed in I Thess. 4:15, that he would still
be living at the Parousia. In II Cor. 5:1 ff. he seems to reckon
with the necessity of passing through the condition of " nakedness," that is, he anticipates that the Parousia will occur only
after his death; this same situation is present in the letter to
the Philippians (ch. 1:23) , where, theoretically at least, he en-
visions the possibility of his immediate death. Here, then, it
might seem that the occasion had arisen for the delay in the
Parousia to change the entire time scheme of redemption. Yet
this change is precisely what did not occur. The hope of Paul
suffered no loss either in intensity or in its firm anchorage,
because from the outset its starting point had been that *the
center, the fixed point of orientation,* lies not in the future
but in the past, and accordingly *in an assured fact which cannot be touched by the delay in the Parousia.*

[3] See, as the most recent treatments of this point, W. Michaelis, *Der
Herr verzieht nicht seine Verheissung,* 1942, pp. 30 f.; O. Cullmann, *Le
retour du Christ espérance de l'Église selon le Nouveau Testament,* 1943,
pp. 23 ff.; and especially W. G. Kümmel, *Verheissung und Erfüllung, Untersuchungen zur eschatologischen Verkündigung Jesu,* 1945, pp. 13, 33 ff.

So also in The Second Epistle of Peter we observe that the delay in the Parousia is indeed recognized as a fact, since here, in the reference to the difference in the divine measures of time (ch. 3:8), a long interval is already taken into account. Here also the hope has preserved its full vitality. This again is possible only because the fixed anchor, the guarantee for the hope of the final victory, lies in the past as an already completed fact.

Therefore it is no contradiction when in the Gospel of John, beside the assertion that the judgment has already occurred (ch. 3:18), there stands the other assertion that it will take place only in the future, "at the last day" (ch. 12:48; cf. ch. 5:28 f.). He who thinks that we have here a contradiction and that therefore the eschatological verses just mentioned (there are still others) must simply be cut out of the Gospel of John as later insertions — an arbitrary solution, which, moreover, from a scientific viewpoint is highly questionable — has simply failed to grasp the inner nature of the entire New Testament thought about time. This thought is characterized by its orientation with reference to the new time center. To be sure, the Gospel of John emphasizes in a stronger way than do the other New Testament writings the decision that has already been reached; it places greater emphasis upon the judgment that has already been executed in man's faith or refusal to believe in Christ's completed work. But the hope of a last judgment is only more firmly grounded by the faith in this decision that has already been reached. Thus also The First Epistle of John cries to its readers with a special urgency: "Little children, it is the last hour!" It "is" (I John 2:18). Precisely because he can speak in the present tense, therefore, and really only for this reason, he can also use the expression "last," which implies the hope in the future. The way into the future has become visible only since the bright mid-point with its brilliant light has illuminated in both directions the previously dark line (John 6:40).

In the light of this Primitive Christian outlook, the entire

complex of questions concerning the expectation of the imminent end and the delay of the Parousia has lost its importance
in Primitive Christianity. It does indeed possess importance
from a psychological point of view, but not in its theological
bearing. This complex of questions can have theological significance only where the center of the time line lies in the
future (as it does in Jewish apocalyptic) ; and the criterion of
the Christian character of an apocalyptic viewpoint is precisely the question whether the center of the line is the crucified and risen Christ or whether it is the returning Christ.
Only where the Christ who died and rose forms the center do
we have Christian apocalyptic.[4] This, of course, does not mean
that the returning Christ has no place at all in the gospel. It
does mean, however, that in the Primitive Christian revelation
he receives his light only from the Crucified and Risen One.
He is no longer himself the source of light as in Judaism.

From the light of the mid-point illumination also falls upon
the line that extends backward. Here again there appears a
significant difference in perspective when compared with Judaism. This difference is connected with the new twofold division. In Judaism the entire history of Israel receives its light
from the future, from the coming Messiah, and this history is
regarded as having truly eschatological character only in the
literal, that is, future, sense. In Primitive Christianity, on the
contrary, the history of Israel is now illuminated from the new
center, that is, it is understood Christologically; but its meaning no longer has to do only with the final history; it refers
rather to the redemptive history. The line of the history of
the people of Israel is drawn down to Jesus Christ the crucified, as is done for example in the speech of Stephen (Acts
7:2–53). For the Jews also there already existed an " Old Testament witness to Christ," to use this expression of Wilhelm

---

[4] It would be interesting to examine once more from this particular
point of view the problem as to the Christian character of the Apocalypse
of John, a question which was so urgently raised by Eberhard Vischer,
in *Die Offenbarung Johannis, eine jüdische Apokalypse in christlicher
Bearbeitung*, second edition, 1895.

Vischer; but it existed only as a reference to the coming Messiah. Primitive Christianity, on the contrary, understands the Old Testament witness to Christ as a reference to the Messiah who has appeared in history with the name of Jesus of Nazareth, who was crucified under Pontius Pilate.

Still farther back, the light from this center falls upon the time before the Creation and upon the Creation itself. It too is no longer regarded only from the point of view of the future, so that Messianic pictures of the future and conceptions of paradise as " the golden age " simply coincide. Rather, the entire time before Creation is now regarded as preparation for the redemption in Jesus Christ; it is the time in which God has already chosen his own (Eph. 1:4), in which the same Logos who later becomes flesh is already with him (John 1:1 ff.), and in which the entire divine mystery of salvation, whose active agent is Jesus Christ, is already hidden in God's counsel down to the last detail of the destiny of the Gentiles (Eph. 3:8 f.). Thus, in Primitive Christianity for the first time, creation itself is regarded wholly in the light of the redemption from sin through Jesus Christ. Therefore everything is already grounded in Christ (Col. 1:16 f.), because through his blood this all will be reconciled (Col. 1:20). The same Christ who is to redeem the world from the sin into which it will fall is the mediator of its creation. Therefore Adam is mentioned as a first Adam, whom Christ follows as the second (Rom. 5:12 ff.; I Cor. 15:45 ff.).

We now understand why the divine Lordship over time, of which we spoke in the preceding chapter, becomes visible in Christ. We understand why there is in Christ the anticipation of the end, and why before the incarnation of Christ there is his pre-existent working. The revelation " now " given to the believers (Col. 1:26) and especially to the apostles (Eph. 3:5), that Jesus Christ the Crucified and Risen One is the mid-point of the process, is the very thing that permits us to recognize the Lordship of God over time. For in this interpreting midpoint of time is gathered up all that takes place (cf. Eph. 1:10:

" to sum up all things ") . This, however, does not bar the fact that this entire process in its earlier and later stages *must nevertheless unfold in time.*

This means that we cannot permit the word " mid-point " to be reinterpreted in a metaphysical sense, as Rudolf Bultmann has done with the word " eschatology." Even in the view that we have set forth, the mid-point, although at the same time it gives meaning to the whole, is conceived primarily in a chronological manner, that is, as mid-point in time. That which lies before it really precedes, and that which lies at a later point actually brings us nearer to the end with every day (Rom. 13:11) ; for even since the resurrection the redemptive time does not stand still.

Once more it becomes clear that we should not say that with Christ calendar time is abolished, so that past and future no longer have their normal calendar sense and so that sin that happens in the future is past.[5] The concepts " sin " and " redemption " are not to be substituted for the time concepts. The really characteristic thing for the New Testament conception is that, for the redemptive history also, the calendar continues in force *after* Christ. It is not " a new time " which is created after Christ,[6] but a new division of time. Because this division refers to the ongoing time of the calendar, or in other words, because the twofold division does not do away with the threefold division, there results the time tension in which we find ourselves. Thus we stand in a section of time in which we are already redeemed through Christ, in which we already have the Holy Spirit, who is characteristic of the new section of time, but in which also the sin characteristic of the entire period before the Parousia is not done away. Just as, before

[5] Thus Karl Barth, *Dogmatik,* Vol. II, Part 1, 1940, pp. 705 ff.

[6] Favoring this view, in addition to Karl Barth, *Dogmatik,* Vol. I, Part 2, 1938, pp. 50 ff.; Vol. II, Part 1, 1940, pp. 705 ff., are G. Delling, *op. cit.,* p. 101, and H. D. Wendland, *Geschichtsanschauung und Geschichtsbewusstsein im Neuen Testament,* 1938. In other respects, however, the latter book contains perceptions which are of great value in the study of our question.

Jesus Christ, the Holy Spirit, in isolated instances, is already present in the prophets upon the basis of the divine anticipation, but really only as anticipation of the final state, just so sin is still present. This is connected with the division of time, not with time itself, which continues to run its God-appointed course. That sin is still present, although the Holy Spirit is already at work, is definite proof that it is a "redemptive necessity" for time itself to continue in order to carry the redemptive history to its goal.

In conclusion, it must further be emphasized that according to the New Testament the new division of time, with Christ as the mid-point, can only be *believed*. To this fact in the last analysis refers the revelation of the "mystery" of the divine redemptive plan, concerning which it is said that it is "now" revealed (Eph. 3:5; Col. 1:26).

It is not correct to say that in Christ "[timeless] eternity invades time," "conquers time." We must rather say that in Christ time has reached its mid-point, and that at the same time the moment has thereby come in which this is preached to men, so that with the establishment of the new division of time they are able to believe in it and in this faith to understand time "in a Christian way," that is, by taking Christ as the center.

6

THE CONNECTION BETWEEN HISTORY AND PROPHECY (HISTORY AND MYTH)

THE SAME REDEMPTIVE LINE includes both historically verifiable occurrences and things beyond the reach of historical testing, such as sagas, which are set in a historical framework, or myths, which deal with the processes of creation and nature. At the outset it must be made clear that between these various items Primitive Christianity makes no distinction. In this respect it considers Adam to be upon the same plane as is Jesus of Nazareth. The genealogy of Jesus, Luke unhesitatingly traces back to Adam (Luke 3:23 ff.). The historical sense is completely lacking in the authors of the Primitive Christian writings, and hence for them a distinction between history and myth is *a priori* remote. This fact must be as clearly recognized as the use in the Bible of a now outmoded world view; nevertheless, it explains only how the placing of history, saga, and myth upon the same level was made easy for Primitive Christianity. It does not explain how it is that this redemptive line, as it is understood by Primitive Christianity, must *by its very nature* unite both things, history and myth. For this union there exists a positive theological ground, which retains its value even when we, in opposition to Primitive Christianity, distinguish between history and myth. We shall have to show, therefore, that while in itself the failure to distinguish between history and myth belongs as much as does the general world view of the Bible [1] to the framework of the limited possibili-

[1] With reference to this world view as framework of the Biblical narrative, see the discussion of W. Zimmerli, *1. Mose 1–11, Die Urgeschichte (Prophezei)*, Part I, 1943, pp. 12 ff.

ties of expression open to the Primitive Christian writers, yet the placing of history and myth together upon one common line of development *in time* belongs to the essential core of the Primitive Christian conception of salvation. The demonstration that a myth is not "historical" does not imply that the happening whose account it preserves is not "temporal."

If the connecting of so-called primal history and eschatological history with actual historical events were *only* a result of the formal inability of Primitive Christianity to separate the two, then the connection would become dispensable as soon as the historical understanding learned how to distinguish the historical elements of the line from the nonhistorical ones. Were the characteristic union of both elements dissolved, however, the line as such would then be destroyed; the history of the primal beginning and of the eschatological drama at the end would then have to be loosed, as being timeless, from that connection with the time development. This, indeed, is often attempted by theologians. The stripping away of mythology, which R. Bultmann consistently undertakes for the entire redemptive history, even the part that concerns actual historical events, is undertaken, when the distinction between history and myth is determinative, only for the actually "mythical" parts of the line, that is, the beginning and the end. Thus, for example, from the Genesis story only the "superhistorical" substance is retained. As the quintessence of the story of Adam there then survives only the ever valid psychological fact of human sin, and in like manner only timeless situations are derived from the other stories of the beginning and the end. But are not those histories robbed of their New Testament significance when they are thus stripped of their character as redemptive *history,* and when no account is taken of their connection with the remaining development? In the New Testament point of view is not the essential thing in the figure of Adam the fact that a second Adam comes *after* him (I Cor. 15:46; see also Rom. 5:12 ff.)?

Thus R. Bultmann has at least a more correct view when he consistently treats the redemptive process as a whole and demands that the same method of " stripping away mythology " be applied also to the section of the line that is accessible to historical study.[2] He thereby recognizes the fact that in Primitive Christianity the line actually forms a complete whole; it must not be torn apart by stripping away the time framework only from the beginning and end while leaving the historical middle section clothed in this time garment. Bultmann has seen that it will not do to limit the redemptive history to these parts that are open to historical testing. To be sure, we do not agree with him when he takes the redemptive history, regarded as a whole, to be as much a dispensable framework as is the outmoded world view of the Bible,[3] and so drops it, in the belief that he nevertheless can hold fast to the essential kernel of the New Testament preaching. Indirectly, however, R. Bultmann concedes implicitly, with a clearness that is seldom found elsewhere in theology, that in Primitive Christianity the connection of the historical events concerning Jesus of Nazareth with the nonhistorical account of the primal beginning and of the eschatological end is so close that the difference between history and myth is unimportant, not because Primitive Christianity possesses no historical sense, but because there exists here a positive theological outlook which transcends the contrast between history and myth.[4]

We now have to inquire concerning the positive principle of this connection. How does the harmonious association of history and myth upon the one redemptive line retain its validity when we know how to distinguish between them? In

[2] See pp. 30 f.

[3] See *Offenbarung und Heilsgeschehen*, 1941, the section concerning the " mythical world view," pp. 28 ff.

[4] Our conception of myth is not the same as that which Fritz Medicus represents in his philosophical study, *Das Mythologische in der Religion*, 1944. It is unfortunate that he does not take issue with Bultmann's demand for the " stripping away of myth," for had he done so the result would have been a closer connection between his philosophical discussion and the question that at this moment interests the theologians.

other words, where is the common bond that constitutes the theological union of history and myth? We shall first have to show that it is the concept of *prophecy*. We have to do with prophecy not only in the "mythical" stories of the beginning and the end, but even in the "historical" sections we are dealing not simply with history but with *history viewed from the prophetic point of view*. In the second place, we shall have to show that the initial process of creation and the eschatological process of the new creation are definitely not understood in Primitive Christianity as timeless mythology, but that rather they are everywhere spoken of only in connection with the historical process of the redemptive line.

The redemptive history as a whole is "prophecy." Here is the point that transcends the contrast between history and myth. By this we do not mean to say that there no longer exists any difference between the events that are narrated, for example, in the books of Kings, the Gospels, and the book of The Acts, and on the other hand those occurrences that Genesis and the Apocalypse of John relate. But from the Primitive Christian viewpoint of "prophecy" this difference is to be otherwise defined than it would be under the viewpoint of the modern distinction between history and myth. Both are prophecy; but the stories of the beginning and the end are only prophecy, while the middle section, which is open in part to historical testing, is prophecy of a kind that refers to facts that can be historically established, and it makes these facts an object of faith.

Martin Kähler,[5] who discerned the problem here treated, uses the word "saga" in approximately the sense that we here give to the word "prophecy." The expression "prophecy" is more in keeping with Primitive Christian thought than are the terms "saga" and "myth."

[5] See especially *Dogmatische Zeitfragen*, I, 1898, third edition, 1937, *passim*.

Narratives concerning the origin and the end of the entire process are *only* prophecy, inasmuch as objectively they are only the object of revelation and subjectively only the object of faith. A confirmation through human historical determination of the facts is not possible here. But that which is related in the Biblical books that are historical in the narrower sense is open, at least in part, to a historical testing that is completely independent of faith.

The most important thing is that in the last analysis even these historical parts are presented in the Primitive Christian writings not as " history " but as " revealed prophecy concerning history." This prophecy of the historical middle section is distinguished from the prophecy of the narratives concerning the beginning and the end only to this extent, that it makes historically verifiable facts the object of faith. Thus we have to do with prophecy in the presentation of the history of the people of Israel as God's chosen people. The facts here used are indeed open to historical testing. But the main fact, that Israel is chosen by God, no historian can test. The same thing holds true of the Gospels, which relate the history of Jesus the Son of God. Here, too, much can be tested by the historian. But the main thing, that this Jesus is the Son of God, remains concealed from the historian as such. Thus the Gospels, as the writings of the form critics rightly emphasize, are not biographies; they are rightly called Gospels. The book of The Acts, which is the history of the working of the Holy Spirit in the Church, is also, in the last analysis, prophecy. Here again we are not dealing with the actual writing of history, for it cannot be historically established that the Holy Spirit was at work in the historical events that mark the life of the Primitive Church and the spread of the gospel. But it is precisely this point that chiefly concerns the author. Without the presupposition of a revelation such a presentation of history is meaningless, and the interpretation which it gives of the history, that is, the thing that is the essential in it and that influences the entire presentation, can only be believed.

We therefore conclude that the entire intention behind the so-called historical narratives that deal with the redemptive history makes of these narratives prophecy, (and in this way corresponds in inner character to the nature of the primal and eschatological history. But to this fact a further bond is to be added.) Apart from the general character of the presentation, the so-called historical books or accounts contain within the historical narrative individual traits which as such are simply not open to historical verification; an example is the Virgin Birth. (In this respect also, therefore, these traits are in a class with the histories of the beginning and the end.) These individual traits, as " mere prophecy," are to be judged in exactly the same way as are those myths of the origin and the end; the only difference is that they are firmly embedded in the midst of the prophetic presentation of facts that are open to historical verification. They are definitely intended to bring out in a special way the prophetic character of this very history. At the same time, the connection is so close that in the Gospels, for example, it is not possible to make a distinction between such individual traits as are prophetically interpreted history and such as are only prophecy. Taken as one whole, they yield the picture of Jesus the Son of God.

Martin Kähler, in *Der sogenannte historische Jesus und der geschichtliche biblische Christus* (2d edition, 1892), distinguishes in this sense between " *historisch* " (verifiably historical) and " *geschichtlich* " (historical), and he correctly writes that facts, even when they are not verifiably historical, can nevertheless be historical. The writings of the form critics take the same standpoint, in that they treat the gospel tradition *as a whole,* that is, as a witness of faith concerning history.[6] To this witness belong also such narrative features as are not open to historical verification.

6 The consistent standpoint which R. Bultmann today represents in his book on *Offenbarung und Heilsgeschehen,* 1941, in which, as we have shown, he treats the whole of the redemptive history in all its parts as on the same plane, is also consistent in so far as he continues to maintain the standpoint of the form historian R. Bultmann (*Die Geschichte der synoptischen Tradition,* 1921, second edition, 1931).

The prophetic element in the so-called historical books thus manifests itself on the one side in the total prophetic interpretation of the entire reported history, and on the other side in the inclusion of purely prophetic individual features which support the total interpretation. It has thereby become clear that from a theological point of view the difference between the historically incomprehensible history of the beginning and the end on the one side, and the historically comprehensible redemptive history on the other, is secondary in importance to the confirmation that in both cases the thing ultimately in question is prophecy, is revelation, which appeals not to historical tests but to faith. The essential thing for the understanding of the Primitive Christian conception is not the confirmation that we, in distinction from the first Christians, know that Adam was not a historical personality in the same sense that Jesus was; what is essential is for us to perceive that the entire redemptive history, in both its historical and its nonhistorical parts, presents a single coherent process which develops upon the same advancing time line, and that on theological grounds this connection, in the view of Primitive Christianity, cannot be dissolved. In the preceding chapter we have seen that from the mid-point of time the light shines both in a forward and a backward direction. Now *this mid-point is itself prophetically interpreted history;* Jesus' death and resurrection are conceived as an atoning death for our justification and redemption from sins. Therefore the entire line must have prophetic character.

Because, however, the entire line gets its light from the mid-point, it in turn must have in all its parts the character of a development in time. As a matter of fact, the events of the primal beginning and the eschatological end are viewed only in this connection, the primal history as tending toward this mid-point, the eschatological history as proceeding from this mid-point. In the prologue of the Gospel of John and in the first chapter of Colossians the story of creation is presented in this Primitive Christian light.

Hence all speech concerning " primal history " is dangerous if by this somewhat confusing expression [7] the story of the beginning and the end are taken together and placed in opposition to the sphere of history, as though they were found, so to speak, " behind " all history in a timeless sphere.

The fact that what occurs in the beginning and at the end does not come into consideration at all apart from its time connection with the mid-point becomes manifest in the further fact that its chief content, the process of creation and nature, is in Primitive Christianity by no means limited to those narratives that portray the beginning and the end; it is also spoken of throughout the entire New Testament. This is possible upon the basis of the solidarity which the New Testament establishes between man and the whole of creation.

This solidarity is already present in the Old Testament and in late Judaism, when the sin of man is regarded as the origin of the cursing of the entire creation. " For the sake of man the earth was made," according to 4 Esdras 7:11 and Slavonic Enoch 58, but on his account it is also cursed (Gen. 3:17; 5:29; cf. Isa. 11:6 ff.; Sibylline Oracles 3:785 ff.; Jubilees 3:25). As the connection between the natural process and history, this solidarity makes its appearance in Ps. 74:13, where the sea monster is related to the Exodus from Egypt; on the other hand, it appears in apocalyptic literature, where the new creation is brought into connection with the significance for salvation of the people of Israel.

In Judaism this solidarity is not anchored in a time line whose mid-point is a historical fact. Therefore the connection

[7] In the use of this expression " primal history," thus interpreted, one has often appealed to Franz Overbeck. From his literary remains, however, it becomes clear that for him this expression is not at all a phrase laden with any theological meaning; he uses it in the purely historical sense to mean the history of the origin of a movement. On this point see Franz Overbeck, *Selbstbekenntnisse,* edited with introduction by Eberhard Vischer, 1941, p. 46.

between the historical process and the process of nature does not play the same role. Only in the Christian preaching does this connection become so close that now the eyewitnesses of that historical fact of the mid-point can assert that they have seen, heard, and handled the same thing that was *from the very beginning* (I John 1:1). Thus, on the other hand, in the Gospels of Matthew and Luke, we hear concerning that decisive moment when Jesus was crucified that the sun became dark and the earth quaked (Matt. 27:51; Luke 23:45).

The solidarity between man and creation is now no longer manifested merely in that primitive myth which deals with the subjection of creation under the man made in the image of God and with the sinful fall of man and the cursing of nature; it is concentrated in a historical act. " For it has pleased God," it says in the Epistle to the Colossians (ch. 1:19), "through him [Christ] to reconcile *all things* with himself, in that he has made peace through the blood of his cross, and through him to reconcile the creatures which are upon earth and those which are in heaven." In this sense it is actually possible from the New Testament standpoint to speak of a " Good Friday charm."

The entire creation now has its part in the special situation that is determinative for the present period between the resurrection and return of Christ. We have previously seen that this time is already eschatological time, although on the other hand it still belongs also to the old age; the Holy Spirit, this factor of the future, is already at work; death and sin are defeated, but not eliminated. It is the time of which it is true that it *still* waits, but on the other hand it is also true that it *already* waits. Precisely this is the situation in which Paul, in the eighth chapter of Romans, which treats of the Holy Spirit, sees the entire creation placed. Because for it also liberation is already decided on the cross, it shares in the present waiting of men; indeed, it shares even in the " groaning " of the Spirit for the consummation (Rom. 8:21 ff.). For even this groaning, according to Paul, expresses both things: the pain at the continued delay of the fulfillment, in which the Spirit will affect even the bodies (Rom. 8:11); and the joyous knowledge of the already decided victory.

That by κτίσις it is really the creation that is here meant,[8] and not man, as A. Schlatter[9] and E. Brunner think,[10] seems to me suggested by the clear reference to the Genesis story in Rom. 8:20. "For your sake," it is said in Gen. 3:17, and in Rom. 8:20 it results precisely from the taking up again of this "for your sake" (διὰ τὸν ὑποτάξαντα) that the *ktisis* whose cursing is here mentioned is really the creation. Moreover, v. 39 in the same chapter uses the expression *ktisis* to designate the invisible angelic powers. This too shows that *ktisis* here seems to designate specifically the creatures apart from man.

Very important for the close connection which exists on one and the same redemptive line between the process of creation and nature on the one hand and historical events on the other is the teaching, taken over from Judaism, concerning the *angelic powers,* the invisible beings who are at work behind all visible occurrences. How important this faith is for Primitive Christianity becomes clear from the fact that in all the ancient confessions of faith, from the first and the opening of the second century, it is said in a decisive place that Jesus through his deed has defeated and subjected these invisible powers. The faith in the existence of invisible powers represents in the New Testament more than merely a "concession to Jewish contemporary thought." We shall have to speak of this in Part III of this book. Here we must point to the significant role which the faith in the subjection of these powers at that historical moment of time plays in Primitive Christianity's close linking of prophecy and history. Since behind all historical present happening there also unfolds the invisible drama where these powers appear, it is clear how on this basis the

---

[8] So correctly also in E. Gaugler, *Der Römerbrief (Prophezei)*, Part I, 1945, p. 299.

[9] A. Schlatter, *Gottes Gerechtigkeit*, 1935, pp. 269 ff.

[10] Emil Brunner, *Offenbarung und Vernunft*, 1941, pp. 73 f. (Eng. tr., *Revelation and Reason*, 1946, p. 72).

line of connection with the primeval time and the final time
becomes particularly plain: with the primeval time when these
powers, " the visible and the invisible," were created in Christ
(Col. 1:16) ; with the end time when they, at least in part, are
destroyed (I Cor. 15:24), and are cast into the pool of fire
(Rev. 19:20; 20:14). In the present "historical" intermediate
period they are at work in the crucifixion of Jesus Christ
(I Cor. 2:8) ; so far as they subject themselves to Christ's Kingdom they also stand behind the legitimate political powers;
they are the "authorities" to whom the believers may and
should be subject, and of whom Rom. 13:1 ff. is probably
speaking.[11] Thus Paul can say that the entire struggle is fundamentally a warfare not against men but against invisible
powers (Eph. 6:12).

Although the existence of such powers is recognized, yet in
Primitive Christianity every dualism is excluded. This results
from the very fact that these powers are never spoken of in a
metaphysical or mythological way, but always and only in connection with all that takes place in time along the redemptive
line. According to this faith, even the devil and his host have
a history; but it is completely subjected to the history of salvation, and has the same center. Even before their subjection the
" powers " are indeed at work, but never as independent powers; rather they operate even here in the setting of their subjection through Jesus Christ, " in " whom they have already
been created (Col. 1:16). From the outset they are destined
to subjection, because in Primitive Christianity they are not
considered as metaphysical powers, but are viewed only in
connection with the redemptive history.

Thus the prophetic character of all historical utterances concerning salvation is shown in this reference to the angelic
powers. But on the other hand, even the Apocalypse, which
indeed is only prophecy and in which the angelic powers operate in a nonhistorical framework, is full of historical refer-

[11] On this point, see pp. 192 ff.

ences to the Roman Empire,[12] and thereby it is indicated that this eschatological drama as well as the initial process of creation is to be thought of as a development in time.

If, in conclusion, against the background of the uniform character that we have shown the entire redemptive line to possess, we nevertheless wish to formulate also the difference between the prophetically interpreted history and the purely prophetic parts of this line, and do so in keeping with the intent of the Primitive Christian preaching, then we shall say that the mid-point of the line *must* be history; indeed, the very reason why it is the mid-point is that here the becoming man, the incarnation, has taken place, and has reached its climax in the historical death on the cross. With this is connected the fact that the parts that lie closest to this mid-point, in a backward direction the history of Israel and in a forward direction the history of the Christian Church as the Body of Christ, are both prophecy and history. The history of Israel and the history of the Church thus really belong to the incarnation of Jesus Christ, the former as preparation, the latter as expansion. In so far as the primal beginnings and the eschatological drama do not belong in the same measure to the incarnation, it may be justified, even on the Primitive Christian view, to distinguish them from the remaining process of revelation.

The chief fact, however, is not this, but rather the recognition that the New Testament faith extends the historical incarnation even beyond the time of the actual preparation into the primal history, and in the other direction extends it past the time of the development in the Church into the history " of the last things," because even for these parts the histori-

[12] Thus the alternative: explanation by mythology or by contemporary history, which E. Lohmeyer, *Die Offenbarung des Johannes,* 1926, resolves in favor of the former, is not correctly stated.

cal event in Jesus is the orienting mid-point. The Primitive
Christian understanding of the history of salvation is correctly
understood only when we see that in it history and myth are
thoroughly and essentially bound together, and that they are
both to be brought together, on the one side by the common
denominator of prophecy and on the other by the common
denominator of development in time.

Only under the condition that this character of development
in time is respected may individual features of the primal and
eschatological history be regarded as mere pictures, which do
not necessarily affect the essence of the Primitive Christian
conception but only serve to give general clarity to the whole.
The difference of primal and eschatological history from actual historical occurrence may and indeed should be taken
into account. But its character as a development in time, which
binds it with the center to form one continuous line, must
not be destroyed. Where the primal and eschatological history
is raised to another, timeless plane, we then have to do with
a transformation of the Primitive Christian faith.

7

THE REDEMPTIVE LINE AS CHRIST–LINE.
THE MANNER OF PRESENTING IT

IT WOULD BE an error to believe that the entire redemptive history, understood in a Christian way, was at once revealed to the first Christians in the chronological sequence of its *kairoi*, as though they had learned it step by step — first that which happened before the Creation, then the Creation itself, then the history of Israel, then the incarnation of Christ, then the history of the Church, and finally the eschatological history. Nor is it the case that they learned to understand the entire process by beginning at the end and working back. Rather, the mid-point is also the starting point of Primitive Christian *understanding;* starting from that mid-point, the divine plan of salvation opened up in both a forward and backward direction. Thus the entire process of this Primitive Christian perception is likewise to be conceived in harmony with that pattern of movement which is presupposed in our way of reckoning time, whereby starting from the year 1 we use a double enumeration, " before and after Christ."

Nevertheless, in what follows we shall attempt to give a brief sketch of this Christ-line of redemptive history as it presents itself in chronological sequence.[1] For, after all, the first Christians did subsequently understand the line as a line running from the beginning through the mid-point to the end. Precisely this presentation of the chronological sequence is

[1] A detailed and masterly presentation of this sort is given by the recently published book of Suzanne de Dietrich, *Le dessein de Dieu,* 1945.

needed to show clearly that the entire line is actually constructed from the mid-point. From the beginning, indeed, it is a Christ-line, so that it is justified to speak of " Christ and time." This presentation confirms the fact that we should not begin to speak of Christ only at some fixed point part way along the line, as though previously one could speak only of God, without reference to Christ. Such a procedure would destroy the line in its magnificent unity of content.[2] The orientation by reference to the mid-point would thereby be surrendered, and there would enter into the divine plan of salvation a dualistic principle, which would completely obscure the very view of salvation that is characteristic of Primitive Christianity.

Even the time before the Creation is regarded entirely from the position of Christ; it is the time in which, in the counsel of God, Christ is already foreordained as Mediator before the foundation of the world (John 17:24; I Peter 1:20).

He is then the Mediator in the Creation itself (John 1:1; Heb. 1:2; and especially vv. 10 ff.; I Cor. 8:6; Col. 1:16). This is indicated by the commanding role that is ascribed to man in the Creation. Thus the Mediator of the Creation is the same one who as man, as " Son of Man," [3] is to carry out on earth the decisive work of salvation.

The election of the people of Israel takes place with reference to Christ and reaches its fulfillment in the work of the Incarnate One.

But the present redemptive movement also is the working of Christ. Christ's role as Mediator continues in his Church,

[2] From this position a special light falls upon the controversy between Emil Brunner and Karl Barth concerning nature and grace.

[3] Jesus' self-designation as " Son of Man " points to the role of man in the created order and thereby to the importance his redemption holds for all created things. Concerning the import of the Son of Man concept see also J. Héring, *Die biblischen Grundlagen des christlichen Humanismus* (*Abhandlungen zur Theologie des Alten und Neuen Testaments*, No. 7), 1946.

which indeed constitutes his earthly body. From it he exercises over heaven and earth the Lordship committed to him by God, though now it is invisible and can be apprehended only by faith (Matt. 28:18; Phil. 2:9 ff.).

Thus Christ is further the Mediator of the completion of the entire redemptive plan at the end. That is why he returns to the earth; the new creation at the end, like the entire redemptive process, is linked to that redemption of men whose Mediator is Christ. Upon the basis of his work the resurrection power of the Holy Spirit will transform all created things, including our mortal bodies; there will come into being a new heaven and a new earth in which sin and death no longer exist. Only then will Christ's role as Mediator be fulfilled. Only then will Christ " subject himself to him who subjected all things to him, in order that God may be all in all " (I Cor. 15:28). At that point only has the line which began with the Creation reached its end.

Thus we see that this is really the line of Christ: Christ the Mediator of the Creation — Christ, God's Suffering Servant as the One who fulfills the election of Israel — Christ the Lord, ruling in the present — Christ the returning Son of Man as the one who completes the entire process and is the Mediator of the new creation. The Pre-existent One, the One who yesterday was crucified, he who today exercises hidden lordship, he who returns at the turn of the ages — they are all one; it is the same Christ, but in the execution of his functions in *the successive stages of time in the redemptive history.*

In the New Testament and other Primitive Christian writings the line just sketched is seldom presented in this systematic way and in its chronological sequence. It is, however, everywhere presupposed, and it gives the key to the understanding of all that is said. Whether the discussion is of theological or ethical nature, it is always to be understood by reference to that line. The line of redemptive history is thus not

drawn completely anew every time a new subject is treated.
Often it forms only the unspoken presupposition; often reference is made only to the one point of the line that stands in
direct connection with the concrete subject that is under discussion at the time. Even where the connected line is fully
drawn, it is presented under the quite particular point of
view of that definite part of the contemporary New Testament
process which is being spoken of at the time and is to be
fitted into its place in that line. This, indeed, is the aim of all
Primitive Christian preaching, to assign to every concrete happening that occurs in the Church its place in the entire redemptive process.

This is the case as early as the Pentecost sermon of Peter;
here the Spirit-caused speaking with tongues is interpreted, in
connection with the prophecy of Joel, as a sign that now the
"last days," the final period, have been inaugurated (Acts
2:17). Stephen's defense deals with the disobedience of the
Jews, which they now manifest in their persecution of the
Christians who have given up the Temple worship, and he
fits their disobedience into the entire redemptive history as
the people of Israel have experienced it.

The discussions in the New Testament letters, especially
those written by Paul, continually point us to this line. For
example, note the discussion that in Romans (chs. 9 to 11) is
devoted to the election of the people of Israel; or the line
Abraham-Christ-Church, which is carried through in a particularly complete way in Gal., chs. 3:6 to 4:7; or the Adam-
Christ line, in Rom. 5:12 ff. Often only a small fragment of
the line is indicated, at times only in the direction of the past,
at times only in the direction of the future. Paul fits his own
calling as an apostle to the Gentiles into the entire redemptive plan.

That the Gospels report the life of Jesus only in the interest
of fitting it into its place in the redemptive history becomes
clear from their entire outline. This is seen when Matthew
places at the beginning a genealogy that goes back to Abra-

ham, and accordingly presents Jesus as the fulfillment of the
entire history of Israel; [4] when Luke introduces a genealogy
that leads back to Adam, and in this way establishes a line
from the Creation to Jesus; when Mark and Luke place at
the beginning the figure of the Baptist, which points both
backward and forward; when the Gospel of John, in the prologue, deliberately goes back to the Genesis expression "in
the beginning," in order to show that he who took part in the
creation of all things is the same One who later became flesh;
when, on the other hand, the Gospel of John as a whole follows the aim of tracing back the line from the Christ who is
present in the Church, and above all in Baptism and the Eucharist, to the history of the historical Jesus; and when Matthew closes his Gospel with a forward look to the world's end.

In thus anchoring the work of Jesus in redemptive history,
neither Paul nor the Evangelists introduced an element that
would have been strange to the historical Jesus. There are, to
be sure, modern presentations that deny that Jesus had any
consciousness that he was fulfilling for his people a definite
divine mission, and thereby was fulfilling the plan of salvation
which was God's purpose for precisely this people. But the
mutilation of the Gospel tradition which has to be undertaken
to make it fit this preconceived opinion is violent and arbitrary. In reality, the teaching and work of the historical Jesus
can be understood at all only on the basis of his consciousness
that he was fulfilling the role of the Suffering Servant of God [5]
as well as of the returning Son of Man. In the execution and
combining of these two tasks, as Suffering Servant of God and
as Son of Man returning upon the clouds, Jesus carries out
God's redemptive plan, which is presented to us as redemptive history. The Suffering Servant of God fulfills the meaning
of the history of the people of Israel, the meaning of which,

4 On this point, see J.-L. Leuba, " Note exégétique sur Matthieu 1:1a,"
in Revue d'Histoire et de Philosophie religieuses, 1942, pp. 56 ff.

5 It is my purpose to deal in a later publication with the fundamental
importance which the Ebed-Yahweh idea has for Jesus' so-called Messianic
consciousness. In my article on "La signification du baptême dans le
Nouveau Testament " (Revue de Théologie et de Philosophie, Lausanne,
1924, pp. 121 ff.) , I have indicated the extent to which the baptism of
Jesus gives us guidance at this point.

as we shall see, is contained in the principle of representation; in his role as the "man," the "second Adam," toward whom as the goal the creation of man in the image of God had moved, the Son of Man coming upon the clouds completes God's work of creation. The words of Jesus presuppose the redemptive history, not indeed as a dispensable framework, but as a foundation which cannot be replaced. That also after Jesus this history continues as a history in time is shown, for example, by the saying in Luke 16:16: "The law and the prophets until John; from then on the Kingdom of God . . ."

We thus confirm the fact that the entire New Testament presupposes a unified conception of the redemptive process. At times this conception is presented more or less completely; at times it is only indicated in passing reference; but it is always the ultimate theme common to all Primitive Christian writers, the theme that, in its various aspects and in all its theological and ethical issues, is unfolded in the individual writings of the New Testament.

The confirmation of the fact that the redemptive line in the New Testament is really the Christ-line, and that Christ does not merely appear for the first time at a definite point somewhere along this line, we find in the earliest confessional formulas that the New Testament contains.[6] These, indeed, possess a quite commanding importance for the fixing of that content of faith which the first Christians regarded as the indispensable and essential common foundation of the Christian message. Not only do these formulas go back to a much earlier time than do the first New Testament texts given written form, but by their nature they present a short summary of the central points of the preaching. When we investigate these earliest confessions, we find that the overwhelming majority are purely Christological, and that in the New Testament there is only a very small number of confessional formulas

[6] Concerning these earliest formulas and their origin, see my work, *Die ersten christlichen Glaubensbekenntnisse,* 1943 (Eng. tr., *The Earliest Christian Confessions,* 1949).

that mention both Christ and God the Father.

We must not be misled by the threefold division that is found in the later creeds, and is first attested about the middle of the second century. This division obscures the original orientation, which is completely Christocentric and is stated in terms of redemptive history. This does not mean that the statements concerning God the Father and the sections enumerated in the third article of the later creed did not also belong to the fundamental convictions of the Primitive Christian faith. However, the sharp separation of the three articles has here created, we may say, a perspective that does not correspond to that in which the first Christians summed up the fundamental features of their faith.

In the later formulation, " God the Father, the Creator of heaven and earth," is placed at the beginning of the creed; this is done in a way that could suggest that this divine work of creating the world stands, so to speak, upon another plane than the occurrence mentioned in the second article. In such a presentation we already have a later systematization, and it is no longer oriented to that completely Christocentric point of view stated in terms of redemptive history, which we encountered in Primitive Christianity's first confessional formulas. These teach us quite clearly that the first Christians did not derive their faith in Christ from their faith in God the Father, the Creator, but that on the contrary they also regarded this faith in the Creator entirely in the light of the Christocentric line of salvation. They teach us that the first Christians fitted even their faith in divine creation into the entire process of redemptive history.

Similarly, in the original summaries of the faith, the sections mentioned in the third article of the later creed, and above all the forgiveness of sins, are more closely connected with what Christ does than they appear to be in the three-part confession.[7]

---

[7] With reference to the forgiveness of sins, see I Cor. 15:3: " Christ died for our sins "; I Peter 3:18: " Christ died once for sins "; I Tim. 2:6: " who gave himself a ransom for all." See also Ignatius, *To the Smyrneans*, ch. 1, " nailed [to the cross] for us." As late as the Nicene-Constantinopolitan

Most of the New Testament formulas of faith, whether they are quite short, as are those of I Cor. 12:3; I John 2:22; Acts 8:37 (according to codex D) ; I John 4:15; Heb. 4:14; etc., or are developed in greater detail, as in Rom. 1:3 f.; Phil. 2:6 ff. (see also Ignatius of Antioch, *To the Smyrneans*, ch. 1; *To the Trallians*, ch. 9) ; etc., contain only one article, the Christological one. Particularly instructive for the question we here are treating, however, is the oldest two-part formula, in I Cor. 8:6, to which go back all the later formulas of more than one part. Here, indeed, is also mentioned the Father, " from whom are all things and we to him," in addition to the " Lord Jesus Christ, through whom are all things and we through him." But it is characteristic that the Creation is here treated in relation to both the Father *and* the Son. The functions of the Father and the Son are not yet separated here, as they are in the later creed, except that it says concerning the Father: *from* him and *to* him, while concerning the Son, the Lord, it says: *through* him. Christ as the Mediator of men is likewise the Mediator of the entire creation; this corresponds to the role that man plays in the creation. Father and Son belong to one and the same line of divine action, and indeed along its entire extension. The ancient confession of faith which Ignatius of Antioch cites in his letter to the Trallians (ch. 9) , and that which Polycarp cites in his letter (ch. 2:1 f.) , also mention the Father in the closest connection with the Christ-event, as the One who raised up Christ.

Thus on the basis also of this evidence we find it confirmed that the redemptive line is a Christ-line.

Creed it is said: " and crucified for us," although here the " forgiveness of sins " is mentioned again in the third article, in connection with baptism. In the great majority of the later creeds of both East and West, forgiveness of sins is mentioned only in the third article; it is no longer mentioned in the second.

8

THE DOUBLE MOVEMENT OF THE REDEMPTIVE
LINE ACCORDING TO THE PRINCIPLE
OF REPRESENTATION

THAT THE CONTINUOUS redemptive line is not a merely formal framework of which the Primitive Christian preaching can be stripped, but really belongs to its innermost nature, is shown finally in the further fact that the movement of this development in time is determined by a notably theological principle, namely, that of election and representation.

The thought of election and representation makes its appearance only in connection with the development that takes place on the time line which we have described. It is not possible to speak in the abstract concerning these central Primitive Christian concepts.

The redemptive line has as its presuppositions the divine revelation and human sin as the act of revolt against this revelation. Sin has a beginning as " fall into sin." This makes necessary a redemptive history in the narrower sense, for the curse that now rests upon man, and upon the entire creation connected with him, is not the last word of the God who is love. In his mercy he brings about a further time process which removes the curse of sin and death, reconciles man with himself, and likewise brings the entire creation to a new creation in which death exists no more.

The principle of this gracious process is that of the *election of a minority for the redemption of the whole*. Otherwise expressed, it is the principle of *representation*.

In his very position within the creation man appears, so to

speak, as the representative of creation. This is shown first of all in his Lordship over creation, but then above all in the fact, of which we have spoken, that the entire creation becomes involved in the curse.

This principle of selected representation determines in a very clear way the further development of salvation. Just as the destiny of the entire creation depends upon the action of man, so now in the first stage of the human drama the history of *one* people becomes determinative for the salvation of *all* men. Out of sinful humanity God chose one community, the people of Israel, for the salvation of the world.

In accordance with the same principle of election and representation the redemptive history develops farther, so that now a *progressive reduction* occurs. Since the people of Israel as a whole do not fulfill the mission assigned to them, there next appears a " remnant " as representative of the people; this is the " remnant " of which the prophets speak.

This " remnant " is further compressed and reduced to *one* man, who alone can assume Israel's role. In Deutero-Isaiah it becomes the " Servant of Yahweh," whose suffering is vicarious; in Daniel it becomes the " Son of Man," who represents the " people of the saints " (Dan. 7:13 ff.) . This One enters into history in Jesus of Nazareth, who executes both the mission of the Suffering Servant of God and that of the Danielic Son of Man; by his vicarious death he first completes that for which God had chosen the people of Israel.

Thus down to Jesus Christ the redemptive history unfolds in the above-indicated sense of a progressive reduction: mankind — people of Israel — remnant of Israel — the One, Christ. Up to that time the many tended to become the one; it pointed to Jesus Christ, who as the Christ of Israel becomes the redeemer of mankind and indeed of the creation. Here the redemptive history has reached its center. We already know that it is not thereby ended, but proceeds farther.

From that point, however, there appears an important change with respect to the principle of movement which we have discerned. This principle is still that of election and representation, but no longer in the sense of a reduction. Rather, all further development unfolds so that from the center reached in the resurrection of Christ the way no longer leads from the many to the One, but on the contrary *from the One, in progressive advance, to the many*. The advance so occurs, however, that this many has to represent the One.

The way, therefore, now proceeds from Christ to those who believe on him, who know that they are redeemed by their faith in his vicarious death. It leads to the apostles, to the Church, which is the Body of the One and now has to fulfill for mankind the task of the " remnant," the " people of the saints." Thus the development advances from this point to the redeemed humanity in the Kingdom of God and to the redeemed creation of the new heaven and the new earth.

Thus the entire redemptive history unfolds in two movements: the one proceeds from the many to the One; this is the Old Covenant. The other proceeds from the One to the many; this is the New Covenant.[1] At the very mid-point stands the expiatory deed of the death and resurrection of Christ. From the facts just established, it becomes still clearer that this is the mid-point. Common to both movements is the fact that they are carried out according to the principle of election and representation. This principle then is decisive also for the present phase of development, which proceeds from the mid-point. The Church on earth, in which the Body of Christ is represented, plays in the New Testament conception a central role for the redemption of all mankind and thereby for the

---

[1] In an unpublished thesis, submitted to the Geneva theological faculty in fulfillment of the requirements for a bachelor of theology degree and entitled *Révélation chrétienne et histoire du salut*, 1943, Jean Burnier notes in connection with a presentation of the theology of C. A. Auberlen that this double movement, which I had first established in *Königsherrschaft Christi und Kirche im Neuen Testament*, 1941, pp. 35 f., had already been observed in an analogous way by C. A. Auberlen, in *Der Prophet Daniel und die Offenbarung Johannis*, 1854. It is not without interest that I have come to a similar conclusion independently of C. A. Auberlen and by another road.

entire creation.

The double movement of redemptive history comes most clearly to expression in the sketch that Paul gives in Gal., chs. 3:6 to 4:7. He takes his start from the promise to Abraham. Then he shows how this promise, which is a promise to the descendants of Abraham, is realized as promise to the One, Christ (ch. 3:16), who effects the ransom by his vicarious death (ch. 4:5). This event has as its result that all men who believe in Christ can become descendants of Abraham (ch. 3:26, 29). Through baptism they all enter into the promise that had been given to the One. The way to the many is now open, but in such a way that the many are " all one," namely, in Christ Jesus (ch. 3:28). Thus they all now become sons and heirs (ch. 4:4-7).

The twofold movement further comes to light in the following two facts: first, the " people of the saints " in The Book of Daniel is designated as " Son of Man " (ch. 7:13 ff.) or, as the correct translation must be, as " Man," who is incarnated in Jesus the One Man; but second, this One " Man " (Rom. 5:12 ff.) is represented after his death in the people of the saints, that is, in the Church, his Body.

Thus in our manner of reckoning time, which numbers the year of Christ's birth as the year 1 and lets the previous period move with steadily decreasing numbers down to this year, while the subsequent period proceeds with steadily increasing numbers from this starting year, the New Testament redemptive line finds an astonishingly adequate symbolical expression; it does so in precisely this twofold movement that we have indicated. We really can find no better scheme to illustrate the Primitive Christian conception of time and history.

PART II

THE UNIQUE CHARACTER OF THE
REDEMPTIVE EPOCHS

ἐφάπαξ

1

THE UNIQUE CHARACTER
OF THE CHRIST–DEED AT THE MID–POINT

IT BELONGS to the nature of the *kairoi* that constitute the redemptive line that each of them corresponds to a unique unrepeatable fact. "Once" means in this case "once for all," for we are dealing with events that in their unique character are forever decisive. From the continuity of the entire line, which was demonstrated in Part I, it results that this uniqueness attaches to all parts of the redemptive history, and indeed we shall show that every point of time and every period of time, as far as it belongs to this line, has its own decisive value for the redemptive history. On the other side, it has nevertheless become clear that to the happening at the mid-point, even when compared with the remaining redemptive process, there attaches a unique significance which no other *kairos* can have in the same way.

From this state of affairs results a special problem, which we must investigate in this Part II, which we have entitled ἐφάπαξ ("once," "once for all"). *On the one side, this unique and "once for all" quality attaches to every point of the redemptive history; on the other side, the redemptive happening at the mid-point is unique and "once for all" in a special way.*

In the linguistic usage of the New Testament the word ἐφάπαξ is applied primarily to the historical redemptive deed of Jesus Christ (Rom. 6:10; Heb. 7:27; 9:12). Similarly used is the synonymous ἅπαξ (Heb. 9:28; I Peter 3:18). In Heb. 10:10 also, where it is said that we are sanctified "once for all" (ἐφάπαξ) by Jesus Christ's sacrifice, the thing in question is the single historical redemptive deed of Jesus Christ. To be sure, we already see here, if we connect the " once for all " not only with the preceding noun but also with the verb, how the *results* also of this unique deed are on their part uniquely decisive. Thus also in Heb. 10:2 mention is made of those " once " cleansed, and again, when in Heb. 6:4 it is emphasized that the benefit of baptism is given only once (ἅπαξ), that is, once for all, there emerges the noteworthy addition which consists in the fact that even after Christ's uniquely decisive deed there are still further uniquely decisive deeds, although this character attaches to them only in so far as they are grounded in the unique deed of Christ.

In the last analysis, we are already dealing here with the situation that is later designated as the problem of " Scripture and Tradition." In this formulation, to be sure, it could not emerge in the Primitive Christian period, since as yet there did not exist a New Testament canon of Scripture. But if the present phase, lying between Christ's resurrection and the Parousia, has its own unique value for redemptive history, and if it nevertheless remains true that the event at the mid-point, which already lies in the past, is uniquely decisive for *all* periods of time, then the theme that is an object of discussion between Catholics and Protestants is thereby implicitly given. We shall have to speak about this theme when we consider the significance of the present in the redemptive history (Chapter 4) .

First of all, however, we must understand the Christ-deed at the mid-point itself, and we must understand it in its unique character, which Primitive Christianity so powerfully proclaimed. The question as to the nature of this uniqueness involves the question of " history and prophecy," which we have already discussed in an earlier chapter.[1] The interrelationship

[1] See Part I, Chapter 6.

of history and prophecy becomes clear in this ἐφάπαξ, which can mean two things at the same time: " simply once as a historical happening," and " decisively unique for the salvation of all men and all times." In other words, it can mean both " once " and " once for all."

The offense of Primitive Christian faith nowhere finds stronger expression than in this assertion that the historically unique events of the years 1 to 30 have in relation to salvation the meaning " once for all." The prophetic view which sees salvation effected in a specific history is a view which, when referred to the entire line, represents " foolishness," but in this mid-point, we may say, it reaches the climax of the foolishness of which Paul speaks. The happening that here is designated as mid-point is concentrated in a very few years, which for Primitive Christianity are in the very recent past. The congregation of disciples which in the first chapters of The Acts we find assembled in Jerusalem is removed by a mere matter of days and weeks from the events that are to be regarded as the actual decision.

It is an added fact that this original congregation also lives in the same geographical setting in which the redemption is said to have been decided. Today that geographical setting has become for us " the Holy Land," and this concept constitutes for us a barrier which prevents us from understanding the complete extent of the offense. For us today the distance that separates us from those events, both the chronological distance of 2,000 years and the geographical distance between West and East, mitigates all too much the offensive nature of the assertion that on those events depends not only our own salvation but that of all men, and indeed of the entire creation! In order to grasp and understand the really astounding character of this statement, in order to appreciate what a difficult thing faith in the divine redemptive history was for Primitive Christianity, but also how overpowering must have been the impulse to this faith, we should overcome this feeling of distance as well as all such concepts as " Holy Land," etc., in order to place ourselves in the situation in which the first Christians found themselves with reference to the events narrated in the Gospels. We should picture to ourselves that this Jesus, who is to mean the salvation of the world, is clothed in such common modern dress as we wear and lives in the same everyday setting of a modern land as that in which we live; that he comes from a family whose relatives we see among us; and that, externally regarded, everything has taken place in just the way that we constantly see things happen among us. Then we could understand the question of Nathanael: "What good thing can come out of Nazareth?" (John 1:46). We need only undertake to put in place of Nazareth the name of any well-known, uninteresting village known to us in our immediate surroundings in order to understand what was demanded of the Jews when they were summoned to "believe" in this Christ, of whom they knew all too well "whence he came" (John 7:27) and who his parents were.

It was infinitely easier to believe in the redemptive history as long as its mid-point was still placed, as in Judaism, in the eschatological future, that is, in a time that could be *only* the object of prophecy and not at the same time of historical confirmation. We see also how very difficult from this point of view was the transfer of the center from the future into the past, and indeed into an *immediate* past. The faith that was asked of the first Christians was something much more difficult than the faith that up until then had been demanded of the Jews. Concerning the Messiah whom the Jews expected it was said that "no one knows whence he comes" (John 7:27; see also Heb. 7:3).

It witnesses, therefore, to a deep comprehension of the essential character of the specifically Christian revelation when the New Testament writers place in the foreground of the preaching precisely this exceedingly offensive point. This The Epistle to the Hebrews does, with its almost pedantically repeated emphasis upon the "once for all" character of the events narrated. This Paul does, when he presents as *the* great truth of revelation the " foolishness " of the preaching of the cross (I Cor. 1:18), the " offense of the cross " (Gal. 5:11); we should really call this the offense of the gallows, since for us even the cross is surrounded with a halo, while in antiquity it represented the most shameful manner of death, as does the gallows today. Furthermore, the Gospel of John actually seeks to scandalize the readers by using the coarsest possible expressions in order to show that the divine Logos really became flesh. Even the statement of the prologue that " the Word became flesh " shows this, when we consider what " flesh " signified for the Primitive Christian readers.

We now understand also that Docetism was *the* great Christological heresy of ancient times. It is really as old as Christianity itself, and is already opposed in the New Testament, not only in the Epistles of John but also in the Gospel of John.[2] It can be shown that the teachings of the opponents whom the letters of Paul attack also show Docetic characteristics. By their Jewish attitude to the law they prove that for them the atoning death of Christ is not the central redemptive event. Docetism, that is to say, did not first appear in the area of Hellenism outside of Palestine. The contrast usually drawn in textbooks between Jewish Christian and Gnostic (Docetic) Christology rests upon a great misunderstanding. For example, the Jewish Christianity with which we become acquainted in sources from the beginning of the second century, the Pseudo-Clementine *Preaching of Peter,* plainly contains Gnostic and Docetic traits;[3] yet in its main teachings it is not different from the heretical Jewish Christianity against which

[2] Concerning the connection between Anti-Docetism and the idea of the sacraments, see O. Cullmann, *Urchristentum und Gottesdienst,* 1944.

[3] The death of Jesus plays no role here. Christ is redeemer as bringer of a *teaching.* He is the " true prophet." See O. Cullmann, *Le problème littéraire et historique du roman pseudo-clémentin,* 1930, pp. 201 ff.

Paul fought. On the other hand, it must also be recalled that the Docetists whom Ignatius of Antioch opposed are likewise Jewish Christians.

It is altogether an error to believe that Docetism was a heretical *system* in which at any given time certain Christians were found united. It has to do rather with a heretical Christology, which we find in the most varied heretical systems. The etymology of the word "Docetism" gives too narrow a basis on which to characterize this attitude. Docetism in the narrower sense, as it is attacked in the letters of Ignatius, is really only one special form of a more general basic tendency which stands opposed to the Primitive Christian conception of Christ. Docetism in that narrower sense, derived from the verb δοκεῖν ("suppose," "seem"),[4] is the special teaching according to which Christ possessed a human body only in appearance. We here have to do with a Christological explanation which, by the very fact that the person of Jesus is discussed apart from his work, is entirely un-Biblical. This in itself, from the standpoint of the New Testament, is a heretical attitude. The New Testament knows only a Christology in which the work and person of Christ are connected and which thus does not consist of an abstract speculation concerning his nature.

Docetism, however, has received still another and quite different formulation, in which it is not limited to the person of Christ but also takes his work into account. The starting point here is not the theory that he had a body in appearance only. Christ's coming into flesh is recognized, but among the events that the Gospels narrate a selection is now made, and only certain ones are recognized as normative for salvation, while others are expressly rejected. To the rejected ones belongs, above all, the death of Christ, which is explained away by all sorts of fantastic theories. Thus in Irenaeus' report of the teaching of Basilides we hear that shortly before the crucifixion there took place a substitution, as a result of which

[4] See Ignatius, *To the Trallians,* ch. 10.

Jesus was able to escape death on the cross; it was Simon of Cyrene who was crucified. Jesus is said to have stood by and laughed at the deluded Jews.[5] Similarly, it is reported concerning Cerinthus that he taught that the Christ first entered into Jesus at the baptism and before the crucifixion left him in order to fly to heaven.[6]

The selection here occurs on the basis of a ready-made ideal view of the Redeemer. Into this ideal view various historical details that are reported concerning Jesus do not fit; this is true, above all, of his death, the great " offense," which in the Primitive Christian revelation represents precisely the central factor. The common root of both formulations of Docetism is thus the failure to respect the historically unique character of the redemptive deed of Christ. The theory of a merely apparent body on the one side, and the arbitrary discarding of historical data on the other side, are only two different means of attaining the same goal, that is, of removing from the center of the redemptive history precisely this offensive and typically unique historical event of the death of Jesus.

There already exists here germinally a position that in its very nature is completely foreign to all redemptive history.[7] That which is decisive for the salvation of man stands fast altogether apart from history. Redemption here is not a thing that occurs in time; it is an abstract teaching. The redemptive history as such is not the central and new revelation. The Docetics of both types already know everything in advance, and on the basis of this knowledge they then come to the redemptive history which has been delivered to them and subject it to their already fixed abstract scheme of salvation. The offense of the " once for all," that in a fact which is open to ordinary historical confirmation is to be seen the center of

[5] See Irenaeus, *Against Heresies*, I, 24, 4. A similar Docetic view is present also in the Koran. In quite another manner Rudolf Steiner distinguishes two natures in Christ.

[6] *Ibid.*, I, 26, 1.

[7] See Part I, Chapter 2, concerning the coincidence of Docetism with the rejection of the Old Testament and of eschatology.

all that occurs, is here completely removed; thereby is removed the very thing that constitutes the essence of the Primitive Christian proclamation.

For this reason the battle against Docetism was for Primitive Christianity the great life-and-death issue. Docetism had
attacked the very foundation with which the entire Christian
revelation stands or falls.

It is not only in Primitive Christianity, however, that we
find Docetism in the wider sense which we have discussed. It
has remained the one great Christological heresy down to this
day. One could show how in the Christological conflicts it not
only emerges again in the Monophysite teachings, but how in
general the Christological conflicts show an extensive slipping
away into Docetic formulation wherever the natures of Christ
are discussed in an abstract way and independently of his
work. Here we must agree with Melanchthon when he insists
that the knowledge of Christ is to be understood only as a
knowledge of his work in redemptive history.[8] Even where the
existence of the Logos with God is under discussion, in the
prologue to John, this is mentioned only with reference to his
role as Mediator at the Creation: "All things were made
through him, and without him was not anything made which
has been made" (John 1:3). And as far as the end is concerned, all speech concerning Christ ceases at the point where
his redemptive work is concluded, when he has subjected
everything to the Father and then subjects himself (I Cor.
15:28). All speculation concerning his natures is therefore
un-Biblical as soon as it ceases to take place in the light of the
great historical deeds of redemption.

One could show how Docetism is also present in P.-L. Couchoud, a modern French denier of the historical existence of
Jesus, who naïvely and in all earnestness believed that he was
doing Christianity a service when he sought to free it from

---

[8] *Hoc est Christum cognoscere, beneficia eius cognoscere, non quod
isti docent eius naturas, modos incarnationis contueri.* (This is to know
Christ, to know his benefits, not as those teach, to view his natures and
the modes of his incarnation.)

the materialism of a historical redemption through a man.[9]

More interesting is the continuing life of Docetism in all those Christological explanations of modern theologians who, instead of making use of all the redemptive facts which are reported concerning Jesus in the Gospels, make a selection among them, in order to recognize only certain ones, but not the others, as theologically normative. In so far as this choice is made on the basis, not of a picture derived from the Gospels themselves, but of an ideal picture which stands complete in advance, we have to do *mutatis mutandis* with the same Docetism as that which we characterized above as the second form of this ancient Christian heresy. In it one no longer has anything really new to learn from the Jesus Christ who appeared in history. Rather, the Biblical witness concerning the Christ-event is made subject to an ideal picture which is derived from some other source. Here again it is precisely the quintessence of the Primitive Christian preaching, the " once for all " aspect, which is set aside in a Docetic manner. It is instructive to investigate from this point of view the modern research concerning the life of Jesus. At the basis of the selection which is here made within the life of Jesus there lies all too often a philosophical, idealistic conception of salvation, which does not know what to make of that fact which for the New Testament itself stands in the center, the fact of the death of Christ.

We repeat in this connection that in rejecting this Docetic attitude we by no means intend to exclude every distinction among the facts that the Gospels report; we do not say that there was no center and no circumference in the Gospel tradition. Quite the contrary; the question as to the center we pose in all its sharpness. For its solution, nevertheless, there is but one way: to derive the criterion for the distinction *from the New Testament itself*. In our study concerning the earliest

[9] P.-L. Couchoud, *Le Mystère de Jésus*, 1924.

Christian confessions of faith we have shown how this is possible.[10] The reason that the establishment of *the earliest formulas of faith* seems to us so very important for all New Testament theology is that in these short confessions, where the concern of the Primitive Church was to formulate briefly only what was central, we possess *the only objective criterion* that permits us to make that distinction, because it is a criterion set up by the first Christians themselves. Every other criterion betrays a more or less hidden Docetism.

[10] *Die ersten christlichen Glaubensbekenntnisse,* 1943 (Eng. tr., *The Earliest Christian Confessions,* 1949).

2

THE PAST STAGES OF REDEMPTIVE HISTORY AND THEIR RELATION TO THE CHRIST–EVENT AT THE MID–POINT

IN SUCCESSIVE CHAPTERS we shall now seek to show that on the one hand the past, future, and present stages of redemptive history are themselves unique redemptive occurrences, but that on the other hand they are such only when related to the mid-point.

The entire past process from the Creation to Christ, as it is set forth in the Old Testament, is already a redemptive process. Before Christ, however, its straight-line orientation to a historical event is not recognized. In Primitive Christianity the Creation story handed down in Genesis continues to hold its place as a revelation of God. To the facts there reported, nothing is added and nothing is taken away; in this respect Christ brought no new revelation. The new feature consists exclusively in the fact that in Christ we are told that this entire event of the Creation is to be *interpreted* from that mid-point. As Paul writes (II Cor. 3:14), a veil lay over the books of Moses as long as this understanding was not revealed; in Christ this veil is lifted, for it is now possible to read and understand Moses from that center in Christ. Thus the New Testament authors wrote no new story of the Creation; they only showed its relation to the mid-point (especially John 1:1 ff.; Col. 1:16; Heb. 1:2, 10). We have seen how the linking of history and prophecy is connected with this latter fact.

The Gospel of John, to be sure, begins precisely as does the Genesis narrative with the words " in the beginning," and yet only an interpretation is offered here. Thus the Primitive Church did not do away with the Old Testament, as Marcion claimed, and hence, from the middle of the second century, there was to be in the Christian Church both an Old and a New Testament, which are both regarded as norm, as Holy Scripture.

The question that has recently been raised by Wilhelm Vischer's book on the witness of the Old Testament to Christ is actually a Primitive Christian problem. In the last analysis it is recognized by all the Primitive Christian writers. It is consciously posed and discussed in all sharpness by the author of the Epistle of Barnabas, in Chapters 1 to 17. He already saw correctly this problem, which results from the fact that the first Christians in their services of worship read the Old Testament and regard it as the canon for the Christian community; they thus treat it in practice as a *Christian* book.

Barnabas seeks a theological justification for the fact that although Christ has come, the Old Testament continues to exist as a Christian norm. He proceeds, to be sure, very arbitrarily in his manner of answering the question. Without attempting to penetrate into the deeper theological meaning of an Old Testament passage, he makes unlimited use of the allegorical method; he continually lays hold of this or that word or image of the Old Testament that is identical with a New Testament word or image. If anywhere in the Old Testament something is said concerning wood or a tree, he at once draws the conclusion that here the cross of Christ is meant. In doing so he pays no attention to the context in which that word appears in the Old Testament. If the Old Testament speaks of water, whether in the literal or in the figurative sense, then for the author of the Epistle of Barnabas it deals with Christian baptism. Chapters 11 and 12 may serve as warning examples.

Thus the author of the Epistle of Barnabas finds all the details of the life of Jesus sketched in advance in the Old Testament: the evildoers who are crucified with Jesus, the giving of sour wine to drink, the mocking, the crucifixion scene itself. When in this way the external, historically unique framework of the entire history of the incarnate Christ has to be found at any cost in the Old Testament, this is a falsely understood witness of the Old Testament to Christ. The Old Testament here becomes a book of riddles, and its content, in so far as it is a revelation of a redemptive history which moves toward Christ as its goal, is deprived of its value. In the conception of the Epistle of Barnabas, the Old Testament no longer offers a revelation concerning the time before Christ, that is, the time of the preparation for Christ, but gives only *a veiled presentation of the events of the life of Jesus himself.*

By such a procedure the view of the Old Testament as redemptive history is completely abandoned. Thereby, indeed, the New Testament has really become superfluous. The unexpressed presupposition of all purely allegorical explanation is that in the books to be interpreted the line of development in time has no importance, but that on the contrary these books contain hidden, *timeless* truths, and that accordingly, in our case, everything that the Gospels report is without exception to be found also in the Old Testament, if only one knows how to use rightly the allegorical method. Thus fundamentally the New Testament writings are made dispensable in advance. The Old Testament already contains the "life of Jesus." By this means not only is the redemptive history that the Old Testament contains dissolved as such, but even the unique incarnation of Jesus Christ and the unique apostolic preaching of this incarnation are no longer taken seriously. In the last analysis, a Docetic attitude is present in the Epistle of Barnabas.[1] For the "new" content of the New Testament there is here no longer any room, since everything is already present in the riddle book of the Old Testament.

It is stimulating to note that one of the modern French deniers of the historical existence of Jesus, Prosper Alfaric,

[1] Recently Karl Thieme, *Kirche und Synagoge*, 1945, has rightly drawn attention to this ancient Christian writing. But he wrongly approves without qualification the undertaking that is therein attempted.

attempts to find the entire content of the Gospel of Mark, down to the very details, in the Old Testament. He holds that the entire Gospel of Mark had its origin in statements of the Old Testament which were later " manufactured into history "; it has no basis in historical occurrence.[2] In this view we have simply the extreme result of an attitude which *mutatis mutandis* is present in the Epistle of Barnabas.

I have purposely dealt in greater detail with the Epistle of Barnabas, because precisely this writing shows us how the past stages of redemptive history, and their relation to the Christ-event at the mid-point, are *not* to be understood when we place them in connection with the general New Testament view of redemptive history. The rejection of the outlook that is present in the Epistle of Barnabas should permit us to determine in a positive way the relation between the past and the mid-point of the redemptive line. In the Epistle of Barnabas the Primitive Christian concept of fulfillment is not taken seriously. *From this standpoint Old and New Testament are interchangeable.*

When Paul says that what is presented in the Old Testament was " written for our sakes " (Rom. 4:24; 15:4; I Cor. 9:10; 10:11), the passage I Cor. 9:10 does indeed contain an idea that could point in the direction of the conception that the Epistle of Barnabas presents. Nevertheless, the original purpose here, after all, is not to obliterate the time distinction between Old and New Covenant; it is rather to refer to the fact that the Old Testament course of events, which as a historical process has its own significance in the redemptive history, constitutes precisely in this its distinctive character a *preparation for Christ;* that is, it prepares for the interpreting mid-point of the entire redemptive process.

The preservation of the Old Testament has its inner justification in the fact that it is regarded as a *preparation in time* for this Christ-event, not in that it is regarded as a parallel

[2] P. Alfaric, *L'Évangile selon Marc,* 1929; *Pour comprendre la vie de Jésus,* 1929.

presentation of the same thing in another form.

The possibility for the false conception to arise that the Old Testament already contains everything that is to be said concerning Jesus of Nazareth may be connected with the fact that in the first period of the Christian Church there did not yet exist a New Testament as a canon. Just because the Old Testament was the only available canon, Christians desired to see preserved in it also the contemporary facts of redemptive history. In reality, however, this procedure does not correspond to the actual understanding that the Primitive Church had of the Old Testament's relation to the redemptive history. This understanding rather takes into account the important fact that the Old Testament speaks, not of the incarnate Jesus, but of the pre-existent one; it speaks of the preparation for the incarnation in pre-Christian redemptive history.

The recognition that *the entire redemptive history of the Old Testament tends toward the goal of the incarnation* is the understanding that should now be possible in Christ. This is the correctly understood witness of the Old Testament to Christ, rather than the assumption that the Old and New Testaments are identical in time reference. The Old Testament offers another part of the redemptive history than does the New. It is itself first of all a unique story of what once happened. But its meaning for redemptive history is recognized only when this entire section of time is placed in relation with the unique, once-for-all event of the mid-point, and this relation may be understood only as a relationship, conceived in a strict time sense, between *preparation* and *fulfillment*.

To find the witness to Christ in the Old Testament does not mean, then, to find the incarnation of Jesus in the Old Testament. It means rather to learn, upon the basis of our knowledge concerning the incarnate and crucified Christ, how to understand the past events of redemptive history as preparation for the incarnation and the cross.

This applies to the history of the Creation as well as to the history of the people of Israel. We have seen how, on the basis of the orientation to the mid-point in time, there results a Christ-line, without the Old Testament being dissolved in allegory. The Creation is preserved as an event, the history of Israel as history, but the whole is interpreted in a prophetic manner, that is, so as to point to Christ. This interpretation, which combines Creation, primitive sagas, and history, has only now become possible, because only now, in Christ, have we gained the criterion for interpreting and orienting the entire process in a concrete way.

Even before Jesus there was, to be sure, a prophetic interpretation of the entire Old Testament process; the election of the people of Israel was already revealed. But the fulfillment of this election came only in the historical event of the death on the cross, and so in the revelation of the New Covenant. Therefore it is only by reference to Jesus of Nazareth, who was crucified under Pontius Pilate, that the entire Old Testament can be interpreted as pointing to Jesus Christ. Only now can it be shown how sin and redemption, which constitute the theme of all the process, make necessary from the outset this particular process, which has as its goal an incarnate and crucified Christ, and which *develops in a time process* to the incarnation and the crucifixion.

Moreover, the expressions "reference" and "indication," and particularly the finger of the Baptist in the famous Grünewald picture which Wilhelm Vischer has significantly included in the first volume of his work on the witness of the Old Testament to Christ, are misunderstood when this element of development in time is not kept in mind. These expressions must not be interpreted as though everything that takes place on the cross were already present — though only in a hidden manner — in the Old Covenant. In the Old Testament it is not the cross itself, but the temporal preparation for the cross, over which lies a veil that only in Christ is removed (II Cor. 3:14).

An objection here appears: How can such a temporal development, which is nothing but preparation, continue to have meaning for the actual salvation of the believer in Christ, after the thing prepared has in the meantime been realized in time? The answer to this is the observation that we have placed at the beginning of this chapter: only both things together, the particular significance of this unique past for redemptive history (preparation) *and* its connection with the unique mid-point (fulfillment), bring it about in the New Testament that this past as such, as " Old " Testament, preserves its actual redemptive value.

The Christ-event at the mid-point, that is to say, is on its part illuminated by the Old Testament preparation, after this preparation has first received its light from that very mid-point. We have to do here with a circle. The death and resurrection of Christ enable the believer to see in the history of Adam and in the history of Israel the preparation for Jesus, the Crucified and Risen One. But only the thus understood history of Adam and the thus understood history of Israel enable the believer to grasp the work of Jesus Christ, the Crucified and Risen One, in connection with the divine plan of salvation. Therefore the Old Testament continues to be actual revelation even for the Christian Church, to which the revelation in Jesus Christ himself has already been given. This is the use that Primitive Christianity makes of the Old Testament in understanding the redemptive history.

It would be the task of a New Testament theology to show in detail how, viewed in the Christian light, it becomes clear from the standpoint of Adam what it must mean when Jesus is called " the Son of Man," and when, with a strong preference for this title as opposed to any other, he thus designates himself in all decisive passages. It would further have to be shown how from the standpoint of Abraham — that is, on the basis of the election of the people of Israel and on the basis of the prophetic designation, conditioned by this election, of a " remnant " and of a Suffering Servant of God — we are to understand what the vicarious character of Christ's atoning death must signify in connection with God's plan of salvation. These two lines, the

Adam-Christ line and the Abraham-Christ line,[3] show how the Old Testament belongs to the Christian revelation. As Son of Man, second Adam, Jesus fulfills the destiny of the man created by God; as Servant of Yahweh [4] he fulfills the history of his people. Both lines permit us to perceive that the entire history in which Christ effects salvation is connected with *human sin*.

The actuality of the pre-Christian past, therefore, does not rest upon an identity in time between the Old and the New Testament; that would amount to an abolition of the time line. On the contrary, it rests upon the successive connection in time between past and mid-point. That Primitive Christianity takes with full earnestness this time quality of the Old Testament events is, finally, also made clear through the lengthening of the line beyond the mid-point and on into the eschatological future. Even where the subject is this last section of time, it is never forgotten that it belongs to the same line in whose earlier section falls the Creation and the election of the people of Israel. On this basis Paul is filled with wondering amazement at the very point where he has recognized the mystery of the divine plan (Rom. 11:33) ; according to this mystery the history of the election of the people of Israel, the Israel " according to the flesh," continues on through the times, in spite of their hardening, and at the end finds its crown in the conversion of this people.[5]

[3] Gottlob Schrenk, in " Die Geschichtsanschauung des Paulus " (*Jahrbuch der theologischen Schule Bethel,* 1932, pp. 59 ff.) , adds for Paul still a third line, the legal line. This, however, can be included in the other two (the Law has " come in between," Rom. 5:20) .

[4] I plan to demonstrate in another publication the fundamental significance that in Primitive Christianity attaches to the Servant of Yahweh prophecy as a reference to Jesus Christ.

[5] Concerning this, see Karl Ludwig Schmidt, *Die Judenfrage im Lichte der Kapitel 9–11 des Römerbriefs* (*Theologische Studien,* No. 13, 1943) and Gottlob Schrenk, *Der göttliche Sinn in Israels Geschick. Eine Erlaüterung zu Röm. 9–11,* 1943.

3

THE FUTURE STAGES OF REDEMPTIVE HISTORY AND THEIR RELATION TO THE CHRIST–EVENT AT THE MID–POINT

WE MUST HERE BEGIN by reminding ourselves of the discussion in the chapter concerning the new division of time, and above all we must recall the fact that in Primitive Christianity the future plays a quite different role from that which it plays in Judaism. Unless we make the necessary limitation, it is false to assert that Primitive Christianity had an eschatological orientation. That is true only of Judaism. On the contrary, even for Jesus, while he is dwelling upon earth, it no longer is true in the Jewish sense.[1] The norm is no longer that which is to come; it is He who has already come. Eschatology is not put aside, but it is dethroned, and this holds true both chronologically and essentially. The stripping away of eschatology, when understood in the sense just indicated, is nevertheless linked with a heightened intensity of expectation for the future;[2] this stripping away coincides with the appearance of Christ, and it is conditioned by this positive fact rather than by delay of the Parousia. The question as to " When " is indeed still asked (Acts 1:6), but it no longer can carry the same theological tone that it does in Judaism, since now another datum is recognized as decisive. Hence the Risen One actually rejects it as a question, and in doing so refers to the bestowal of the Spirit, which will follow upon the basis of what has already occurred.

The question concerning the future is now no longer stated

---

[1] See pp. 71, 83 f.   [2] See pp. 86 f.

in this general form: In what way does our salvation depend upon that which is still to come? It is rather put in the way we have expressed it in the title of this chapter: In what relation does the future stand to that which has already been done for our salvation? How does the future bring the *completion* of that which has already been decided?

In point of content the future is no longer, as in Judaism, the *telos* or " end " which gives meaning to the whole. Even C. A. Auberlen, who in other respects powerfully established the viewpoint of redemptive history as the center of Christian theology,[3] failed to see this correctly; he thought that the meaning of the redemptive history is disclosed by the prediction of the end. The " end " as the meaning of redemptive history, however, is Jesus Christ, who has already appeared. What Paul says in Rom. 10:4 concerning the law, that Christ is its " end," may be applied to all features of the redemptive process; its " end " is the Christ who died on the cross and rose.[4] While the " end " was previously only expectation, it is now acknowledged as fulfillment.

In spite of this dethronement, however, eschatology continues to possess, as do the other sections of the redemptive line, its own significance for redemptive history. Indeed, no part of that line can be torn loose from it. Primitive Christianity does indeed think eschatologically; but it now no longer thinks in a " consistently," that is, an exclusively, eschatological manner — not if we understand the word " eschatologically " in the futuristic sense, as we must do, since all other speech concerning eschatology is a reinterpretation of the thing involved.

[3] C. A. Auberlen, *Der Prophet Daniel und die Offenbarung Johannis,* 1854.

[4] All history is prophecy for Joh. Chr. K. von Hofmann, *Weissagung und Erfüllung,* 1841 and 1844. Every prediction becomes history. See p. 184. Christ's incarnation he rightly sees to be the meaning of the entire history, inasmuch as he sees in it the last and therefore final prediction, the prediction, that is, of the Parousia. Thus it is not the end that here gives meaning to the whole; it is rather the incarnate Christ.

But what is now the eschatological future's peculiar value for redemptive history? Wherein does the completion which is still to come differ from the decision which has already been reached? Wherein does the once-for-all uniqueness of this section consist? Is it possible to assert here too this uniqueness? One could indeed be tempted, from the viewpoint of redemptive history, to devalue the entire eschatological future, on the ground that the decision has already been reached. Everything that is still to come could be regarded as irrelevant. But thereby the redemptive history would again be dissolved.

Just as the "Victory Day" does in fact present *something new* in contrast to the decisive battle already fought at some point or other of the war, just so the end which is still to come also brings something new. To be sure, this new thing that the "Victory Day" brings is based entirely upon that decisive battle, and would be absolutely impossible without it. Thus we make for the future precisely the same confirmation as we did for the past. It is a unique occurrence; it has its meaning for redemptive history in itself; but on the other hand it is nevertheless founded upon that one unique event at the mid-point.

The new thing that the "Victory Day" brings, in addition to the decision already reached, is that the Holy Spirit, the πνεῦμα, lays hold of the entire world of the flesh (σάρξ), of *matter*. In Christ, according to the Primitive Christian faith, only his own body had previously risen to become a spiritual body. Other spiritual bodies do not as yet exist. At the end, however, the Spirit, which already dwells in us, will also "lay hold of our mortal bodies" (Rom. 8:11). Therefore it remains true for the Primitive Christian eschatology just as for the Jewish one that it does not occur in a purely otherworldly sphere. Indeed, we must actually say that particularly for Primitive Christianity the eschatological drama must take place in a setting that includes the earth, because here the new thing that the final completion adds to the already reached decision consists in the fact that the Spirit, which in a preliminary way, in baptism, lays hold only of the inner man, now creates anew the whole of matter which has fallen into the state of sinful flesh.

As long as this final completion is still to come, the Holy Spirit penetrates into the world of the body only temporarily; only temporarily are sickness and the power of death repelled. The raisings of the dead that are narrated in the New Testament have nothing final about them. The young man at Nain, Lazarus, and Tabitha are not raised to live in a spiritual body; they will again have to die as do all men. It is the unique meaning of the eschatological drama that only then will the dead really rise to live in a spiritual body, that only then does a creation emerge in which there is no longer any withering and decay. Just as the decision in Jesus Christ has already occurred upon earth, so even more must the completion take place precisely upon earth. Hence Mark 13:31, as well as Rev. 21:1 ff. and II Peter 3:13, emphasizes the fact that that completion will affect both heaven *and earth.* The Son of Man appearing in glory will " descend " to the earth.

Thus the adornment of the material side of the final happening, such as occurs when Papias, for example, describes the " new creation " in crude colors,[5] does not signify a Jewish relapse. A relapse ensues only where the question as to the " When " receives an exclusive emphasis. For in Primitive Christianity this question has lost its justification. Where the certainty rules that the decisive battle has been fought through to victory, then only in the circle of understandable human curiosity is it still of importance to know whether the " Victory Day " comes tomorrow or later. Theologically, that is, for salvation, this latter question has no further significance.

This very expectation of that which is still to come, namely, the laying hold of the body by the Spirit, roots entirely in the already fulfilled fact that upon the basis of the resurrection of Christ this Spirit " already dwells in us." Paul expressly em-

---

[5] Irenaeus, *Against Heresies,* V, 33, 3 ff.

phasizes this guarantee of the hope of the resurrection (Rom. 8:11; II Cor. 5:1 ff.).[6] The important Pauline discussion concerning the resurrection in I Cor., ch. 15, develops precisely this central theme, that all hope of the still future resurrection of the body rests solely and alone upon the already completed resurrection of Jesus Christ. Thus in this point also we find it confirmed that every section of the redemptive line has its own unique significance, and yet only because it is determined by the event at the mid-point.

[6] Concerning the resurrection of the individual Christian's body, and its relation to the present possession of the Holy Spirit, see Part IV, Chapter 3.

4

THE PRESENT STAGE OF REDEMPTIVE HISTORY AND ITS RELATION TO THE CHRIST–EVENT AT THE MID–POINT

THE PROBLEM of the significance that the present has for redemptive history and of its relation to the mid-point is posed in a much more complex manner than is the case for the past and for the future. On the other hand, the judgment passed on the post-Easter present is the real test of the correct understanding of the Primitive Christian conception of time and history. Here also we confirm the fact that for the Primitive Church the redemptive history is by no means a mere theory; on the contrary, this very vivid consciousness of the first Christians that they are instruments of a special divine process finds its only possible explanation in their faith in this redemptive history, within which a particularly important significance attaches to the present time in which the Church of Christ now lives. Not without point does the primitive confession "*Kyrios Christos*," "Christ rules as Lord," relate itself to the present time in which the Church is living.

If the later Church has lost so much in vitality, if the workings of the Spirit, measured by those of the Primitive Church, are so very few, this is connected with the fact that this consciousness of standing as a Church in redemptive history's quite definite plan, and of being on the way from the resurrection to the Parousia, has been lost or in any case greatly weakened. As soon as the line is no longer taken in full earnest in its time character, the present necessarily loses in significance. All speculations concerning eternity, even when its " invasion

into time " is ever so much emphasized, deprive the present
of the mighty significance that the faith of Primitive Christianity attaches to it in the setting of redemptive history. In the
final analysis, that is to say, these speculations have as their
result only the reduction of all epochs to the same level, and
the unique character which the present also possesses is treated
as commonplace.

On the grounds both of the complexity and of the importance of the problem we must devote more time to the question concerning the present stage of redemptive history than
we did to the past and the future.

The complexity is connected first of all with what we discussed in the chapter concerning the division of time, that is,
with the tension between " this age " and the " coming age."
This tension results from the fact that the mid-point of time
no longer falls at the end of the section which lies between the
Creation and the Parousia; it now falls rather in the middle
of this period, so that the present of the Church already lies
in the new age, and yet is still before the Parousia, and so
before the actual end time. We must here refer back to the
illustration on page 82.

The result of this tension is that the particular significance
of the post-Easter present lies in a special relation not only
to that mid-point, but also to the future. It stands in a different relation to the end from that of all the preceding epochs
since the creation of the world; it is *the final time before the
end* (I John 2:18), because, no matter what its still undetermined duration may be (Acts 1:7), the mid-point has been
passed.

It is already the time of the end, and yet is not *the* end.
This tension finds expression in the entire theology of Primitive Christianity. The present period of the Church is the time
between the decisive battle, which has already occurred, and
the " Victory Day." To anyone who does not take clear account
of this tension, the entire New Testament is a book with seven
seals, for this tension is the silent presupposition that lies be-

hind all that it says. This is the only dialectic and the only dualism that is found in the New Testament. It is not the dialectic between this world and the Beyond; moreover, it is not that between time and eternity; it is rather *the dialectic of present and future.*

If, however, the post-Easter present is thus determined on the one side entirely by the mid-point, which already lies in the past, and on the other side entirely by the future which is still to come, does there still remain any room for the present to have its own significance for redemptive history? We have seen how Irenaeus has the tendency to overleap this present period in his survey of redemptive history.[1] In his view everything hastens from the mid-point to the end.

In quite another way Kierkegaard, with his conception of "contemporaneity,"[2] mistakes the significance of the present for redemptive history. According to him, faith transfers us back into the time of the incarnation; it makes us contemporaries of the apostles. In this view it is correct that faith permits us actually to survey the entire redemptive line and to share in its fruits, as we have explained in the chapter concerning the divine Lordship over time. But the concept of contemporaneity presupposes that basically time as redemptive time has already come to a standstill with Jesus Christ; hence, we can only go back to him in order to enter the realm of salvation. But is this the conception of Primitive Christianity? When the first disciples utter their original confession: "Christ reigns as Lord," this means rather that *Christ the Crucified and Risen One comes to us.* The redemptive history continues; *Christ sits at the right hand of God,* now, today.

If in what follows we seek to determine more closely this meaning that the present, that is, the period of the Church, has in redemptive history for Primitive Christian faith, then the later Catholic absolutizing of this period of the Church *appears* to be justified. And indeed, we do emphasize — in con-

---

[1] See p. 57, footnote 10.
[2] See Kierkegaard, *Der Augenblick.*

trast to the extreme conclusion of Protestantism, as it has been drawn, for example, by Kierkegaard — that the return to the Christ-event at the mid-point must not so mislead us that we fail to recognize that the post-Easter present signifies a continuance in time of the redemptive process. But with reference to the Catholic absolutizing of the period of the Church, it is to be said that when the Catholic Church fails to subject the " tradition " to the " Scripture," it does not sufficiently observe the necessity of constant orientation to the event at the mid-point. Thus here also the Primitive Christian redemptive line, with its distinctive relation of the different sections to one another and of all sections to the mid-point, is not preserved. That in general this strictly temporal conception of the present stage of redemptive history, as a period lying between past and future, is much weakened even in Catholicism is further shown in the fact that what Primitive Christianity says of the future is in large part transferred into the present. The reference of the thousand-year Kingdom (Rev. 20:4) to the Church, a view that goes back to Tyconius, is characteristic in this respect.[3] It could also be shown that in later Catholicism the relationship between time and eternity is not determined in the same way as in the New Testament.

The Primitive Church bases upon the conception of time that we established in Part I its strong consciousness of being the instrument of the redemptive history, which continues to unfold along the same time line. In its relation to the present, this conception nowhere comes more clearly to expression than in Rom. 13:11: "We know concerning the *kairos,* namely, that it is time to wake out of sleep, for our salvation is *now nearer than when we first believed."* In view of this text, all philosophical reinterpretations of the Biblical redemptive history, with its eschatologically future goal, should be impos-

[3] In this connection the recent decision of the Congregation of the Holy Office, according to which faith in the visible return of Christ no longer is regarded as obligatory (it can " not be taught as certain "), should also be noted. (See Martin Werner, *Schweizerische Theologische Umschau,* 1944, p. 117.)

sible. Every passing minute brings us nearer to the end point, and from the viewpoint of redemptive history every passing minute, when seen from the center, is important in the Church.

Before we go on to define this period of the Church according to its foundation as the time of the reign of Christ, and according to its meaning for redemptive history as the time of preaching the gospel to all peoples, we must first ask a preliminary question: Did Jesus himself, according to the Synoptic testimony, expect such an intermediate period between his atoning death and the Parousia? Albert Schweitzer has answered this question in the negative. He is of the view that Jesus, in the first phase of his ministry, when he sent out the disciples (Matt. 10:1 ff.), still expected the end in his lifetime; then, in the second phase, he regarded the date of his death as the time of the coming of the Kingdom of God. Such a distinction, however, finds no real support in the New Testament texts. It is, on the other hand, correct to say that the expectation which Albert Schweitzer assumes only for the second phase of Jesus' life is actually attested in the Gospel records. Jesus really regarded his death as the point of time decisive for redemptive history, even if it is nowhere expressly said that his death coincides with the final end.

Now, however, thanks particularly to the discussions of W. G. Kümmel,[4] we know it to be characteristic of Jesus' thinking about redemption that what we have called the Lordship of God over time becomes visible in him in such a way that in his work the end is already anticipated. From this it results that the question may not be put as though the identification of the decisive point of time with his death excluded the assumption of a time interval between this death and the Parousia. As a matter of fact, indeed, we find that equally well attested sayings of Jesus can be cited for *both* views, namely,

4 See pp. 71 f., 83 f.

that in the moment of his death the decision already occurs, and that the Son of Man will come only at a later time.

It should no longer be disputed that Jesus regarded his own death as the decisive point in the divine plan of salvation. This fact can be refuted only by an unrestrained application to the gospel tradition of the arbitrary and all too easy method of amputation, and this procedure can scarcely be scientifically justified.

In addition, however, to the numerous texts that might here be cited which clearly attest Jesus' knowledge of the necessity of his death for salvation, there is a whole series of sayings that show that according to Jesus' own expectation an interval of time, even if a short one (this we fully concede to Martin Werner), lies between his death and the Parousia. Here we must point to Mark 14:62, where Jesus, standing before the high priest, distinguishes between the moment when the Son of Man will take his seat at the right hand of God and the one when he will come again upon the clouds of heaven; we must further point to the saying of Mark 13:10, according to which the gospel must be preached to all the Gentiles before the end comes.[5] W. Michaelis [6] emphasizes particularly that in Mark 9:1 it says that $\tau\iota\nu\epsilon\varsigma$, accordingly only " some," will not taste of death until the Kingdom of God comes with power. This presupposes that the others will have died. Above all, mention should here be made of the often mentioned writing of W. G. Kümmel.[7] He brings forward a great number of additional texts, above all the words concerning fasting (Mark 2:18 ff.), and also Mark 14:28: " But after I am risen, I will go before you into Galilee."

The question whether Jesus himself expected an intermediate period is thus to be answered in the affirmative. For the

---

[5] These passages I have already cited in *Le retour du Christ*, second ed., 1945, p. 25.

[6] *Der Herr verzieht nicht seine Verheissung*, 1942, p. 30.

[7] *Verheissung und Erfüllung*, 1945. See the entire chapter entitled " Die Erwartung einer Zwischenzeit zwischen Jesu Tod und Parusie," pp. 38 ff.

problem that concerns us this conclusion suffices. In the light of this answer, the fact that Jesus did not measure the intermediate period in centuries and millenniums any more than did the Primitive Church, but probably looked forward at the most to decades, is of no import, since it makes no change in the division of the stages of redemptive history.

If, however, Jesus actually assumed a time interval between the two events, between his atoning death, decisive for salvation, and his Parousia, then he must have intended that in this intermediate period — whether it is of longer or shorter duration is here not essential — his disciples were to play a role. From this insight light falls upon the saying concerning the Church in Matt. 16:18; there is no longer any substantial reason to deny its genuineness,[8] when we go back to the Aramaic equivalent for " church " ($\grave{\epsilon}\kappa\kappa\lambda\eta\sigma\acute{\iota}\alpha$) .[9]

For the Primitive Church, at any rate, it is a fixed fact that the present stage of redemptive history is the period of the Church, the earthly Body of Christ. Even at the present time, however, the redemptive history is not simply identical with the events of the present. To be sure, in the present as in the past, the entire process of events is closely bound to the redemptive process, as we shall show in Part III of this book. But even now, when the mid-point of time has already been reached, it is only a *small line,* namely, the line of things that occur in the Church of Christ in connection with Christ's present Lordship, that constitutes redemptive history in the true sense.

The Primitive Church had from its first hour the conviction that it stood in a segment of time that was exactly defined and precisely determined in content; this segment is the time between Christ's ascension and his Parousia. This becomes especially clear in Acts 1:11, in the narrative of the ascension itself. There, in the proclamation of the two men, it is said with

8 I say this in opposition to W. G. Kümmel; see p. 7, footnote 3.

9 On this point see K. L. Schmidt, article on $\grave{\epsilon}\kappa\kappa\lambda\eta\sigma\acute{\iota}\alpha$ in Kittel's *Theologisches Wörterbuch zum N. T.,* III, pp. 502 ff. See also his " Die Kirche des Urchristentums," in *Festgabe für A. Deissmann, 1927.*

emphasis that Christ will return in the *very manner* in which he has just been taken up into heaven, that is, upon a cloud. By the similarity of the event that marks the later limit of the period, the unity of this segment of time is indicated.

This unity has its factual ground in the particular Christ-event that fills this segment: *Christ rules over all things in heaven and on earth. The spatial center of this Lordship is the Church, which constitutes his Body upon earth.* In my book entitled *Königsherrschaft Christi und Kirche im Neuen Testament,*[10] I have endeavored to show precisely this time-limited character of the kingly rule of Christ. In chronological respect (although not in the spatial) [11] the kingly rule of Christ and the Church completely coincide. Like the Church, this Lordship of Christ began with the ascension. While the Kingdom of *God* will begin only at the end of the revelatory process, when Christ shall have subjected himself to God (I Cor. 15:28), we already stand in the Kingdom of *Christ* (Col. 1:13). Like the Church, therefore, the Kingdom of Christ has a beginning and an end.[12]

The present reign of Christ is described by the Primitive Church with the use of expressions from Ps. 110, interpreted to refer to Christ: " Christ sits at the right hand of God," " all enemies are subjected to him." The unusually large number of passages in which this " sitting of Christ at the right hand of God " is expressed [13] shows how great an importance the first Christians plainly ascribed to this faith. We here find confirmation of the fact that this redemptive action of the present intermediate period, the period of the Church, particularly interests Primitive Christianity.

---

10 *Theologische Studien,* No. 10, 1941.

11 *Königsherrschaft Christi und Kirche,* pp. 24 ff.

12 I have already indicated, in *Königsherrschaft Christi und Kirche,* pp. 14 f., how the end of this intermediate period already extends into the initial stage of the new creation (the reference here is to the millennial Kingdom).

13 Rom. 8:34; I Cor. 15:25; Col. 3:1; Eph. 1:20; Heb. 1:3; 8:1; 10:12; I Peter 3:22; Acts 2:34; 5:31; 7:55; Rev. 3:21; Matt. 22:44; 26:64; Mark 12:36; 14:62; 16:19; Luke 20:42; 22:69; I Clem. 36:5; Barn. 12:10.

This is proved above all by the already indicated fact that in the earliest confessions of faith this present reign of Christ is regularly mentioned. If it is correct in point of method to see in the earliest formulas of faith the authentic summary of the essential content of the message, whose more detailed form the first Christian generations have handed down to us in the books of the New Testament, then a commanding importance attaches to the confession "*Kyrios Christos,*" " Christ rules as Lord," in our effort to determine the essential content to which the main interest of the Primitive Church is directed. This interest in the present does not at all mean that the post-Easter present is the center of the time line. We have seen, indeed, where the unique center of this line is to be sought. But of all the segments of time that are illuminated from this center, it is precisely the present one that interests the first Christians more than does any other. They still stand so near to the center in point of time that for them the conviction that their intermediate present period is completely anchored in this center is still much more lively and strong than will be the case in later times.

If this present, rather than the future, commands the chief consideration in the Primitive Christian summary of the Christian faith, then it must be repeated in this connection that the so-called " consistent eschatology " is not correct when it regards the eschatological future as the object of Primitive Christianity's chief interest. This becomes clear from the fact that wherever the desire is to sum up in a very brief formula the content of faith, nothing is said as yet about the future. By this, to be sure, we do not mean to say that the hope has lost any of its intensity. It is, however, expressed only in prayer, not in confession; "*Maranatha*" is almost certainly to be understood as an imperative (" Our Lord, come! "), not as an indicative, even if philologically this latter interpretation is possible.[14] The confession of the Christ-event in the present

[14] See K. G. Kuhn in *Theologisches Wörterbuch zum N. T.,* Vol. III, p. 500.

includes in itself the reference to the past and to the future; it points to the entire redemptive line.

The simplest expression of the confession of the present Lordship of Christ is that formula " *Kyrios Christos*," " Christ rules as Lord." It was uttered in times of persecution before the pagan authorities, as well as in worship and in exorcism. Its unusual importance comes to light in Rom. 10:9, where the apostle Paul designates every " confession with the mouth " as a confession of " *Kyrios Christos*." It signifies nothing else than that utterance which goes back to Ps. 110: " Christ sits at the right hand of God. All enemies are subject to him." The mention of the " enemies," which is also taken from the psalm, is referred in Christianity to the quite diverse invisible powers which are regarded in part as the earlier world rulers.[15] Their subjection is the result of the victory that has been gained through Christ's death and resurrection. To be sure, this subjection at the moment is rather merely a " binding," for they must once again be defeated at the end. Here again the tension which is so important for characterizing the present redemptive period emerges into view. In I Cor. 15:25 and Heb. 10:13 it is said that the hostile powers are subjected at the end, while in other passages the saying from the psalm is referred to their subjection which has already occurred; indeed, in II Tim. 1:10 the same verb, καταργέω (" render inactive," " abolish "), that Paul uses in I Cor. 15:25 to designate the future final annihilation of death as the last of these enemies is used to describe the victory over death as already accomplished through Christ's death and resurrection.[16]

Most of the more developed confessions of the first period are not limited to the statement that Christ sits at the right hand of God, but regularly emphasize that the invisible " powers " are subjected to him. The concern of these confessions is to give particular emphasis to this wide scope of the Lord-

[15] Concerning this, see Part III, Chapter 3.
[16] Hence Luther here translates the verb thus: " He has deprived him of his power."

ship of Christ, for in it is made clear the relation between the Church, or Body of Christ, and the universal Lordship of Christ.

In this connection we must refer above all to the confession of Phil. 2:6 ff., which reaches its climax in the formula " *Kyrios Christos,*" " Christ rules as Lord "; this formula is uttered by the creatures in heaven, by those upon the earth, and by those under the earth. The confession of I Peter 3:22 states: " He is at the right hand of God, after he has ascended into heaven and the angels, authorities, and powers have been subjected to him." The confession cited in the letter of Polycarp, ch. 2:1, does not forget to add, after mention of the resurrection, that the glory and the throne at the right hand of God are given to Christ and " that all heavenly and earthly things are subjected to him and everything which therein breathes serves him." The further developed confession of Ignatius of Antioch (*To the Trallians,* ch. 9:1) shows the regularity with which both the heavenly things, the earthly things, and those under the earth appear in the most ancient creeds.[17] We still find traces of this in the middle of the second century. The confession cited by Justin in his *Dialogue with Trypho,* ch. 85, names Christ " Lord of the Powers."

The relation of tension between mid-point and end, which is so characteristic of the present intermediate period, is manifested in *the Church* in a manner that exactly corresponds to the Lordship of Christ, since Church and Kingdom of Christ coincide in time. The Church is the earthly center from which the full Lordship of Christ becomes visible. It is the Body of Christ as the Crucified but also Risen One. It is the " spiritual body " of Christ, and through participation in it in worthy enjoyment of the Lord's Supper the believer already appropriates the fruits of the Holy Spirit, even in the area of

17 See O. Cullmann, *Die ersten christlichen Glaubensbekenntnisse,* 1943, p. 55 (Eng. tr., *The Earliest Christian Confessions,* 1949, p. 60).

his earthly life (I Cor. 11:30) . The Church is the place where
the Spirit, this feature of the eschatological period, is already
at work as " earnest," as " firstfruits." The constitution of the
Church by the Spirit became visible at Pentecost. In the
Church, through this Holy Spirit, miracles typical of the eschatological period already occur. And yet the flesh, the great
opponent of the Spirit, still rules. The time tension is manifested in the Church through the continuance of sin, which
nevertheless has already been defeated by the Spirit. The
Church is God's highest gift of salvation in this intermediate
period, and yet it is composed of imperfect, sinful men. Just
as the entire redemptive history as such can only be believed
but not proved, so above all the Church also can only be believed, and it really takes a quite special courage of faith to
see the center of the present Lordship of Christ in this Church,
which from its very beginning is so imperfect and all too human. Even in the Primitive Church there are conflicts from
the first hour, even between its greatest members, Paul and
Barnabas, Paul and Peter (Acts 15:39; Gal. 2:11 ff.) ; there
were " murmurings " of believers against one another on account of quite material affairs (Acts 6:1) ; etc. The Primitive
Christian writers are well acquainted with all these unpleasant
things; yet they write such powerful things concerning this
same Church, in which indeed there actually occur eschatological miracles, speaking with tongues and healings of the
sick, miracles in which the resurrection power of the Holy
Spirit even now, although only partially and provisionally,
repels the power of death even in the physical sphere.

The eschatological miracle of the Church, however, is realized above all in the assemblies for worship, which find their
crown in the Supper celebrations. Here happens even now
what really will take place only at the end. Christ returns already to the assembled congregation, as he one day will come in
a way visible to all. We have seen [18] that " *Maranatha* " means
both: " Come to us who are assembled in thy name," and

[18] See p. 74.

" Come finally at the end." In the Supper celebration there is
concretized, so to speak, the present's entire situation in redemptive history: its simultaneous and particularly close relation to both the mid-point and the end. In the Lord's Supper
there is a pointing back to the Last Supper of Jesus before his
death and to the Easter suppers that were eaten with the Risen
One, and there is a pointing forward to the Messianic Banquet,
which Christ will eat with his people in the Kingdom of God.
We have seen how particularly in the Apocalypse of John the
Supper is thought of as an anticipation of the Kingdom of
God (ch. 3:20).

When Peter, interpreting the Pentecost miracle on the basis
of the citation from Joel (Acts 2:16 ff.), characterizes what is
occurring as that which happens " in the last days," this likewise means that the present days are already " the last days "
and that they are *preliminary signs* of the end. The nature of
the preliminary sign corresponds to the tension character of
the intermediate period. To be sure, it is only in the apocalypses, in the Synoptic ones as well as in the Johannine one and
in the apocalyptic fragments of the letters of Paul, that we
find mention of real preliminary signs in the narrower sense:
cosmic catastrophes, wars, persecutions, final call to the world
to repent. They appear at the end of the present intermediate
period, where the final section of the redemptive line will already be undergoing the birth pangs, which are, so to speak,
particularly concentrated at that moment. But in so far as
everything that will happen there, at the border limit of the
present time phase, nevertheless forms a unity with all that occurs in this intermediate period, it is possible to call this entire intermediate process a preliminary sign in the wider sense.
This is the way the first Christians looked upon the events of
their days.

The anti-Christian feature in the apocalyptic evaluation of
events in time, as we find this evaluation in later apocalyptic

sects down to the present day, is not the fact that such events are in some way interpreted as "preliminary signs," but that from them the time of the end is reckoned. Such a reckoning stands in contradiction to the Primitive Christian belief that the fixing of the *kairoi* belongs solely to the sovereign power of God, and that men, even by their knowledge, have no control over it. Viewed from this standpoint, it is not a falling away from the Primitive Christian attitude when ever and again, in the course of the centuries, this or that phenomenon is judged to be a manifestation of the Antichrist; but it is such a falling away when such a phenomenon is regarded as his *final* manifestation and so is used to reckon the date of the end.

Above all, however, the one great task that is assigned to the Church to do in its period, namely, the missionary preaching of the gospel, is likewise evaluated as a preliminary sign of the end. It is connected with the above-indicated double character of the Church, which on the one side is God's redemptive gift to the world (Body of Christ) and yet on the other side is composed of sinful men, that the Church's activity in redemptive history represents both a task for its members and an eschatological divine grace.

This missionary proclamation of the Church, its preaching of the gospel, gives to the period between Christ's resurrection and Parousia its meaning for redemptive history; and it has this meaning through its connection with Christ's present Lordship. This is the unique character of the present. Even this uniqueness is completely anchored in the uniqueness of the Christ-event at the mid-point. It is indeed the preaching of that which happened back there at the mid-point of time. But it also shares in the characteristic connection with the future; it points directly to the time of fulfillment.

It is effected by that element of the final period, the Holy Spirit. This is shown by the Pentecost story, which is the foundation of the mission. This is the meaning of the Pentecost miracle, where all suddenly understand one another. To this relation points also that answer of the Risen One to which we shall return later: " Ye shall receive the power of the Holy Spirit, and ye shall be my witnesses in Jerusalem, Judea, Samaria, and unto the end of the world " (Acts 1:8) .

The conception of the mission as the mark of redemptive history's intermediate but final phase, in which we stand since Easter — this Primitive Christian idea seems to me particularly important in our connection. For this reason I here reproduce the results of my earlier investigations on this subject.[19]

The conception that the gospel preaching is an integral part of the divine plan of salvation, and is a part that makes clear that the redemptive line continues on in the present time, assumes in Primitive Christianity the precise form that we shall here follow through the entire New Testament: the end will come only when the gospel shall have been preached to all peoples. Here at the outset we emphasize that it does not say that the end will come only when all are converted. On the contrary, it is a further conviction of the Christian eschatological expectation that wickedness will increase in the last time. The thing that here concerns us is the fact that the gospel is *preached* to all. Thus during the period of the Church the preaching of the gospel itself becomes the sign of the end. It appears here as the gracious gift of God which belongs to the unfolding in time of his plan of salvation.

The origin of this idea can be traced back to Judaism, where, to be sure, it appears in a quite different form. Pre-Christian Judaism is indeed familiar with the mission, but not as a preliminary condition of the coming of the Messianic Kingdom. We do, however, find another teaching, which prepares for that New Testament faith in the mission as a sign of the end time, and is likewise corrected by it. In Judaism there is a constant attempt to reckon the date of the Messianic

[19] " Le caractère eschatologique du devoir missionaire et de la conscience apostolique de S. Paul (Étude sur le κατέχον (-ων) de 2. Thess. 2:6–7) ," in *Mélanges théologiques publiés à la mémoire de G. Baldensperger,* 1936, pp. 210 ff. In what follows I reproduce in essentials the summary and the other arrangement of the material which I undertook in the *Evangelische Missionsmagazin,* 1941, pp. 98 ff. (" Eschatologie und Mission im Neuen Testament ").

Kingdom. We cannot here cite the computations and the quite divergent solutions to which men came. Ever and again these efforts were found to give false results. The Kingdom of God did not appear at the dates computed. Hence there arose the view, which is often attested in the Talmud and in the Apocrypha for the Judaism of the New Testament period, that the Kingdom of God can come only when all Israel shall have repented. In this connection there often appears in the Talmud the question: " Who is delaying? Who is delaying the Messiah? " [20] For judging the New Testament conception of the mission it is characteristic that in Judaism, according to the rabbinical texts, there were two different schools, which answered that question differently, and in so doing both did violence to the idea of God's omnipotence, which nevertheless is the constitutive element of all eschatology. The school of Eliezer renounced all further efforts to reckon that date. They taught that the Messiah will come when *all Israel shall have repented*. Thereby, however, the coming of the Kingdom is made dependent on the moral attitude of man, and the divine omnipotence is curtailed. The coming of the Kingdom is no longer a sovereign divine act. In opposition to this view stands that of the school of Rabbi Jehoshua, who seeks to fix a definite date, namely, A.D. 240, which comes as the end point independently of men. To the question: " Who is delaying the Messiah? " he does not answer: " The still unfulfilled repentance," but, " The fact that the date is not yet due." [21] Thereby he also, but in another way, does violence to the divine omnipotence, in that he binds the coming of the Messiah to this reckoning which is accessible to men. In the New Testament conception, of which we are now to speak, the divine omnipotence is on the contrary fully preserved, since here man controls this date neither by his action nor by his knowledge. Full justice is done to this fact in the particular conception of the mission which we are here studying and after which the end will come, when once the gospel shall have been preached to all nations.

We must further point to two other lines within Judaism

[20] *mî mĕakkēb,* Sanh. 97b. See Strack-Billerbeck, *Kommentar zum Neuen Testament aus Talmud und Midrasch,* Vol. II, 1924, on Acts 1:7 (p. 589).

[21] See p. Taan. 1, 6 (63d) and b. Sanh. 97b; also P. Volz, *Die Eschatologie der jüdischen Gemeinde im neutestamentlichen Zeitalter,* 1934, p. 103, and Strack-Billerbeck, *op. cit., Excursus II,* 1928, pp. 992 f.

which in a more direct way prepare for the Christian conception of the mission as a sign of the end time: first of all, that one according to which Elijah will preach repentance at the end of the times (Mal. 3:1; Jesus ben Sirach 48:10, 11); and further, the other one, according to which the Kingdom will come only when the number of the elect is complete (I Enoch 47:4; Syriac Baruch 30:2; IV Ezra 4:35 f.).

As far as the relevant New Testament passages are concerned, we must take our start from the two parallel passages in the Synoptic Apocalypse, Mark 13:10: "And the gospel must first be preached to all the Gentiles," and Matt. 24:14: "This gospel of the kingdom shall be preached to all the Gentiles in the whole world for a witness, and then shall the end come." In both texts we should note particularly the clear chronological determination. In Mark: "First" (in what follows, the discussion concerns the appearance of the Antichrist). In Matthew still more clearly: "*Then* shall the end come"; and this end is likewise introduced by the appearance of the Antichrist. In both passages the mission is named as a divine *sign*, along with the eschatological "woes": wars, famines, cosmic catastrophes, persecutions, etc., and the increase in the wickedness of men. Thus it is not the case that the coming of the Kingdom depends upon the success of this preaching; it depends rather upon the fact of the preaching.

We find a further attestation of the same conception in The Revelation of John, in the famous chapters concerning the "apocalyptic horsemen" (Rev. 6:1-8). What the second, third, and fourth horsemen there signify is clear. In each of these cases we have to do with one of the characteristic eschatological "plagues," which these sinister figures personify. Their external appearance corresponds completely to this disaster-bringing task which they accomplish on the earth. But what does the first horseman signify? Many interpretations have been given. We must first take note of the fact that the description of him has nothing in common with the ominous appearance of the other three. On the contrary, he is rather a

luminous figure; he rides a white horse, and when one recalls
that throughout the Apocalypse the color of white appears as
a heavenly attribute, doubts must arise, even on this basis, concerning the interpretation according to which this first horseman, like the three following ones, is sent to spread disaster
and inflict an eschatological plague upon the earth. Moreover,
the crown with which he is adorned gives to him the character
of a beneficent power. Finally, it is said, that " he went forth
as a conqueror and to conquer." Now the verb " conquer "
does not have in the Apocalypse the bad secondary meaning
" conquer through violence "; on the contrary, it designates
divine action. It is therefore very unlikely that this first horseman stands, as the usual exegesis asserts, for some warlike
power, the Romans or the Parthians. This also seems excluded
for the reason that in such a case this horseman would have
the same task as does the second one, who rides a red horse
and carries the sword, and of whom it is expressly said that his
task is to take peace from the earth, that is, to spread war.

Who, then, is meant by this first horseman? This becomes
clear when we take note of the other passage of Revelation
(ch. 19:11 ff.) in which a horseman appears upon a white
horse. In that passage the figure is explained thus: " He is
called faithful and true; the name by which he is called is The
Word of God." In other words, he has the task of preaching
the gospel to the world. This must also be the mission of the
first horseman; moreover, it fits quite well the description
which is given of him.[22] But what does the preaching of the
gospel in the world have in common with the plagues represented by the three other horsemen? It, like them, is a divine
sign of the end, and as a last offer of salvation it runs parallel
to all those terrors which are specifically connected with a particular form of men's wickedness. Moreover, the necessity for
repentance to be preached before the end is emphasized at another place in The Revelation of John. In ch. 11:3 we meet

[22] K. L. Schmidt, among others, represents a contrary view; see his
Aus der Johannes-Apokalypse, 1944, pp. 18 ff.

the two witnesses (Elijah and Moses), who prophesy. In ch. 14:6 f. the angel appears with the eternal gospel, and he directs to all pagan tribes, tongues, and peoples a last call to repent.

That in this expectation of the eschatological "sign" of missionary preaching we do not have to do merely with a peripheral viewpoint becomes particularly clear, however, from the already mentioned passage of The Acts (ch. 1:6 f.). There the Risen One, when questioned by his disciples, rejects all questions concerning the "When" of the Kingdom of God; he regards them as encroaching upon the omnipotence of God. This, however, the disciples should know, that until the Kingdom comes they must carry on the mission. This task results from the bestowal of the Holy Spirit, which they have received. The period between the resurrection and the unknown date of the return must be occupied with missionary preaching "from Jerusalem unto the end of the earth." It is indeed the time of grace which is now granted to men; all should have an opportunity to hear the gospel during this time. Here again this reference to the mission before the end is presented, not primarily as an imperative, but as an indicative, as an eschatological utterance: "Ye shall be my witnesses." It is God who through his messengers introduces this sign; it is he who offers the gospel to the world. In this work the apostles are only the executive instruments of the eschatological plan of salvation.

But this view meets us also in the form of a missionary command to the apostles, in the well-known saying at the end of the Gospel of Matthew: "Go ye into all the world and teach all peoples." This command, too, applies to the expressly defined last phase of this age, that is, it covers the period that lies between the resurrection and the Parousia. This becomes clear in the promise connected with it: "I am with you all the days until the end of this age." This is not so vague a chronological statement as we usually interpret it to be when we take it to mean "always." It is rather a clear reference to the eschatological character of the mission, which must take place precisely in the intermediate period and which *gives to this period its meaning.*

In Paulinism the motif of the Gentile mission as the precondition for the coming of salvation runs through the entire theology of the apostle, and stands in the closest connection with his own consciousness of mission. The latter is clearly determined in Paul by his knowledge concerning the plan of salvation and the meaning of the present for redemptive history. He has the firm conviction that he himself is in the present an instrument of the eschatological plan of salvation. In this connection we must first point to Romans, chs. 9 to 11. These chapters are really a commentary on the saying in Mark 13:10: "The gospel *must* first be preached to all the Gentiles." In Rom., ch. 10, the apostle emphasizes most strongly that God is indeed following his exact plan, but that nevertheless the responsibility of men continues in full force, for all receive an opportunity to hear the gospel: "How shall they believe if they have not heard? How hear if no one is sent?" (v. 14). To all must be offered an opportunity to *hear* the gospel. The Jews have already had it; "but not all have received the gospel," and therefore the call now goes to the Gentiles before finally, at the end, the Jews do enter. Thus the word of the gospel, which must first be preached to the Gentiles, has for Paul a particularly concrete meaning, in which the chief emphasis now lies upon the word "Gentiles." But here again the character of the missionary preaching, as determined by the redemptive history and as a sign of the end, is clear. It is only that Paul, as an instrument of this plan, views this sign first of all from the standpoint of his own apostolic obligation. With reference to God's eschatological plan of salvation, Paul repeatedly emphasizes that he is called to preach particularly to the *Gentiles*. Even in Rom., ch. 11, where he speaks of the mystery of that divine plan, he mentions his own office, which he honors as an apostle to the Gentiles (v. 13). In Col. 1:22–29 he underlines the narrow bond between his personal office and the divine economy which has to do with the "mystery among the Gentiles." When we remember that Paul knows

himself to be given a place in a plan on whose execution God
makes the coming of his Kingdom dependent, then we also
understand better the " compulsion " (I Cor. 9:16) to which
he knows that he is subjected; he is a " debtor " in relation to
" Greeks and Barbarians " (Rom. 1:14). He regards himself
as a " prisoner of Christ for the Gentiles " (Eph. 3:1). On this
basis we also understand better his haste in continually seek-
ing out new " places," from Jerusalem unto Illyricum, where
the gospel has not yet been preached, and when his work in
this part of the world is completed, he turns to Spain. " The
time is short." " Woe unto me, if I preach not the gospel "
(I Cor. 9:16).

Hence it is very probable that also in the much discussed
passage II Thess. 2:6, concerning that " which still restrains
the coming of the Antichrist," there is a reference to the missionary preaching as a sign pointing to the end.

The passage is usually interpreted as referring to the Roman
State, but no other passage can be produced from the New
Testament to support the view that the State delays the end
and the manifestation of the Antichrist. On the contrary, in
Jewish as well as in Primitive Christian apocalyptic, the Antichrist is ordinarily presented in the form of some kind of
Satanic empire. Precisely in II Thess. 2:3, 4 it is described with
images from Daniel, where they certainly refer to the Syrian
empire. Is it likely that Paul, in the very place where he uses
these images to sketch the Antichrist, has at the same time
introduced the State as the power that is to restrain the Antichrist? He thereby would have introduced into the eschatological conceptions a remarkable confusion; in the same passage he would have spoken of the State as the opponent of the
Antichrist and as a Satanic power.

In opposition to this there is a great deal to say for the assumption, which was first expressed by the Church Fathers
Theodore of Mopsuestia and Theodoret, and later also by
Calvin, according to which it is the mission preaching of the
final time that II Thess. 2:6 means by " that which restrains."
In the first place, the Greek verb for " restrain " ($\kappa\alpha\tau\acute{\epsilon}\chi\epsilon\iota\nu$) has
a temporal meaning in the sense of " retard," " delay." The
thing in question is the " When " of the Kingdom of God.

Now nowhere is such a relation found between the State and the " When " of the end, but we do have such a relation clearly established between the preaching to the Gentiles and the question as to the date of the Parousia. According to the Synoptic passages Mark 13:10–14 and Matt. 24:13–16, it is this very *Antichrist* who comes after the preaching to the Gentiles, just as, according to II Thess. 2:6 ff., he will come after that which " still restrains."

Furthermore, this assumption connects directly with that Jewish rabbinical question of which we have spoken: " Who is delaying? " [23] We have seen that the most frequent Jewish answer to that question ran: " The still unfulfilled repentance of Israel." This answer tends clearly toward the Christian view of the eschatological necessity of the preaching to the Gentiles, and it is likewise, as we have seen, corrected by this view, inasmuch as here the essential thing is the *presentation* of the call to repentance.

Moreover, the entire connection in which the passage stands speaks in favor of the reference to the mission to the Gentiles, and shows why the gospel must be preached to all before the appearance of the Antichrist. In vs. 9–12 we read of those who will not receive the love of the truth which would have saved them. In vs. 13 f. Paul contrasts with those who reject the preaching of the apostle the readers themselves, and of the latter he says that the Lord has chosen them to give them salvation: " Thereto has he called you through our preaching." The entire immediately preceding ch. 1 has already treated of the relation of the eschatological events to the acceptance or rejection of the gospel heard: " We boast . . . concerning your endurance and faith . . . as a sign of the righteous judgment of God, namely, that you should be counted worthy of the Kingdom of God, for which you suffer. . . . When the Lord is revealed from heaven with the angels . . . , when he brings recompense upon those who . . . do not accept the gospel of our Lord Jesus."

In the passage under discussion there stands first the neuter " that which restrains " (v. 6, τὸ κατέχον), then the masculine " he who restrains " (v. 7, ὁ κατέχων). If the restraining thing is the missionary preaching, then it is natural to take the reference to the restraining *person* as a self-designation of the apostle. This would agree entirely with what we have said

[23] See p. 159.

concerning Paul's lofty consciousness of mission, which indeed is determined by that eschatological conviction that the gospel must be offered to the Gentiles. Moreover, the fact that Paul would then speak thus of himself in the third person would cause no difficulty, since elsewhere also, with a similar reference to a gift of grace that has been granted him, he uses the third person: " I know a man in Christ who was caught up into the third heaven " (II Cor. 12:2) .

Even if this explanation of II Thess. 2:6 f., which seems to have the best foundation, and in support of which, moreover, one can also cite passages from the ancient Christian literature of the second century,[24] should not prove true, nevertheless all the other New Testament passages would sufficiently attest the faith's fundamental viewpoint, according to which the mission constitutes the real meaning of the present period of redemptive history. This view of the last time, as the time of grace which God in his long-suffering grants us for repentance, leaves undiminished the omnipotence of God. That is to say, it does not make the coming of the Kingdom of God dependent upon men, and it excludes all reckoning of dates; on the other hand, precisely with reference to the present time of salvation, it increases to the highest degree the responsibility of man, and in the period which we call the period of the Church it gives to the Church its definite commission to carry out in the name of Christ the redemptive work by proclaiming the gospel to the Gentiles.

As is the case with all signs, so also this one of the mission permits of no calendar reckoning and also of no limitation to this or that generation, since it is characteristic of the last period, in which we live, that as a whole it is characterized by " signs." From this it results that the Reformers took a false attitude when they believed that they could do away with the mission to the Gentiles by saying that the gospel had already been offered to all Gentiles by the apostles. It belongs rather to the nature of the sign that to the very end it *appears in*

[24] See O. Cullmann, " Quand viendra le Royaume de Dieu," in *Revue d'Histoire et de Philosophie religieuses*, 1938, pp. 174 ff.

every generation that belongs to the present intermediate period in the final phase of redemptive history. From this, however, it follows that the missionary obligation also must fill the entire time that still remains until the unknown final limit, and that every generation must proclaim the gospel anew to the nations of their time, without being troubled by the question as to whether their ancestors had already had the opportunity to hear it. On the basis of this Primitive Christian conception, therefore, the Church must proclaim the gospel to the entire world in every generation.

Only now do we completely understand the lofty consciousness that filled the Primitive Church. The Church was conscious that every day it was carrying forward the divine redemptive history; it was the instrument of the divine redemptive activity; it was taking part in a process that is as much a redemptive process as was that which took place before the incarnation, and as will be the final period which is still to come. In different ways the first Christians gave expression to this consciousness, for example, by speaking of " reigning together" (with Christ; I Cor. 4:8) or by designating themselves as the royal people (Rev. 1:6; I Peter 2:9) . Speaking with this consciousness, Paul's speech in Acts 13:16 ff. gives a sketch of the history of God's people; it shows the line that leads to Christ, but connects with it, as a continuation of that same line, what is occurring in the present, namely, the rejection of the proclamation by the Jews and its acceptance by the Gentiles.

It has become clear that the integration of the present into the redemptive history is here effected in quite a different way than is possible in Judaism; precisely this is the point where Primitive Christianity carries through the time line much more consistently than is done in Judaism. In the Primitive Church the present can be appraised in terms of such a " consistent viewpoint of redemptive history" because the fixed orientation point, the Christ-event at the mid-point, no longer lies in the future, but is known as historic fact.

Now that we have learned, however, to recognize in all its aspects the notable and specific significance of the present, we must once more, and on this very basis, reject all those transformations of the Primitive Christian conception of time that play with the concept of " eternity invading time." Moreover, all talk concerning a " contemporaneity " which faith should establish with the incarnate Jesus lacks support in the writings of the New Testament. Kierkegaard, who has emphasized most strongly this contemporaneity, thereby implicitly destroys the redemptive line, inasmuch as he really abstracts the present from it. He emphasizes the necessity of an " overleaping," because otherwise, as our distance in time from Christ's death continues to increase, we would also be removed ever farther from this event's essential meaning, that is, its significance for salvation. But he thereby overlooks the fact that, according to the New Testament faith, Christ now rules invisibly over heaven and earth, and works visibly in and through the Church; his function in every relation, including his high-priestly work, is now continuing, in that he intercedes for us with the Father and brings all our prayers before him (John 14:14 ff.).

It is, however, correct that precisely in this knowledge of the Lord Jesus we are constantly referred back to the unique deed at the mid-point; it constitutes the foundation of this present Lordship of Christ and also of our faith in it. In this respect that which has taken place and still takes place in the Church, that is, the ecclesiastical " tradition," may not be regarded as of equal importance with that which then took place at the mid-point. So to regard it would be to make the same error, with reference to the present, as that which " consistent eschatology " makes with regard to the future. The center is neither the present nor the future, but rather the earthly work of Christ. The danger of such an absolutizing of the present exists, as we have indicated, in the Catholic Church, where, in dealing with the problem of " Tradition and Scripture," the post-Easter present period of the Church is elevated to the central position. The necessity, which we have indicated in this work, of constant orientation to the unique, once-for-all event of the mid-point is indeed granted throughout; nevertheless, in the last analysis it is misunderstood, inasmuch as this unique feature is *realized* in the Church in such a way that it is now, so to speak, bound to the present, and ceases to be a unique past. Ultimately this fails to take seriously the time character of the whole process, and herein lies, in all probability, the deeper ground for the Catholic attitude to the uniqueness of Christ's death on the cross.

To be sure, leading Catholic theologians have protested, perhaps not unjustly, against the Protestant misinterpretation according to which the offering of Golgotha is " repeated " in the Mass. In actual fact, the thing in question is not a repetition but a "realization" of the unique happening. But from the basis of the Primitive Christian conception of time, as we have here presented it, this concept of " realization " does not seem to me to do justice to the uniqueness. I too emphasize strongly that the Primitive Christian worship service, with the Eucharist as its indispensable climax, points back to the Crucified and Risen One and forward to Him who comes at the end. But he who now appears in the assembled congregation does *not* appear as " one being crucified " and rising, any more than he appears as returning for the eschatological Parousia; he appears rather as the one *sitting at the right hand of God,* who *has been* crucified and *has* risen and *will* return. As such he now offers the forgiveness of sin, which he has effected,[25] and promises the completion, which he will bring. If in Kierkegaard the time from the present to the Christ-event at the mid-point is, so to speak, overleaped in a backward direction, in Catholicism, on the contrary, the leap is made in a forward direction from the Christ-event to the present. If in Kierkegaard the peculiar significance of the present for redemptive history is undervalued, here, on the contrary, in relation to that past central happening, it is overvalued.

[25] I Cor. 11:25 and Luke 22:19: " Do this *in remembrance of me.*"

The Ancient Church, which about A.D. 150 created the canon as a norm in order to subject to its control all further tradition, proved thereby its understanding of the necessity of subjecting the tradition to the Scripture *from a certain moment on.* This was the moment where the distance in time from the mid-point became so great that it was no longer possible to regard the entire post-Easter process as belonging to this mid-point. About this time, that is, about the middle of the second century, Papias wrote his " Explanations of the Lord's Sayings," and he boasts that in so doing he relies less upon written tradition than upon the " living voice," that is, the oral tradition. The latter was actually still living at that time. But that which he transmits to us from it is sufficient to prove what value the oral tradition still possessed at that time. Let one read, for example, the legendary narrative of the Papias fragments concerning Justus Barsabbas,[26] or, above all, let one compare his obscene legendary narrative concerning the death of Judas Iscariot with the New Testament accounts concerning the same event (Matt. 27:3 ff. and Acts 1:18 ff.) .[27] Then one will understand why the Church developed a distrust of the tradition, and on this ground subordinated it to the norm of a canon. With the removal in time from the mid-point, the tradition, taken alone, no longer offered any guarantee for a legitimate development of the gospel.

At the proper moment, while there was still time, the Ancient Church by forming the canon took a firm hold of the previous apostolic tradition, which in its entirety was still connected with the mid-point and almost belonged to it. The Church also added to that tradition, as a principle of interpretation, the ancient rule of faith. By so doing it made the decisive distinction between the ancient tradition, which was now codified as Scripture, and the now beginning *further* tra-

[26] *Patrum apostolicorum opera,* ed. Gebhardt-Harnack-Zahn, Pap. fragm. III (Eusebius, *Church History,* III, 39, 9) .

[27] *Ibid.,* fragm. V (*ed. minor,* fragm. III). The narrative of Acts 1:18, to be sure, already shows clear signs of a development in the direction of the Papias legend.

dition, which was to be controlled and judged on the basis of that earlier one. It should never be forgotten that it was the developing Catholic Church itself that about this time created this specific norm; this step could have no other meaning than that the Church thereby placed the Scripture over all tradition that might develop after that time.

In opposition to the Protestant narrowing of the Primitive Christian faith, however, it must be emphasized that the Ancient Church, by thus setting up the canon, did not intend to prevent completely the rise of a further Church tradition; it believed, of course, that the redemptive history would continue to develop, but it also believed that only from the fixed orientation point at the mid-point could one recognize where this redemptive history really continues. This orientation to the center is meant to protect the Church against taking false ecclesiastical developments as redemptive history.

Thus *the Scripture itself must, so to speak, be regarded as also belonging to the center.* The fact that these books were written in the apostolic age was at a later time necessarily included in the redemptive happening of the mid-point. The result of this was that from the second half of the second century the entire apostolic age was regarded as the time of the unique *foundation* of the Church, and that this foundation, which, to be sure, already belongs to the post-Easter present period, was nevertheless still understood as an event of the mid-point itself. The apostles, and the New Testament Scripture traced back to them, thus received a place in the unique event at the mid-point, although on the other side they already belonged to the unique events of the period of the Church. However, in this latter connection they occupy an exceptional position, namely, as foundation.

Since this is so, a saying that in the New Testament has reference to the apostolic calling cannot from the standpoint of the Ancient Church be referred without further ado to the bishop's office. The apostolic calling is unique (ἐφάπαξ); it is not transferable. For in the New Testament the apostle is the

witness to the resurrection of Jesus Christ, the One who appeared in the flesh. This the later leaders of the Church can
no longer be. The preaching, as we have seen, must indeed
continue to the end, but the *foundation* of this preaching,
namely, the witness of the apostles who "have seen the Lord,"
cannot continue.

The undeniable fact that Primitive Christianity, in the first
period, did not take into account that the present time phase
would continue on beyond the time of the work of the apostles does not deprive of value the distinction between the
preaching of the Church and the apostolic foundation of this
preaching. The distinction, to be sure, became meaningful
only from the moment when this expectation was proved to
be erroneous (see pp. 87 f.). We know that Paul, for his part,
put aside this limitation while his active ministry was still in
progress.
The Ancient Church created the New Testament canon
when it became clear that the Church was continuing while
the apostles were all dead, and precisely in this Scriptural fixing of the apostolic witness it remained true to the original
evaluation of the apostolate as a unique function.

The Church is "built upon the foundation of the apostles
and prophets" (Eph. 2:20). The foundation can be laid only
once. Therefore even the famous saying of Jesus concerning
the Church, in Matt. 16:18, cannot furnish Biblical justification of the papacy.

It is with this question and only with this question that the
Protestant-Catholic discussion concerning Matt. 16:18 should
deal. Protestant exegesis has often made its task too easy when
it has believed that in an *a priori* and radical way it can
completely get rid of the problem by declaring the passage
spurious or by denying the residence of Peter in Rome. On
the one side, the arguments that are drawn from literary
criticism and the saying's content in order to deny the genuineness are not sound enough; that the saying is present only in
Matthew does not in itself say anything,[28] for, after all, many

[28] Literary comparison of the Synoptic accounts, to be sure, shows
that the saying is certainly not introduced in the right setting when

sayings whose genuineness has never been doubted belong to the material found only in Matthew; the claim that the mention of the " Church " is impossible on the lips of Jesus cannot be regarded as any more convincing, especially when one goes back to the Semitic equivalent.[29] On the other side, the attempt recently made by Karl Heussi, in opposition to Hans Lietzmann, to deny the residence of Peter in Rome [30] cannot be held to be any more successful than the attempts of his predecessors. In this connection, however, we should note that even the acceptance of the view that Peter died in Rome as a martyr does not prove that he was the bishop of the Roman Church.

The Reformers, to be sure, endeavored to explain the saying as directed by Jesus to Peter, but their attempt to refer the words concerning the rock to the faith of Peter instead of to his person is not at all suggested by an unprejudiced exegesis; it betrays all too much influence of the polemical tendency to rob the papacy of the possibility of supporting itself by this saying. In actual fact, the saying is directed to the person of the apostle, but only to him, and indeed to him in so far as he is the once-for-all established foundation of the Church. The foundation of a house is laid but once, namely, at the beginning.

Thus in this problem also we find confirmed the double character which is determinative for the present period as for every section of the redemptive line; each phase of the redemptive history has its own significance, but only in connection with the Christ-event at the mid-point. In opposition to Catholicism we have emphasized that according to Primitive Christian faith the present, from the viewpoint of redemptive

---

Matthew connects it with the narrative of the event at Caesarea Philippi (Mark 8:27–33), whose point cannot be harmonized with Matt. 16:17. This, however, by no means proves that the saying is not genuine.

[29] See p. 150.

[30] Karl Heussi, *War Petrus in Rom?*, 1936. In *Petrus und Paulus in Rom*, 1915, 2d ed., 1927, H. Lietzmann had already demonstrated on the basis of archaeological evidence that the martyr death of Peter at Rome cannot be denied. The appearance of K. Heussi's pamphlet provoked a controversy in 1936–1937 between K. Heussi and H. Lietzmann, into the details of which we need not enter here.

history, is rightly evaluated only in its subordination to the mid-point in time, and this means, from the standpoint of the post-Apostolic Church, in subordination to the Scripture; in opposition to a cramped Protestantism we have emphasized that the redemptive history has been advancing continuously ever since the ascension of Christ, and that our present period has its particular meaning for redemptive history.

PART III

REDEMPTIVE HISTORY AND THE GENERAL COURSE OF WORLD EVENTS

" Through whom are all things"

1

REDEMPTIVE HISTORY AND CHRISTIAN UNIVERSALISM

IN WHAT PRECEDES we have sought to determine both the redemptive line as a whole and the manifold relations of its parts to one another. It is now necessary to establish, so to speak, the radiations of this line into the area of the happenings that do not constitute redemptive history in the special sense. Is there a real justification for such an attempt, from the standpoint of the New Testament? Is it not the intention of Primitive Christianity to withdraw quite consciously and in extreme concentration to the slender line of salvation? Is it not the case that only this small strip is brightly illuminated, while no light falls upon the broad surrounding surface, which is shrouded in black darkness? " The light shines in the darkness, and the darkness has not received it "; thus reads the prologue of the Gospel of John. With these words the concentration, to be sure, is most strongly emphasized, but on the other hand it is presupposed that the light has the tendency to shine forth, and that therefore in principle a conflict must occur. " He came unto his own." The world is, after all, the possession of Christ (John 1:11) .[1]

Great significance is ascribed to the mediatorial activity of Christ in Creation, both by the earliest two-part formulas of faith (I Cor. 8:6) and by the New Testament authors in decisive passages (John 1:3; Col. 1:16; Heb. 1:2,10) . This in it-

---

[1] τὰ ἴδια is interpreted by R. Bultmann, *Das Evangelium des Johannes*, 1941, p. 34, to refer to the " world of mankind."

self is sufficient to prove that Primitive Christianity, in spite of all its concentration upon the redemptive line in the narrower sense, or rather on the basis of this concentration, has in view the *entire world process*. The primitive confession " *Kyrios Christos*," " Christ rules as Lord," whose primary reference is to the present, expresses at the same time Christ's universal Lordship, for *Kyrios*, interpreted on the basis of the Hebrew *Adonai* (Lord) as well as on the basis of the Hellenistic usage of the Greek word, includes a radical totalitarian claim. This fact also confirms the view that, paradoxical as it may seem, the concentration upon redemptive history signifies the very opposite of indifference toward the world process.

We recall what was said in Part I concerning the double movement of the line of salvation.[2] We there established the fact that the principle of this movement is that of election and representation. It takes its start from the broadest conceivable basis and narrows steadily until it reaches that center from which it again broadens out: Creation — mankind — Israel — the remnant — the One — the apostles — the Church — mankind — the new creation. The Primitive Christian universalism is bound to this concept of *representation*. With this is connected the redemptive line's unity, so characteristic of the New Testament revelation; it is the Christ-line not merely from a certain point on, but in its entire extension. All dualism between creation and redemption is here excluded. In the New Testament there cannot be, in addition to the Christ-line of redemption, another and separate God-line of creation. Rather, the redemptive process receives its world-wide significance not only from the broad base of departure and the broad final goal, but also from the universal outreach of the event at the mid-point, the event in which the narrowing reaches its climax precisely for the sake of the redemption of all. For Primitive Christianity, there is only the one line of divine activity; it is that one of which it is said from beginning to end: everything *from* God and *to* God, and everything *through* Christ,

---

[2] See Part I, Chapter 8.

through the Word, " through him."

Is the " offense," the " foolishness," of New Testament thinking about redemptive history, to which we made reference in the Introduction, removed or even lessened by the fact that the concentration of redemptive history is universalistic? Even the paradoxical conjoining of words to which we had to turn, " universalistic concentration," shows that this question is to be answered in the negative. Indeed, this redemptive line, from the standpoint of secular thinking, cannot serve as a platform for the comprehension of the universal process; it must still appear not only much too small, but also much too arbitrarily drawn or, better, selected. The thing to do is to let the entire paradox stand as such, and not attempt to resolve it, for example, in any rational way. We really have to do here with both things: with the most extreme concentration and with the widest universalism, which includes not only all secular human happenings but also the entire natural process in one and the same view.

There is according to the New Testament a *Christian universalism*. This word formation points again to the paradox which we here want to point out. For " Christian " specifically means limitation to a slender Christ-line.

In the three decisive stages of the Christ-line of salvation the general process is drawn into the redemptive process. It is so in Creation: everything is created through Christ. It is so in Christ's death and resurrection: everything is reconciled through him. It is so in the eschatological completion: everything is subjected to God, who is all in all.

It is clear that in the sections that lie between these three main points of the line, the general process of events cannot simply vanish from the field of vision of the redemptive history, even if that process does unfold outside of this history. Indeed, the narrowing of the process before the incarnation of Christ, as well as its broadening out after his resurrection,[3] occurs for the sake of those who remain outside.

3 See pp. 116 f.

Since the time of Abraham there has been occurring a course of events which, to be sure, develops outside of the real redemptive history, but which nevertheless has proceeded from it and will again enter into it; indeed, since Christ's death and resurrection it already has begun to enter into it again. The human figures in this process are the Gentiles, that is, precisely those people who do not figure in that development in redemptive history which began with Abraham.

The frequently cited passages Rom. 1:18 ff., Rom. 2:14 ff., and Acts 17:22 ff. show only how these Gentiles indirectly still remain within the horizon of the redemptive process; this is true inasmuch as it is also on account of *their* guilt that Christ must die, since they react negatively to the revelation that has been given them (Rom. 1:18 ff.), and inasmuch as on the other hand, in comparison with the guilty Jews, they will suffer no disadvantage because they were not included in the giving of the law through Moses (Rom. 2:14 ff.).

The problem of the relation between the Christian redemptive revelation and a non-Christian revelation is not under discussion at all in these passages; it will emerge only later in the apologists, above all, in Justin. The revelation to the Gentiles which is here presupposed is none other than that which, at the very beginning of the historical process, went forth to all mankind as a demand for the recognition of human impotence (Rom. 1:21); it accordingly belongs to the Christ-line. But now, as before Abraham, this revelation leads to guilt, because God is indeed recognized but is not glorified as such, so that in spite of this recognition there is only " blinding and darkness " (Rom. 1:21).

The concept of " natural revelation," which emerges only later, is still foreign to the New Testament. In the passages mentioned the discussion concerns the Gentiles from the point of view of their relation to the *redemptive process,* not primarily from the point of view of the revelation which is given to them. The latter is mentioned only as a function of that process. The intention is to show that even those who, in the time since Abraham, have no role in the redemptive process, nevertheless have preserved their relation to this process, inasmuch as even their attitude to the revelation which has been given to them can have as its result only human guilt and divine "wrath" (Rom. 1:18 ff.). On the other hand, however, even though they do not pass through the stage that the law occupies in redemptive history (Rom. 2:14 ff.), their attitude can become the presupposition of faith in the single way of salvation.

In the context of Rom. 1:18, therefore, the mention of the divine revelation to the Gentiles among the works of Creation cannot have the aim of providing a basis for a natural revelation in addition to the Christian revelation given in redemptive history. It rather has only the meaning of showing that the Gentiles, like the Jews, are "inexcusable." For in the face of this revelation they, precisely like the great majority of men before Abraham, have rested content with a purely theoretical knowledge of God, and this has led them to place the Creation in the place of the Creator, instead of glorifying God as God (v. 21). Had they recognized themselves in their creatureliness and acted accordingly, the same result would thereby have been achieved that faith in the atoning work of Christ must now effect. But that did not happen and does not happen upon the soil of paganism. Paul merely confirms the fact that the revelation through the works of Creation, although when viewed in the light of Christ it is already a revelation of Christ, does not effectually lead the Gentiles to Christ. For them it only prepares for the revelation in the cross; it shows their guilt and makes it known that for them also, because of their guilt, the only way open is the way of Christ's death on the cross (as it is for the Jews, who in like manner have taken their revelation of the law as an occasion of human presumption; see Rom., ch. 2).

On this point R. Bultmann, in *Offenbarung und Heilsgeschehen*, 1941, p. 23, writes quite correctly: " But why does he [Paul] speak of this? In order to set forth ' natural theology,' that is, in order to show God's revelation in the world? In order to open men's eyes for God's revelation outside of Christ? Rather, in order to open their eyes solely for the revelations of God in Christ! And therefore in order to bring an accusation, so that they have no excuse! For wherein does the natural theology consist? In this, that the Creation teaches man to understand himself as a creature, so that he becomes conscious of his limits and knows himself as the recipient of gift and demand."

The fact that the Gentiles are not drawn into the redemptive process which moves forward from Abraham is, however, not only no excuse for them, but also signifies, on the other hand, that they are at *no disadvantage* in the judgment. This latter point, if τὰ ἔθνη in Rom. 2:14 ff. means the Gentiles,[4] is the meaning of this passage, where the discussion concerns the law written in the hearts, which manifests itself as "conscience" and as "accusing and defending thoughts." In any case, here also we have to do with the establishment, not of a natural theology independent of Christ, but of a condition which the Gentiles have in common with mankind before the election of Israel. This revelation in the heart does not stand unrelated beside the fact that Christ had to die also for the Gentiles. The judgment of which v. 16 speaks is indeed the last judgment, which for Paul is not conceivable apart from Christ and of which it is expressly said that it takes place "according to my gospel through Jesus Christ." At that moment the Gentiles, in comparison with the Jews, will suffer no disadvantage because they were not chosen to pass through the stages of the redemptive history; that is, they will not suffer because they did not belong to the people of Israel, to whom the divine law was imparted through Moses. There is here present no contrast between natural and Christian revelation; the contrast is rather between revelation without and revelation with the Mosaic law. To the Gentiles at their conversion is granted what we may call an "overleaping" of the legal stage of redemptive history; this is because *Christ is indeed the fulfillment of the law and so includes this stage.*

Here too, therefore, the revelation in the hearts is not introduced as one that leads to salvation independently of Christ. There is also no word to indicate that it prepares for the revelation in Christ. It is only said that those who were not chosen to take part in the redemptive revelation in history need not pass through the preceding stage of the law in order finally to attain to salvation (which it is understood they can do only

---

[4] On philological grounds, to be sure, a reference to Gentile Christians is quite possible. See Rom. 16:4; Gal. 2:12; Eph. 3:1. If this view is accepted, what is said above is so much the more true.

through Christ!).

How and when the revelation of the Crucified One is given to those who died as Gentiles we do not learn at all from Paul. Moreover, the remaining writings of the New Testament give us no information on this point, with the exception of I Peter (chs. 3:19; 4:6). The preaching to the dead which is there mentioned probably contains an answer to this question. Later the Book of Hermas was busied with it in a similar manner, in that it extends the preaching activity among the dead even to the apostles.[5]

In Paul's Areopagus speech (Acts 17:22 ff.) the point is in the fact that the apostle preaches what the Gentiles "ignorantly" have worshiped (v. 23), and shows that the God who remained unknown to them is the same one who raised Christ from the dead (v. 31). God now reveals this while he "overlooks the times of ignorance" (v. 30). If Paul in Athens had simply placed a natural revelation of God beside the Christian one, there would have been no laughter. The failure of his speech is explained by this very fact, that he permitted the offense to stand; he preserved the unity of the redemptive line which begins with Adam (v. 26) and ends with the resurrection of Christ. That the Gentiles of Athens, according to Acts 17:32, reject Paul's Areopagus speech can be regarded as a confirmation of that which Paul set forth in Rom. 1:18 ff.; that is, the Gentiles after Abraham, just as previously, close their minds to the revelation of God in the works of Creation, so that all their knowledge of the fact that we are his offspring (v. 28) is nevertheless only "ignorance" (v. 30).

It is not the relation of the Christian revelation to a "natural revelation" independent of Christ that interests the writers of the New Testament books, but rather the significance that the Gentiles have in the light of the redemptive process. If the idea of the advancing preparation of salvation through election and representation is intended to have a meaning, then those who are represented must remain in the field of vision of the redemptive line. It thus is shown why they must be represented, but also how this representation, through the hardening of Israel (Rom. 11:11), leads in a positive way to

[5] Similitudes, IX, 16, 57.

the result that they "enter" into the redemptive movement
of the Church (Rom. 11:25). Therefore all so-called "secular"
occurrence stands in relation to the redemptive history. The
two areas are different, indeed, but not separated. To place
them beside one another in separation — for example, to assign one to Creation and only the other to redemption through
Christ — would mean a failure to understand correctly the
Primitive Christian universalism.

Hofmann, the already mentioned Erlangen theologian and
a brilliant representative of the so-called " theology of redemptive history " in the nineteenth century, seeks an explanation
of the relation between the redemptive movement and the
general process of history that would preserve the particular
character of the New Testament redemptive history. He bases
his explanation upon the concept of *prediction*. (See p. 140.)
Everything that occurs is a prediction of an occurrence to
come. Thus he so connects the secular history that it forms
one line with the Biblical course of events, but nevertheless
he does not thereby do justice to the specific claim of the Biblical revelation.

The general process of history takes its start from the same
line as does the redemptive process, and it finally passes over
into the same line. The present stage of redemptive history,
since the resurrection of Christ, is already on the way back to
that junction. Christ already rules over all things, but in a
way visible only to faith. In proclaiming this fact, of which it
knows by faith, the Church fulfills the task of carrying the
development on to the goal where the now invisible Lordship
of Christ will be visible to all. Because the present is the time
in which everything in heaven and on earth is already committed to Christ, it is particularly at this point in the faith of
Primitive Christianity that the general process of history appears with particular clarity to join unconsciously in supporting the narrower redemptive process. The way in which this
happens is to be indicated in the next two chapters.

2

THE COMPLETE LORDSHIP OF CHRIST AND THE REDEMPTIVE PROCESS

THE RESULT of Christ's death and resurrection is that the Lordship over all things is committed to him. The entire creation is affected by this redemptive event. Ever since the ascension Christ sits at the right hand of God, and everything is put under his feet. With this is connected the fact that since reaching this mid-point the world process is drawn into the redemptive history in a decisive manner. To be sure, this history, until the completion of the new creation, must still travel the prescribed way from the central One to the many. Because, however, the decisive victory has already been won for the entire world, interest in the world process is concentrated in the New Testament upon the present which develops from this victory.

Even in this period the difference between the narrower redemptive history, as it unfolds in the Church, and the universal process is not obliterated. The peculiar, complex relationship in which each stands to the other during this period of time, and which is connected with the intermediate character of the present, finds a more precise definition in the two New Testament concepts " sovereign Lordship of Christ " and " Church." I have investigated this relationship in an earlier publication,[1] and for all details must refer to that study. Here I select and present that which requires consideration in connection with the problem we are now facing.

[1] *Königsherrschaft Christi und Kirche im Neuen Testament*, 1941.

We have already cited the texts that speak of the subjection of the invisible powers by Christ.[2] Hence we may here limit ourselves to placing those that speak of Christ's present Lordship over all things in contrast to those that speak of his Lordship exercised only over that small section which is the Church.

It is not only the general history of mankind, but also the process of nature, that stands in this noteworthy relationship to the slender course of events in the Church.

To Christ is committed everything in heaven and on earth (Matt. 28:18); the knees of all creatures, of those in heaven and upon earth and under the earth, bend before him (Phil. 2:10). Likewise, the confession *Kyrios* (= *Adonai*) *Iēsous Christos*, "Jesus Christ rules as Lord," which "every tongue" utters, says that there is no being and no place in the entire creation over which he is not the Lord. This is what it must mean when it says that God has given to him the name that is "above every name" (Phil. 2:9), that is, his own name, Lord = *Adonai*.

On the other hand, the Church is named in the closest connection precisely in the passages where the discussion deals with this Lordship of Christ over the entire visible and invisible world. In Col. 1:18 the apostle, after he mentions the creation of visible and invisible things, the "thrones, dominions, principalities, and powers, through Christ and unto him," writes that Christ is the head of the body, the Church, and immediately thereafter, in v. 20, he speaks of the fact that God through the blood of Christ the crucified has reconciled with himself *everything* that is on earth and in heaven. Likewise we read in ch. 2:10 that Christ is the *head of every principality and power*. How can Christ be designated at the same time as head only of the small Church and as head of all things? The same astonishing connection appears in Ephesians. According to Eph. 1:10, God determined that in Christ he would bring under one head everything that is in the heavens and on

2 See pp. 153 f.

earth, and according to v. 22 he put *everything* under Christ's feet and gave him to the Church as *head over all things*. Moreover, the already mentioned saying of the Risen One concerning the power given him over all things stands in the closest connection with the immediately following command to baptize, which indeed is equivalent to a command to found the Church (Matt. 28:18 f.).

In Colossians and Ephesians the relation Christ — Church — World is expressed by the concepts head and body. In that connection we should note that Christ is designated as head of everything *and* of the Church. On the contrary, here, as also elsewhere in the New Testament, only the Church is the body of Christ upon earth. The use of the term *"corpus christianum,"* which emerges later in Church history, thus finds no support in the New Testament.

This idea that Christ from the time of his resurrection is head of the Church and likewise head of all visible and invisible beings, but that his body, on the contrary, is represented only by the Church, helps us to understand better the close relation that Primitive Christianity presupposes to exist in the present period between redemptive process and general world process. The Church as Christ's body continues his work on earth. What here happens is decisive for all beings: "Through the Church the manifold wisdom of God is proclaimed to the lordships and powers in the heavenly world" (Eph. 3:10). From this center Christ rules the world of the visible and invisible. It is the heart and center of his Lordship. To be sure, he also rules over the Church, for he is also its head, but in such a way that the Church, in so far as he takes form in it (Gal. 4:19), likewise rules with him (II Tim. 2:12).

Church and world are not two circular surfaces that lie beside one another, so to speak, or perhaps only touch or intersect. They also are not identical. We must rather conceive two concentric circles, whose common center is Christ. The entire circular surface $(r_1 + r_2)$ is the reign of Christ; the inner circle (r_1) is the Church, the surface lying between the two circumferences (r_2) is the world.

The inner surface stands in closer relation to Christ than does the outer one, and yet Christ is the common center. Thus the alternative between two areas or one area [3] does not exist in the New Testament. The relation is more complex. This will become clear especially in the Primitive Christian attitude to the State.

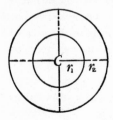

C = CHRIST
r_1 = CHURCH
r_2 = WORLD
$r_1 + r_2$ = REIGN OF CHRIST

The inner area, to be sure, is also made up of sinful men, but nevertheless of such as believe in the redemption in Christ; by this faith they know concerning Christ's rule over them and over the entire world. The rest of the visible and invisible world is also ruled by Christ, but for the time being does not know it. It can stand *unconsciously* under the Lordship of Christ, since it is indeed subjected to him. But the Church has to proclaim to all the world that all stand under the same Lordship, whether they belong to the Church or not. Because the Church alone knows of this *Kyrios Christos,* it must preach this Lordship to those who, without knowing it, are also subjected to it and fulfill the function assigned to them.

Therefore the Church must be interested in everything that happens in the world outside its bounds; the redemptive history has reached a point where, according to the New Testament revelation, the world process has already begun to enter again into the redemptive process, without, however, being as yet identical with it. But this interest, if it roots in the New

[3] See Emil Brunner, " Zur christologische Begründung des Staates " (*Kirchenblatt für die reformierte Schweiz,* 1943, pp. 2 ff., 18 ff., 34 ff.) . For a criticism of these discussions that Brunner presents, see pp. 206 ff.

Testament, must of course have its grounding in redemptive history, in Christology.[4]

Up to this point we have spoken only of the present stage of redemptive history. To what extent does the world process stand in an analogous relation to the other sections of the time line of redemption? We have seen that at the beginning all redemptive occurrence is likewise world occurrence. It is also clear without further discussion that at the end, according to Christian faith, the redemptive history again becomes world history, for indeed the meaning of the consummation is that " all Israel " enters in, both the Gentiles and the previously elected people of Israel (Rom. 11:25 ff.) , and that a new heaven and a new earth are created.

Concerning the time from Abraham to Christ, however, the Primitive Christian writings contain very few references that deal with this point. As far as this period's " secular " history as such is concerned, we are thrown back upon deductions. We may perhaps assume that in this respect Primitive Christianity appropriated the Old Testament outlook, in which, on the one hand, the secular process is considered as a foil of the redemptive process, while on the other hand Gentile peoples and rulers can be, even this early, direct but unconscious instruments of the redemptive process. It is sufficient here to point to the role of the Assyrians in the older prophets and of Cyrus in Deutero-Isaiah. In some such way the first Christians may have conceived the preparation for the Lordship of Christ in the course of secular events in the Old Testament period.

In the New Testament also the secular " contemporary history " is still at first only the " background " of the redemptive process, as for example when the emperor Tiberius is mentioned in Luke 3:1. The census which the emperor Augustus

---

[4] Karl Barth's utterances dealing with the events of the years 1938 to 1945 are to be evaluated as an attempt to interpret the most recent course of events in this sense. See *Eine Schweizer Stimme 1938–1945*, 1945.

causes to be made (Luke 2:1) is already of more significance; here the pagan emperor is already, though unconsciously, an active instrument in the redemptive process. Pilate, particularly as presented in the Gospel of John (ch. 19:11), is completely and in an outstanding way the involuntary instrument of the Christ-event, which he brings to its very climax, to the decision on the cross.[5] Thus the mention of Pontius Pilate in the Apostles' Creed not only corresponds to a definite historical situation of the Church,[6] but also has a theological significance, inasmuch as it shows by way of example how the course of even the so-called secular events stands in relation to the redemptive history.

In the Pauline estimate of the role of Pilate, on the other hand, a still more concrete connection becomes clearly recognizable. It will permit us in the following chapter to give a more specific statement of the way in which Primitive Christianity fits the world process into the redemptive process.

[5] See Karl Barth, *Rechtfertigung und Recht,* 1938. Concerning the historical circumstances of the trial of Jesus, to be sure, I hold a different opinion. The legal responsibility for the sentence of condemnation seems to me to lie entirely on the side of the Romans. But this is not the place to prove this statement.

[6] Following G. Baldensperger, " Il a rendu témoignage devant Ponce Pilate " (*Revue d'Histoire et de Philosophie religieuses,* 1922, pp. 1 ff., 95 ff.) , I have sought to show in my work on *Die ersten christlichen Glaubensbekenntnisse,* 1943, pp. 20 ff. (Eng. tr., *The Earliest Christian Confessions,* 1949, pp. 25 ff.) , that, speaking historically, the mention of Pontius Pilate in the Creed owes its origin to the fact that the earliest formulas of faith were spoken in persecution, before pagan courts, where the Christians were encouraged to give their witness by the reference to Christ's own witness before Pontius Pilate (cf. I Tim. 6:13) .

3

THE SUBJECTION OF THE INVISIBLE POWERS AND THEIR RELATION IN REDEMPTIVE HISTORY TO THE WORLD PROCESS (STATE AND REDEMPTIVE HISTORY)

In I Cor. 2:8, in the course of his discussion concerning the "wisdom" destined by God unto our glory, Paul writes that the rulers of this world had not recognized this wisdom. "For had they recognized it, they would not have crucified the Lord of glory." By "the rulers of this age" Paul manifestly means *both* the invisible "princes of this world," who are often mentioned as such, and their actual human instruments, Herod and Pilate. We thereby are directed to an eminently important relation, which gives us the key for the deeper understanding of the problem of redemptive history and history. This problem we now take up.

As we saw above,[1] the assertion that God is also the creator of the invisible things — an assertion taken up into the later Church confessions of faith in the Orient, as, for example, the Niceno-Constantinopolitan one known from the liturgy of the Mass — has its foundation in the New Testament. On the other hand, we have established the fact that Primitive Christianity does not stop with this statement concerning the creation of the *invisibilia,* but proclaims the victory of Christ over these powers, and we have shown that they are particularly mentioned in every place where his complete Lordship is being discussed.

The existence of these powers Paul regards as certain, even

---

[1] See pp. 103 f.

if they have no significance as mediators between God and us
(I Cor. 2:8). As far as their character is concerned, he indeed
presupposes much as known, since he here is dealing with
views current in late Judaism. His readers obviously know
better than we do what is meant when he speaks of " principalities, powers, rulers, thrones, lordships." Hence we should
pay more attention than is usually given to the late Jewish
teaching concerning these angelic powers.

It is connected with an arbitrary distinction between central
and peripheral statements of the New Testament when, in the
commentaries and presentations of New Testament theology,
this entire complex of questions is regarded as more or less
unimportant, as nothing but a framework " conditioned by the
contemporary situation." We must repeat here that there is
but one objective criterion for determining what is essential,
namely, the earliest formulas of faith. We have seen, however,
that in these quite brief summaries of the Primitive Christian
revelation the invisible powers are almost invariably mentioned. Whatever our personal attitude toward this view may
be, we must conclude from this fact that these powers, in the
faith of Primitive Christianity, did not belong merely to the
framework " conditioned by the contemporary situation." It is
these invisible beings who in some way — not, to be sure, as
mediators, but rather as executive instruments of the reign
of Christ — *stand behind what occurs in the world.*

We must regard the late Jewish teaching concerning the
angels, and especially concerning the angels of the peoples, as
belonging to the solid content of faith in the New Testament.

It is the merit of Martin Dibelius that in *Die Geisterwelt im
Glauben des Paulus,* 1909, he pointed out for the first time
the importance of the faith, widespread in Judaism, that there
is a particular angel for each people. Günther Dehn, in his
essay, " Engel und Obrigkeit, ein Beitrag zum Verständnis von
Röm. 13:1–7 " (in the testimonial volume, *Theologische Aufsätze für Karl Barth,* 1936), has taken up this reference and
developed it in greater detail.

This abundantly attested late Jewish belief that all peoples are ruled through angels is present particularly in The Book of Daniel, in The Wisdom of Jesus, Son of Sirach, and in the Book of Enoch, and it can be shown to be present also in the Talmud and Midrash. It explains the fact that in the already mentioned Ps. 110 the subjection of the pagan enemies of Israel which is there promised to the king of Israel can be unhesitatingly referred to the invisible powers. This faith further explains how, in the well-known ancient confessional psalm, Phil. 2:10, the Old Testament saying of Isa. 45:22 f., " To me every knee shall bow," which originally had in view the Gentiles, could be referred to the " beings in heaven, on earth, and in the underworld."

We understand on the basis of this faith how the existing earthly political power belongs in the realm of such angelic powers. They stood behind the State authorities which had brought Christ to the cross. They are the " rulers of this age," whom we mentioned at the beginning of this chapter. Moreover, I Cor. 6:3 proves that according to the Primitive Christian view these invisible angelic powers stand behind the earthly states. For it is only on this assumption that it has any meaning when Paul justifies his admonition to the Church, to avoid the State courts in trials among Christians, by reference to the fact that the members of the Church will judge the " angels " at the end of the days.

Thus the so-called " Christological grounding of the State " is not at all based, as is usually presupposed by the opponents of this view, merely upon the interpretation given to the " authorities " (ἐξουσίαι) of Rom. 13:1. It is based rather upon the very specific late Jewish teaching concerning the angels of the peoples; this teaching is taken up into Primitive Christianity and actually plays there a very important role in connection with the significance that attaches to the *subjection of the angelic powers through Christ.*

Therefore it will not do to transfer this conception of the

angels and powers to the periphery of the Pauline theology, as is done by G. Kittel, in *Christus und Imperator, Das Urteil der ersten Christen über den Staat*, 1931, p. 51, and by F.-J. Leenhardt, in *Le chrétien doit-il servir l'État?*, 1939, p. 36; on these and other grounds [2] they reject the reference of the "authorities" of Rom. 13:1 to angelic powers.

The famous passage Rom. 13:1 ff. contains rather a confirmation of this conception. We shall see that only when this conception is found there does the entire section become really clear; only then does it fall into harmony with the entire outlook of Paul.

It is, indeed, entirely correct that in the usual interpretation a discrepancy exists between this passage and everything that we know of Paul's attitude; as a result it has often been thought that the entire section cannot have been written by Paul (so most recently Chr. Eggenberger, "Der Sinn der Argumentation in Röm. 13:2–5," in *Kirchenblatt für die reformierte Schweiz*, 1945, pp. 243 f., written in connection with the series of articles in the same journal by W. Mögling on "Anspruch, Grenze, und Aufgabe des Staats," 1945, pp. 162 ff., 178 ff., 194 ff., 212 ff.; see also the answer to Chr. Eggenberger, *ibid.*, 1945, p. 278).

For everyone who comes from the other Pauline passages to Rom. 13:1 and considers it without prejudice, uninfluenced by the usage of the word in secular history and by the familiar translation into modern languages,[3] it is by far the most natural thing to give to the plural ἐξουσίαι no other sense than that which it always has for Paul, that is, the meaning of "angelic powers."

When G. Kittel, *op. cit.*, p. 50, argues against this that in some eighty out of ninety instances where the New Testament has the word ἐξουσία, we find only the ordinary meaning of "any power which someone has," it must be replied that this

---

[2] See below in this chapter.

[3] We should become accustomed to translating thus: "Let everyone be subjected to the supreme powers."

usage of the singular is not under discussion here. We here are dealing with the *plural form* ἐξουσίαι or with the pluralistic usage of the singular πᾶσα ἐξουσία (" all authority "), and with reference to it the result of New Testament statistical study is quite clear.

To be sure, it becomes crystal-clear from the context that the passage is speaking of the State. This, however, only proves that the conception that we have found in the other two Pauline passages and that is abundantly attested for late Judaism is also found here, the view, namely, that the actual State authority is thought of as the executive agent of angelic powers. The fact that in ordinary Greek usage the singular and the plural (even when used together with ἀρχαί, " principalities ") designate only the earthly magistracy,[4] may not be cited in proof of the view that also in Rom. 13:1 ff. only this meaning can be considered.[5] The ordinary Greek usage is not familiar with the late Jewish and New Testament teaching concerning the angelic powers. Accordingly, and as a matter of course, the corresponding use of the word ἐξουσίαι is also foreign to it. But that Paul, for whom this word elsewhere always designates angelic powers, thinks of them here too, but specifically as *the invisible angelic powers that stand behind the State government,* is naturally suggested by the very use of the word in secular history, a usage that was indeed known also to him and with which he connected the late Jewish and New Testament usage. Thus as a result the term has for Paul a double meaning, which in this case corresponds exactly to the content, since the State is indeed the executive agent of invisible powers.

The analogy to I Cor. 2:8 is complete with respect not only to content but also to language. For here also, where it is quite plain that by ἄρχοντες τοῦ αἰῶνος τούτου are meant both the invisible " rulers of this age " *and* the visible ones, Pilate and Herod, there stands in characteristic fashion a term that in

[4] See W. Förster, *Theologisches Wörterbuch zum N. T.,* article on ἐξουσίαι, II, p. 560.

[5] This false conclusion is drawn by G. Kittel, *op. cit.,* p. 50.

secular Greek naturally designates only the actual human rulers, while in the New Testament it designates also the invisible ones. In I Cor. 2:8 as well as in Rom. 13:1 the expressions are purposely so chosen that they make clear the *combined meaning* that is typical of the conception we have indicated.

This explanation of ἐξουσίαι, which is quite compelling, was represented later in antiquity, outside of the New Testament, by Gnostics in their interpretation of Rom. 13:1; this we learn through Irenaeus (*Against Heresies,* V,24,1). To be sure, we know nothing more definite concerning their interpretation of the entire passage. It is probable that these heretics, in the context of their dualistic outlook, conceived these " authorities " that stand behind the State simply as evil powers and nothing more; in this case, to be sure, it is not clear how they may have interpreted the demand of Paul for obedience to those powers.

In any case, it is an established fact that Irenaeus himself, the opponent of the Gnostics, only rejected the interpretation of " authorities " as angelic powers because he took into consideration merely this false dualistic understanding, and on this view to interpret the " authorities " to mean the invisible powers that stand behind the State would make of this State itself an institution hostile to God. The New Testament conception of " authorities," however, is definitely not dualistic in this sense. By their subjection under Christ the invisible powers have rather lost their evil character, and they also now stand under and within the Lordship of Christ, as long as they are subject to him and do not seek to become emancipated from their place in his service. Since Irenaeus probably, like his Gnostic opponents, reckons only with a false dualistic conception of the angelic powers, he must reject as heretical the connection with them of the " authorities " of Rom. 13:1.

That Irenaeus thus makes this mistake in explanation is due to the fact that in his battle against Gnostic dualism he exaggerates the straight line of development from the Creation to the redemption, and that he altogether fails to take account of the present stage of redemptive history (see p. 57). So it is typical for him that even in a confessional text handed down to him (*Against Heresies,* I,10,1), he refers to the eschatological future that which is there said concerning the *present* Lordship of Christ, namely, his Lordship over the invisible powers. From such a standpoint Irenaeus can understand the explanation of the "authorities" as the angelic powers only in the dualistic form in which it no doubt was actually represented by Gnostic heretics. For the complex situation of the present, where these powers are already subjected and nevertheless are not finally overcome, there is indeed in Irenaeus no room.

Interestingly enough, G. Kittel, *op. cit.,* pp. 48 ff., by his rejection of the reference of "authorities" to these powers, finally falls into precisely the same mistake, when on p. 50 he sees in this interpretation a discounting of the State *"in malam partem."* It is from this false presupposition that G. Kittel proceeds when he thinks that the passage I Peter 2:13–17, which has reference to Rom. 13:1 ff. and offers, so to speak, the first exegesis of this Pauline passage, certainly excludes that interpretation. He thus thinks because in the context so high a dignity is ascribed to the "human institution" (ἀνθρωπίνη κτίσις), in which the author of I Peter includes the State government. This dignity, however, is entirely harmonious with the character of the angelic "authority." In Rom. 13:4 the designation of the State as servant of God is to be taken in full earnest, in its scarcely surpassable dignity, even when and precisely when we know that behind the State stand the angelic powers, which on their part are responsible before God. Moreover, the text in the *Martyrdom of Polycarp* 10:2, which is cited by G. Kittel, proves nothing at all against the interpretation of the "authorities" of Rom. 13:1 as angelic powers, when we take into account the fact that by it the State is not discounted but on the contrary is honored, under the condition, of course, that the powers remain in their position of subjection.

In the Primitive Christian faith in the conquest of the invisible powers through Christ, the significant thing is the very fact that while this faith holds firmly to the existence of powers originally hostile to God, it nevertheless does not concede to this existence any independent significance, and so it avoids all dualism. The strongly Christocentric attitude is in no way endangered by this faith; " even if there are such beings," Paul writes in I Cor. 8:5 f., " Yet *we* have only *one* God and *one* Lord." To him, indeed, all these powers are now subjected. They are bound. That which the Apocalypse of John says of the binding of Satan in the end time (Rev. 20:2) holds true somehow for the Pauline conception of the present situation of the angelic powers. In the time between the resurrection and the Parousia of Christ they are, so to speak, bound as to a rope, which can be more or less lengthened, so that those among them who show tendencies to emancipation can have the illusion that they are releasing themselves from their bond with Christ, while in reality, by this striving which here and there appears, they only show once more their original de- monic character; they cannot, however, actually set themselves free. Their power is only an apparent power. The Church has so much the more the duty to stand against them, in view of the fact that it knows that their power is only apparent and that in reality Christ has already conquered all demons.

A certain freedom, however, is left to the angelic powers within their subject position. This explains how, in the pres- ent stage of redemptive history, it still is not possible for the Church to take without qualification or criticism the view that the State is divine, even though, on the other hand, the State too belongs within the Lordship of Christ. The situation is thus in this respect quite complex, and every simplifying pres- entation of it fails even in this point to do justice to the Primi- tive Christian conception. The complexity is connected with that of the entire intermediate situation of the present time. On the one side, the angelic powers are already subjected, and in this respect are placed in the service of Christ, so that of them it can be said in the most positive manner that al- though they had formerly been enemies they have now become " ministering spirits sent forth for ministry " (Heb. 1:14); hence obedience toward them is demanded from the Christians in Rom. 13:1 ff., where their agents are designated by precisely the same expressions as "God's minister" (Rom. 13:4) and as "servants of God" (Rom. 13:6). On the other side, however, the apostle Paul still remains critical toward this State; the Christians should keep away from the State courts and settle their cases among themselves (I Cor. 6:1 ff.). Not so very much later the same Roman state of which Paul speaks so positively in Rom., ch. 13, can be designated the "beast" by another New Testament writer (Rev. 13:1 ff.).

This apparently contradictory attitude extends through the entire New Testament. But of this contradiction also it holds good that it appears as such only for him who has not recognized the complexity of the situation in the redemptive history. We have seen that this complexity has its roots in a temporal but not in a metaphysical dualism. We know the ground of this temporal dualism. That tension between present and future, between "already fulfilled" and "not yet completed," which contains the key to the understanding of the entire New Testament, shows itself when applied to our problem in the fact that the angelic powers are already made the "footstool" of the feet of Christ, and yet must once more be overcome at the end. The Kingdom of Christ is indeed already present; in it both areas, the Church and the world, are placed under Christ; nevertheless they are distinguished, since they will merge into one only in the Kingdom of God, when at the end Christ's mediatorial role has been fulfilled (I Cor. 15:28).

If in the "authorities" of Rom. 13:1 as well as in the "rulers of this age" of I Cor. 2:8 we see both the invisible powers and their executive agents on earth, there results a completely unified view of the State in the New Testament, and the apparent contradiction within Paulinism between I Cor. 6:1 ff. and Rom. 13:1 ff., or the still greater one within the New Testament between Rev., ch. 13, and Rom., ch. 13, vanishes. For it becomes discernible that, in spite of all the positive statements of Rom. 13:1 ff., the State here, as in the entire Primitive Christian conception, is not an ultimate but only a penultimate institution, which will vanish when this age does;

the Christian believer will always place over against the State
a final question mark and will remain watchful and critical,
because he knows that behind it stand powers which do indeed have their place in the divine order determined by the
victory of Christ, but which nevertheless for the time being
still have a certain possibility of permitting their demonic
strivings for independence to flare up into apparent power.

I would go so far as to assert that precisely in Rom. 13:1 ff.,
according to the entire context, and even independently of the
meaning of the word "authorities," Paul starts from the
principle that the State has attained to such a dignity that
obedience is due to it, not by reason of its original nature, but
only because it has been given its place in the divine "order."
The context, that is to say, is usually not sufficiently taken
into account. The passage concerning the State, vs. 1–7, is embedded in a larger section, over which one could place the
title "Recompense and Love"; this section begins in ch. 12
(see especially vs. 17 ff.) and is continued in ch. 13:8. The
basic concepts of vengeance, of the vindication (ἐκδίκησις) and
the wrath (ὀργή) of God mentioned in ch. 12:19, recur in the
section concerning the State (ch. 13:4).[6] The readers are commanded not to avenge themselves, since, as it stands written,
vengeance belongs to God and only God has the right to exercise wrath. On the other side, the apostle, making use of the
same words, says that the State exercises vengeance "unto
wrath." This, however, says that the State does the opposite
of that which the fellowship of believers are commanded to
do; they are not to take vengeance on one another but to love
one another (v. 8). The apostle's intention is to explain
how *nevertheless* these very members of the Church have to
obey this State. Against this chiefly negative background we
must understand according to the context the positive command to be subject to the State. The entire context shows that
at the outset the word "nevertheless" must be placed above

---

[6] I see in this the proof that the passage concerning the State is not
to be regarded as an interpolation. See p. 194.

this discussion. Although the State applies a principle that is opposed to the essential Christian law of love, we should nevertheless obey it; indeed, rather, we should obey it precisely for this reason; for when it appears as an avenger, it does so only in its function as servant of the God to whom vengeance belongs. The obligation of this servant is to carry out the divine vengeance and the righteous judicial wrath of God. (The Christian knows that this divine vengeance is anchored in the divine love in Christ.)

From this point the apostle now goes a step farther: this commissioning of the State has as result that the State agrees with the Christian Church in its judgment concerning good and evil (vs. 3 f.). Indeed, recompense, punishment, and reward presuppose the capacity for this judgment. This agreement Paul simply confirms; the State rewards the good and punishes the evil. This accord with the Church in spite of the completely opposed fundamental position — here recompense, there love — comes from the fact that the State stands in a divine order in which it becomes the agent of the divine recompense. How important this concept of the divine " order " (τάξις) is to the apostle appears at the beginning of the chapter in the heaping up of the words that contain this root: ὑποτάσσεσθαι ("be subject"), τεταγμένος ("ordained"), ἀντιτάσσομαι ("resist"), διαταγή ("ordinance"). We thus confirm the fact that even apart from the significance of the word "authorities" in Rom., ch. 13, a view is here presupposed according to which the State, not by nature, but only by its being placed in a definite order, is God's servant and fulfills his will.

In this case, however, the context yields a complete confirmation of the interpretation, much disputed in recent years, that the "authorities" are the subjected angelic powers. On the other hand, this interpretation gives to the entire section a particular emphasis; it does so by giving the section a place in the article of faith, so very important for the Primitive Church, concerning the subjection of all invisible angelic powers; it thus builds the State into the structure of that order which Primitive Christianity regards as the *present sovereign reign of Christ*. The so-called "Christological foundation" of the State is thereby proved to be correct. It is in the position to explain satisfactorily the parallelism of I Cor. 6:1 ff. and Rom. 13:1 ff., and on the other hand of Rom. 13:1 ff. and Rev., ch. 13, which all refer to the same Roman State. The angelic powers are placed in the service of the Kingdom of Christ, not by their original nature, but only by being bound; they are, however, elevated to the highest dignity by the function that is here assigned to them. Nevertheless, they can for a time free themselves from their bound condition and then show their demonic character. But the final Christian criticism of the State can never be omitted, not even where a State remains in its completely bound situation; because in its original nature it is not divine, it can never be regarded as an ultimate fact. Hence the negative attitude in I Cor. 6:1 ff. toward so completely legitimate an institution as the State courts of justice. In view of this passage, which is also Pauline, Rom. 13:1 ff. cannot and must not be understood in so uncritical and unthinking a way as is often the case. Neither of the two passages may be explained without reference to the other.

The New Testament leaves unsettled a series of questions. It does not give us the criterion that permits us in every case to recognize whether a State does or does not remain within its own limits in the divine order. To be sure, we do learn in a specific case where a State oversteps its limits. We know from the Apocalypse of John that the State claim to emperor worship is irreconcilable with the confession *Kyrios Christos,* "Christ rules as Lord." On this basis we can further deduce that a State falls out of the area ascribed to it within the divine order when it does not content itself with that "which is Caesar's"; this happens, in other words, where the "authorities" seek to free themselves from their subjection under Christ's Lordship, and so again, with their apparent power, become demonic. But even where the State does not thus over-step its limits, it can happen that within the district assigned to it it ceases to be a just State and declares right to be wrong and wrong to be right. Primitive Christianity knows no instance of this case, for the Roman State was indeed a just State. Therefore the Primitive Christian opposition to it really appears only at the one place, where the disciple of Christ is asked to confess the emperor as the divine *Kyrios,* and where he is hindered from making his confession to his only *Kyrios,* Jesus Christ. In other respects Primitive Christianity is fully loyal in its attitude toward the Roman State; for where this State fulfills its own function it is really a "just State," to which what is said in Rom. 13:1 ff. applies.

The events of recent years, to be sure, have shown us with particular emphasis that a falling away from the divine order can also occur in the region that " is Caesar's."

In so far as this does not apply to the Roman State, the parallels that Christians in recent years have drawn between the Roman Empire and the Germany of National Socialism are not correct. By such comparisons too much honor has been given to National Socialism. Only the Roman State's surpassing of its limits in the imperial cult and the therewith connected aggression against the Christians, but not its general exercise of its functions as a State, can be compared with the State demonism that we have experienced in the most recent past.

The New Testament, since it nowhere foresees this case and reckons only with that relapse of the State into demonism which shows itself in the overstepping of its limits in the imperial cult, contains no sort of teaching concerning the tasks of the State. In this regard it simply confirms the fact that the State (the Roman State), in its judgment concerning good and evil, agrees with the Christian judgment. In what way this agreement is essentially possible is not explained. On this point the New Testament offers no theory, least of all one in terms of natural law.[7] In Rom., ch. 13, Paul simply traces this agreement back to the fact that the State stands in God's " order "; it should not be disputed that for Paul there is since Christ no other divine order than that of the Kingdom of Christ. This therefore is the sole foundation of the State.

This undoubtedly holds good not only for the Christian State but precisely for the *pagan* one. Indeed, the New Testament has no acquaintance with any but a pagan State. Even in Rom., ch. 13, Paul speaks of the pagan Roman State, which thus can be truly a member of the Kingdom of Christ, even when it does not know it. A Gentile State can be a just State, which both respects its limits and is God's servant in its judgment concerning good and evil and in its execution of the divine recompense. As a pagan State, to be sure, it does not know that it is a member of the Kingdom of Christ. The Church of Jesus Christ knows this and must always proclaim it, particularly when it perceives that the State is in danger of falling out of the divine order.

We thus see that the State is honored upon the basis of its position in the divine order, and only for that reason, but that it nevertheless does not have the same significance as does the Church. State and Church both belong in the Kingdom of Christ, and yet not in the same way, since only the Church knows it, while the State, in so far as it is a pagan State, does not know it.

The " Christological foundation " of the State which is here championed has been accused of making the subjection of the

---

[7] F.-J. Leenhardt, *Le chrétien doit-il servir l'État?*, 1939, has made the interesting attempt to explain the agreement, not by reference to natural law, but rather, in connection with Rom., ch. 13, by regarding love as the Christian basis of all secular law. In this view it is at least correct that the *Christian* statesman, who *knows* that Christ is Lord also over the State, is not " divided," as Emil Brunner thinks; as a Christian he does not make decisions in any other way than he does, for example, as a judge; rather, even within the State, he must in the last analysis stand in Christian love and carry out the will of Christ, which in the outer circle is no other than it is in the inner one.

powers simply identical with a "commissioning." [8] Yet, it is objected, the New Testament speaks only of a subjection. This, however, is not quite correct. As we have seen, The Epistle to the Hebrews in particular speaks, in a way similar to late Jewish teaching concerning angels, of the "ministering spirits, sent forth to minister" (λειτουργικὰ πνεύματα εἰς διακονίαν ἀποστελλόμενα; Heb. 1:14). In this connection it seems to me particularly noteworthy that in this passage these "ministering spirits" are expressly identified with the "enemies" cited in Ps. 110, the enemies whom the Christ who sits at the right hand of God "makes the footstool of his feet." And it is furthermore of the greatest significance that precisely in our section of the thirteenth chapter of Romans, introduced with the mention of the "authorities," we find applied to these "authorities" who stand behind the actual State the same expressions "minister" (διάκονος; v. 4) and "ministers" (λειτουργοί; v. 6), that are contained in the designation of the subjected powers in The Epistle to the Hebrews.

We thus come to the conclusion that the relation that we have indicated between the State and angelic powers agrees in every respect with the little that we hear concerning the State in the New Testament. If we here champion with special emphasis this relation and the Christological foundation of the State that is therewith given, this occurs in the context of this book for the reason that from this standpoint the relation that Primitive Christianity assumed between the redemptive process and the present secular process becomes clear.

We mentioned above the fact that the interpretation of the "authorities" of Rom. 13:1 ff. that is here supported is already found in Martin Dibelius, *Die Geisterwelt im Glauben des Paulus*, 1909. It was later commended by H. Schlier, "Mächte und Gewalten im N.T.," in *Theologische Blätter*,

[8] Thus Emil Brunner, "Zur christologischen Begründung des Staates" (*Kirchenblatt für die reformierte Schweiz*, 1943, p. 4). Concerning this series of articles, see pp. 206 ff.

1930, p. 292; it was demonstrated in a more comprehensive way by Günther Dehn, "Engel und Obrigkeit," in *Theologische Aufsätze für Karl Barth,* 1936, and was accepted by Karl Barth, *Rechtfertigung und Recht,* 1938, and K. L. Schmidt, "Das Gegenüber von Kirche und Staat in der Gemeinde des Neuen Testaments," in *Theologische Blätter,* 1937, pp. 1 ff. G. Kittel strongly opposed it in *Christus und Imperator, Das Urteil der ersten Christen über den Staat,* 1939, in a special appendix (pp. 48 ff.) ; so did F.-J. Leenhardt, *Le chrétien doit-il servir l'État?,* 1939, pp. 36 ff. Otto Eck, *Urgemeinde und Imperium (Beiträge zur Förderung christlicher Theologie,* 42, 3) , 1940, p. 35, considers it sufficient to say in a footnote (3) , when citing G. Kittel's work, that these theories of the "authorities" as angelic powers may be characterized as "fantastic" and "completely perverse"; he presents no proof of this summary judgment.

I have attempted to refute the objections of G. Kittel and F.-J. Leenhardt in my *Königsherrschaft Christi und Kirche im Neuen Testament.* More recently Emil Brunner has taken an emphatic position against the Christological foundation of the State. In his book *Gerechtigkeit,* 1943, he declares in footnote 34 on p. 321 (Eng. tr., *Justice and the Social Order,* 1945, p. 272) that the "fantastic character" of the "derivation of the order of justice and the State from the Christ-event, from the cross of Christ," is "clear without further argument to every unprejudiced person." But that Brunner misunderstands this derivation becomes clear from his further assertion that it must necessarily lead to a "fanatical intermixture of Church and State, of the message of love and the teaching of righteousness." This assertion he seeks to establish in greater detail in a series of articles in the *Kirchenblatt für die reformierte Schweiz.*[9] To prevent similar misunderstandings of the interpretation we here represent, we must pause for some further study of the discussions in these articles of Emil Brunner, especially since the debate with them is suited to make clear the foundation of the State in a Christological view of redemp-

[9] 1943, pp. 2 ff.; 18 ff.; 34 ff.

tive history.

Brunner explicitly recognizes that *State and Church, with their two different basic laws, both stand under the Lordship of Christ*.[10] On this basis it really should be possible to reach an understanding, for this statement lies at the basis also of the Christological foundation of the State. Unfortunately, Brunner contents himself with the mere confirmation of the Lordship of Christ, to which both realms, with their appropriate laws, are subordinated, but he takes no further interest in this fact which is so important for the New Testament. He is much more concerned with the difference between the laws basic to each realm; he thus deals with that which is really obvious, for this difference is by no means disputed, as Brunner thinks, by the champions of the Christological foundation. The only divergence is that they, on the contrary, do not place the accent upon this quite obvious difference in character; they put it rather upon that which from this standpoint is not obvious. They ask: How can two realms that are so different as are State and Church both stand under the *one* Lordship of Christ which is also recognized by Brunner? The " Christological foundation of the State " thus asks *the* question, which is the chief question in the New Testament itself, where the difference between the two basic laws is simply presupposed. It is undoubtedly the right of the dogmatic theologian to take as an object of thought a question that is present in the New Testament only as a presupposition. But in this case he must remain conscious of the fact that by reversing the way the New Testament puts the question, so that the assertion of the one Lordship of Christ is now placed at the beginning as though it were no problem and hence receives no further attention during the discussion, he creates for the entire discussion a perspective that is different from that of the New Testament.

The objection of Brunner, that the Christological foundation

[10] *Kirchenblatt für die reformierte Schweiz*, 1934, p. 34: " These two spheres, which both stand under the one Lord Christ."

of the State mixes the two realms, seems directly opposed to
that which G. Kittel raises against this foundation. G. Kittel
objects to it, as we have seen, because it introduces a dualistic
separation of the two! In reality, however, both Brunner and
G. Kittel fail to note that here in the New Testament a *complex* state of affairs exists, which cannot be violently simplified by the concepts intermixture and separation.

We have established that in the relationship between
Church and world, which both stand under the sovereign
Lordship of Christ, justice is done to the difference between
both while at the same time no dualism is taught. I here recall the figure of the large circular surface, which was used
above (p. 188) as an illustration and presented in a drawing;
this circular surface represents the Kingdom of Christ as a
whole, with Christ the Lord as center and with the smaller
concentric circle representing the Church. Christ rules over
the Church, and he rules over the entire world. The Church
stands nearer to him, for it is his Body. The State also belongs
to the same "order," to his Lordship, but it stands at a greater
distance from him, since its members do not know of the
Lordship of Christ. This duality reminds us of the fact that
the Kingdom of Christ, when we speak in respect of *time,* is
not yet the Kingdom of God, which only at the end, when
Christ shall have subjected all things to God, will succeed the
Kingdom of Christ. Only in the Kingdom of God will there
no longer be two realms, for there God will be "all in all"
(I Cor. 15:28).[11]

Because the Church knows about this entire situation, it
has to subordinate itself to the State, even the pagan State,
that remains within its limits. But nevertheless it must regard
that State as something provisional.

The argument of Brunner, that the positive attitude of
the New Testament toward the *pagan* State is a proof that in

[11] On the distinction between the two Kingdoms, see O. Cullmann,
Königsherrschaft Christi und Kirche im Neuen Testament, 1941, pp. 11 ff.,
and Jean Héring, *Le royaume de Dieu et sa venue,* 1937, pp. 171 ff.

the State we have to do only with God, not with Christ, seems to me rather to prove that Brunner has too narrow a concept of the redemptive history of Christ.

For redemptive history, as we have been concerned to present it in this book, the idea of representation is basic. Fundamentally, therefore, nothing exists that stands outside of the redemptive history of Christ. There is in the New Testament no dualism between a realm where God is Lord and a realm in which Christ is Lord. The pagan State does not know that it belongs to the Kingdom of Christ. Nevertheless, according to the New Testament, it can discern its task. When the question, which is not put in the New Testament, as to how this is really possible comes up for solution, the answer can be found only in the framework of the New Testament outlook we have presented; it cannot be found, if we are to give the answer upon the basis of the New Testament, in the framework of a theory of natural law. The New Testament itself, in any event, knows only that the State also stands within the redemptive history. This is shown on the one side in the fact that in the divine order it knows how to distinguish between good and evil (Rom. 13:3 ff.), but also in the fact that Pilate has Christ crucified and yet even so becomes the unconscious instrument of the redemptive history.

The question which has forced itself upon us in all these discussions and has often been asked of me in connection with my study of " Christ's Sovereign Lordship and the Church in the New Testament," the question, namely, whether in the time *before* Christ's death and resurrection the angelic powers and their executive agents were able to exercise an unlimited authority, is nowhere directly asked in the New Testament. We therefore can only attempt to answer it in line with the mind of the New Testament. On the basis of the knowledge of the Christian revelation concerning the decisive mid-point, it must be said in retrospect that the demonic beings, even in

the time before Christ, never possessed a power independent
of God, in the sense of metaphysical dualism, since even at
that time they were *destined to be subjected through Jesus
Christ*. Thus that question may be answered by saying that
the angelic powers, before their conquest through Jesus Christ,
could only exercise their pernicious work with reference to
this their coming subjection. This answer, indeed, is implicitly
contained even in the New Testament, when in the already
mentioned passage of Col. 1:16 it is said that these beings also
were created from the beginning *in Christ*. This, then, means
that from the beginning they did not exist as metaphysical
independent powers in the sense of dualism, but only in connection with the redemptive history, and that consequently
from the outset they were destined for subjection under Christ.

4

THE QUESTION OF WORLD AFFIRMATION OR WORLD DENIAL IN THE LIGHT OF THE NEW TESTAMENT REDEMPTIVE HISTORY

IF THE CENTER of the Primitive Christian redemptive line had lain in the future, as it does in Jewish apocalyptic, then Franz Overbeck and Albert Schweitzer would be right when they declare that the attitude of Primitive Christianity to the world was world denial. But we have now seen that in reality the center does not lie in the future, but is already in the past, and that the meaning of the present, although it stands in a particularly close relationship to the future, is nevertheless to be determined from that center which lies in the past. The end of the world is impending — this, to be sure, is the conviction of Primitive Christianity. But we know that this represents neither the only nor the central statement of its faith. On the contrary, in the foreground of the Christian message stand those other statements, that Christ is risen, after having conquered powers and authorities, that *Christ rules as Lord over all things in heaven and on earth!*

It is only when men fail to recognize the significance that the present phase of redemptive history has for Primitive Christian faith that the question as to the attitude of the first Christians to the world is solved by the all too simple label " world denial." Moreover, it is only when Christianity really falls back upon the standpoint of Jewish apocalyptic, where the absolutized hope floats in the air and is not anchored in faith in what has already been fulfilled, that the world is really denied. This has happened in the fanatical apocalyptic movements of all times, and continues to happen. Even in the New

Testament period we meet this hope which is sickly because it is separated and isolated from the Christian redemptive history; so, for example, in Thessalonica, where the people, in connection with this false hope, stop working (II Thess. 3:10). This is not the eschatology of redemptive history, but rather eschatological fever. It is possible to make the test in any given case by observing that to a hope that is false, because isolated from the redemptive history, there regularly corresponds a false, that is, an ascetic ethic. But the New Testament ethic likewise runs the risk of being misinterpreted as ascetic wherever the hope is regarded as the center of the Primitive Christian line of salvation and as a result the significance of the present for redemptive history is not recognized.

For this present period, however, according to Primitive Christian faith, the characteristic thing is precisely the fact that *the "world" has already been drawn into the redemptive process* in the manner which we have indicated. Consequently world denial cannot be an adequate expression for the Primitive Christian attitude. Here again we must be on our guard against all forced simplifications, for the New Testament situation is definitely not simple.

On this ground, to be sure, it would also be false if one were to speak here of "world affirmation." The situation in redemptive history of the present, which lies between Christ's resurrection and Parousia, is a complex one; it is determined by the noteworthy tension between past and future, between "already fulfilled" and "not yet fulfilled." The world is already ruled by Christ, and yet its present "form" is passing away (I Cor. 7:31).

Therefore no alternative of world denial or world affirmation can here exist, and ascetic world denial is as remote from Primitive Christianity as is a naïve contentment with culture. Even in the passage that seems most strongly to justify the assertion of world denial, I Cor. 7:29 ff., we must hear not only the negative conclusion: "As though they made no use of the things of the world," "as though they had no wife," "as though they wept not," "as though they did not rejoice," "as though they possessed it not," but we must also hear the compelling reference to the fact that they nevertheless use the things of the world, nevertheless have a wife, nevertheless weep, nevertheless rejoice, nevertheless buy. We know, indeed, that all these things pass away with the form of this world; but now they are still present, for it belongs to the very nature of the present that they are still there, and that the believer lives in this framework as one who knows that his way goes from the resurrection of Christ to his Parousia.

When Albert Schweitzer speaks of interim ethic, the expression is to be approved, for the present is in fact an interim in the redemptive history; but it is so in the sense we have just stated rather than in that of an ethic which therefore can have no application for the generations that follow Primitive Christianity. The confirmation of the fact that the present is an "interim" is independent of the question as to the duration of the interim.

The believer lives in a world concerning which he knows that it will pass away, but he knows that it still has its divinely willed place in the framework of redemptive history and is ruled by Christ. In so far as he knows that it will pass away, he denies it; in so far as he knows that it is the divinely willed framework of the present stage of redemptive history, he affirms it.

That in Primitive Christianity this affirmation also is to be taken with all seriousness is connected with the fact that in the sequence of redemptive history the time character of the present is taken seriously. Where one takes his point of departure from the opposition, not found in the New Testament, between "time" and "eternity," the result, when this opposition is carried out to its ultimate consequences, is ascetic world denial. Where, on the contrary, time is conceived as a line upon which every section has its significance in the divine economy, then in the present, on the one hand, simple world denial is not possible, but world affirmation is also limited by the line's goal, of which the believer knows and at which the form of this world passes away.

PART IV

REDEMPTIVE HISTORY AND THE INDIVIDUAL MAN

" Your life is hid
with Christ in God."

1

THE INDIVIDUAL MAN AND THE PAST STAGE OF REDEMPTIVE HISTORY (FAITH AND ELECTION)

THE ERRONEOUS CONCEPTION could arise that the entire redemptive history, in the form in which Primitive Christianity regards it as revelation, concerns only mankind as such, and that in it interest for the individual man emerges, at the most, only on the margin. We know, however, that the worth of the individual man is immeasurably enhanced in the New Testament writings, and this very point is often regarded as a chief distinguishing mark of the Christian proclamation in contrast to Judaism, which considers man more as a member of the people. Does this interest for the individual man stand alongside the viewpoint of redemptive history without any connection? We propose to show in what follows that in this point also the faith of Primitive Christianity is completely unified and consistent, and that everything that is said concerning the individual man is built into the structure of the entire redemptive history.

Where the discussion deals with the individual, the entire redemptive history stands behind it. But the reverse is also true; the redemptive history has as its goal the individual; this entire happening concerns him: *tua res agitur*. The revelation of the development of the great divine plan of salvation makes a personal claim on each one; it determines his life.

He who wishes to understand the " personal ethics " of the New Testament must here again renounce all modern viewpoints. Even the New Testament ethic is such as to be an "offense." This consists in this case in the fact that our personal life is anchored in the time line of the Christ-event, which comprehends past, present, and future!

This dependence of the individual life on a process which unfolds in time, a process which at first glance seems to have as its object only the general development of mankind and the world, forms the presupposition of every New Testament statement concerning the individual. In a particularly compact form, in a very few verses of Colossians (ch. 3:1–4), the different stages of the Christ-line of salvation are placed in relation to our personal life: "If ye now be *risen* with Christ, seek that which is above, where Christ sits at the *right hand of God;* set your mind upon that which is above, not upon that which is upon earth. For ye have *died,* and your life is *hid* with Christ in God. When Christ, our life, shall be revealed, then shall ye also be revealed with him *in glory.*" One can even say that the main points of the second article of the later Creed are here connected with the life of the individual: with Christ he dies, with Christ he rises, with the Christ who sits at the right hand of God he makes his home "above." With Christ he takes part in the present hidden state of glory upon earth. With the Christ who returns in manifest glory he himself will one day be glorified.

The statement, which is made also in Phil. 1:21, that Christ is our life, is characteristic for the question that concerns us in this last part of our book, just as are the expressions "to die with" and "to rise with" and "to be glorified with" Christ, which are also used in Rom. 6:2 ff. and Rom. 8:17. "Christ lives in me" (Gal. 2:20) also belongs here.

If the Primitive Christian conception of time were not so strongly linear as we in the preceding parts of this book have shown it to be, there would exist, in the presence of all these statements, the danger of a mystical misinterpretation. This, however, is excluded by the inherent time quality of the redemptive history. The participation in a timeless myth bears a necessarily mystical character, a fact that we verify in the Hellenistic mystery religions. In a time happening of the *past,* if the past is actually and seriously taken as such,[1] there is only such participation as rests upon faith in the redemptive significance of these facts of the past.

Faith in the New Testament sense is the way by which the past phase of redemptive history becomes effectual for me. In this connection it is, to be sure, necessary for me to believe that this entire process concerns me personally, me as the individual, as sinner and as redeemed in Christ. This presupposes that the consciousness of sin and guilt is not only a " general " thing which applies to " mankind," but that it is real, and it is real only when I am conscious of my own sin and my own guilt.

The faith of Primitive Christianity in the redemptive process presupposes such a consciousness of sin and guilt. Only on this basis can the redemptive history be related to the individual. The entire redemptive history, indeed, is intelligible only on the basis of this consciousness of sin; for it is on account of the sin of man that this entire process is necessary. Here is the reason why redemptive history not only *can* be related to the individual but *must* be so related. Without this relation it cannot be understood at all.

Our task here is not to present the entire New Testament teaching on justification. It is sufficient to point to the fact that essentially it is nothing but the application of the redemptive process to the individual. It shows how the individual man is decisively affected in his individual life by what occurred in past time. *The connecting link is faith.* Faith in the New Testament sense means to be convinced of the fact that this entire happening takes place *for me,* that Christ died on the cross for me, that for me also this central event represents the mid-point. Inasmuch as the history of the people of Israel finds its fulfillment in the cross, it too affects my individual salvation.

[1] That is, when it is not interpreted in the sense of a " present realization " and so robbed of its true past character. See p. 169.

This relation of the redemptive history to me finds its concrete expression in faith in my own election. Indeed, this faith signifies that we as individual men belong from the beginning in the divine providential administration (οἰκονομία). The election of the individual is no less emphasized in the New Testament than is the election of the people of Israel and the election of the fellowship of those who are called. In the New Testament predestination means both. In Rom., chs. 9 to 11, Paul speaks of predestination with reference to the history of both the people of Israel and the Gentiles. When the apostle speaks of himself as a " called apostle " (Rom. 1:1) and knows that he has been " set apart from his mother's womb " (Gal. 1:15), this election belongs to precisely the same line of salvation as does the election of Israel. Although the apostle has to fulfill a unique function within the redemptive history, the election as such is not a prerogative of the apostle. Rather, every single member of the Church is elected as an individual " from the beginning of the world " (Eph. 1:4). He who says election, predestination, says thereby election of each individual; this belongs to the New Testament conception of election. To this points the spiritual gift, the *charisma*, which is different for every believer in his relation to the Church, the Body of Christ (I Cor. 12:4 ff.) composed of many individual members, of which every one has his special destiny. By predestination the life of every individual believer is given its place in the Christ-line, and indeed along its entire extension in time. The individual election consists in the fact that the individual as such participates in the entire redemptive process. Accordingly, the certitude of being elected includes the conviction of being a fellow bearer of the redemptive history even in the most remote past, " before the foundation of the world." So it is not to be wondered at that in the New Testament the election of Christ is spoken of in precisely the same way as is the election of the believers. Christ too was " loved before the foundation of the world " (John 17:24); he was " foreknown " (I Peter 1:20). In Rom. 8:29 it is explicitly said that upon the basis of predestination the believers are foreordained to be " conformed to the image of the Son."

Thus the individual man stands related to the past phase of redemption in a twofold way. On the one side, it is precisely for him, the sinner, that this entire process has occurred, and there is salvation for him only if he believes that this past concerns him in a quite personal way. On the other side, he, as one foreordained to this faith and thereby to redemption, is chosen from the beginning to become an active fellow bearer of the redemptive process, and in view of this role he belongs in the past phase of redemptive history; *it is his own past*. The active participation, to be sure, emerges only in the Church, and so in the present phase of redemptive history. Through baptism, on the occasion of his entrance into the Church, there becomes real for the individual, on the one side, the " dying with " and the " rising with " Christ, and so the participation in what occurred in the past, and on the other side, the impartation of the Holy Spirit, and so the participation in the redemptive occurrence of the present and the future. The sacrament of Baptism is distinguished from that of the Lord's Supper precisely by the fact that it assures the individual once for all of this participation, while in the Lord's Supper the Church as such places itself ever anew in the redemptive history of past, present, and future.[2]

[2] See O. Cullmann, *Urchristentum und Gottesdienst (Abhandlungen zur Theologie des Alten und Neuen Testaments,* No. 3) , 1944, p. 77.

2

THE INDIVIDUAL MAN AND THE PRESENT STAGE OF REDEMPTIVE HISTORY (THE GIFT OF THE SPIRIT AND THE COMMANDMENT OF GOD)

THE REDEMPTIVE LINE manifests for the individual man of the Primitive Church all the narrow but complex relationships of the different sections of time which we have indicated in the first two parts of this book. Thus we have seen that the already past central event of the cross and resurrection rules also the individual life. On the other hand, however, the man who lives in this present period naturally lives in a particularly close relationship to the present phase of redemptive history, which in an invisible way is marked by the Lordship of Christ and visibly by what takes place in the Church. Thus the individual shares also in the temporal tension that is characteristic of the present.

Since the present is the time of the Church, the fact of belonging to it assigns to the individual his exact place as one actively sharing in the redemptive history. Therein, as we have seen, lies the significance of baptism. It has two effects. On the one side it mediates to the individual believer forgiveness of sins, that is, the fruit of redemptive history's " past " phase, the death and resurrection of Christ; on the other side, however, it mediates the Holy Spirit, that is, the gift that marks the present and future stages of redemptive history. The place in which the Holy Spirit is now active is the Church. Therefore the spiritual gifts, the *charismata* which are bestowed upon the individual through the Holy Spirit, are destined for the service of the Church. With reference to the " *one* body

into which we all are baptized in *one* Spirit" (I Cor. 12:13),
the apostle enumerates the varied individual spiritual gifts
(I Cor. 12:4 ff.). On the one side, individualism finds here its
strongest expression, and yet on the other side, since it is conceived as the working of the Holy Spirit, it must serve the development of the redemptive process as it unfolds in the present in the Church, which is the Body of Christ. As a member
of this Body, each one expresses his own individuality in his
own way. Thus we can actually say that it is only the placing
of the individual in the redemptive process that gives him his
individual significance, since indeed, according to Primitive
Christian faith, the charismatic endowments are only awak-
ened through the Holy Spirit.

In this way is explained also the powerful apostolic consciousness of Paul. In the case of the apostle the thing in question is the unique role in redemptive history, that of laying
once for all the Church's unique foundation, which it will
have until the end. The apostle knows that his office carries
forward the divine redemptive process in a special way, that
it belongs in the divine "stewardship" of the "mystery." In
this sense Paul, making use of the characteristic expressions,
designates himself as "steward of the mysteries of God" (I
Cor. 4:1), in which connection we must think not only of
an administration of the divine teaching about salvation but
also of the active realization of the redemptive history. We
know, indeed, that in this connection "stewardship" (οἰκονομία)
and "mystery" (μυστήριον) are the New Testament designation for that which we call redemptive history or revelational
history.

This apostolic task which Paul performs in the redemptive
history is exactly defined. It deals with the conversion of the
Gentiles in the framework of the entire redemptive process;
on the basis of the "dispensation" (οἰκονομία) of God he,
Paul, is entrusted with the "mystery among the Gentiles"
(Col. 1:25 ff.; Eph. 3:3 ff.). We can scarcely conceive his apostolic consciousness in too strong a way. It is not characterized

with even approximate correctness when we simply speak of his "calling" and in so doing think only in a general way of the call to convert the Gentiles. We must rather keep constantly before our eyes the fact that this call to convert the Gentiles stands in closest connection with the revelation of the divine plan of salvation, in which the Gentiles have a quite definite place, definitely fixed in time.[1] Everything that Paul writes in Rom., chs. 9 to 11, concerning the divine plan in reference to Israel and the Gentiles stands in closest relationship to his own apostolic office. By this we do not mean to give a "psychological" explanation of the important section, Rom., chs. 9 to 11. On the contrary, we mean to emphasize that *the apostolic consciousness of Paul is founded in redemptive history*. The apostle and his office belong in the redemptive history.

But even *the most modest service in the Church of Christ belongs in the redemptive history.*[2]

Thus also the divine command, which is directed to the individual believer of the congregation, is completely determined by the Christ-event. Hence in Primitive Christianity ethics without theology is absolutely inconceivable. All "Ought" rests here upon an "Is." The imperative is firmly anchored in the indicative. We are holy; this means that we should sanctify ourselves. We have received the Spirit; this means that we should "walk in the Spirit." In Christ we already have redemption from the power of sin; this means that now as never before we must battle against sin. This apparently contradictory joining of imperative and indicative is nothing else than the application to ethics of the complexity, here shown in different ways, of the present situation in redemptive his-

[1] See p. 163.
[2] See the significant work of Eduard Schweizer, *Das Leben des Herrn in der Gemeinde und ihren Diensten, eine Untersuchung der neutestamentlichen Gemeindeordnung* (*Abhandlungen zur Theologie des Alten und Neuen Testaments*, No. 8), 1946.

tory. We are dealing with the working out of what we have called the " tension between already fulfilled and not yet fulfilled." Thus we see that the new division of time created by Christ's earthly act determines also the question of individual sanctification.

It is connected with the situation in the present, which is characterized as " intermediate period," that new general ethical commandments are not set up by Primitive Christianity, but that in every moment of the present the ethical decision is made on the basis of the concrete situation, and specifically on the basis of the knowledge concerning the event at the mid-point, concerning the present Lordship of Christ, and concerning the goal toward which the redemptive process moves. Because the believer knows that in the present he is on the way between the resurrection of Christ and his Parousia, between the fulfillment which has already occurred, in which all imperatives are removed, and the consummation still to come, therefore the Primitive Christian " ethic " cannot consist of new commandments. It consists rather of the demand that the believer, on the basis of the fulfillment and with reference to the consummation, should recognize ever anew at each moment the commandment that the situation at that time presents. He thus " fulfills " the old law.

Knowledge of the importance for redemptive history of each *kairos* of the present must guide the ethical judgment and all of the believer's action which proceeds from it. The certainty that all his actions are connected with the advance of the redemptive history, with Christ's present Lordship, is the firm ground upon which his concrete decision rests. Thus is the time " redeemed " (Col. 4:5; Eph. 5:16) ; it is " served " (Rom. 12:11).[3]

In the mission charge, in Matt. 10:7, Jesus gives to his disciples as the content of their proclamation, not an imperative, but only an indicative; it is a statement concerning redemptive history in the present: " The Kingdom of God has come

[3] See p. 42.

near! " Thus in his own preaching Jesus does not at first define the imperative " Repent," but he adds, " For the Kingdom has come near "; from this fact all imperatives are to be drawn in each individual case. Fundamentally it is nothing different from the Church's proclamation after Christ's resurrection: *Kyrios Christos,* " Christ now rules as Lord."

No new commandment is set up, but the old and long-known commandment is to be fulfilled, that is, radically observed on the basis of that indicative. The ancient commandment is to be taken seriously.[4] This is what Jesus means when he speaks of the fulfillment of the law. The law known of old is to be applied to every concrete situation, not in literal fashion, but *radically,* so as to fulfill God's will of love which is embodied in every commandment. Thus it is not possible to regard this or that Old Testament commandment as done away because it does not foresee the present situation. The Old Testament deals throughout with a situation different from that of the New, and the ethical task, according to the New Testament, is precisely this, that in every new situation one is to fulfill the Old Testament in the light of the New, and so in accordance, not with the letter, but with the divine will. Along with the letter the law also is done away, because one can say that the letter does not fit the concrete situation. The New Testament ethic is *an ethic of redemptive history* in the sense also that it applies to the Old Testament commandments the idea of the " fulfillment " of the times.

Everything that stands in the antitheses of the Sermon on the Mount is proclaimed by Him who, by his authority which introduces the end time and by his " but I say unto you," sets the Old Testament Decalogue in the light of the imminent Kingdom of God, that is, sets it in the situation in which one must be radically obedient to the divine will at every moment.

---

[4] This is well worked out by R. Bultmann in *Jesus,* 1926 (Eng. tr., *Jesus and the Word,* 1933). On the question of the New Testament conception of the divine commandment, see also Karl Barth, *Die Kirchliche Dogmatik,* Vol. II, Part 2, *Die Lehre von Gott,* 1942, pp. 364 ff., and Alfred de Quarvain, *Die Heiligung, Ethik,* I, 1942.

In this situation one can no longer think that he is following the commandment, " Thou shalt not kill," while he says " Raca " to his brother and goes to the altar without being reconciled to his brother (Matt. 5:22 f.) .

It would be a dangerous error to make the concrete examples, the " paradigms " that Jesus gives, into a new general law. It would be false thus to misunderstand the word concerning the offering of the cheek (Matt. 5:39) , instead of seeing in it a concrete example of a situation in which God's command is to be thus fulfilled. Only where this paradigmatic character of the instructions of Jesus has not been recognized have opponents of the Christians been able, even in antiquity, to derive a special satisfaction from discovering the contradictions in the words of Jesus.

If all the words of Jesus are to be understood from their concrete situation, then an important significance attaches to the specific setting in which they are spoken. It is therefore so much the more to be regretted that in most cases the historical setting has not been transmitted to us or has been transmitted only in an uncertain form. We know, indeed, that the oral transmission of the gospel tradition has handed on as a rule only separate, unconnected items.[5]

On the other hand, however, the parables of Jesus, when seen in this light, possess particularly great importance, because in them Jesus himself has created the narrative framework.

How much each word of Jesus is to be understood, not as a law, but in its concrete application, is shown by that profound word concerning the Sabbath, which unfortunately is preserved only in the Western text and therefore is lacking in most modern translations, although it is certainly genuine: " As Jesus saw a man working on the Sabbath, he said to him: ' Man, if you know what you are doing, you are blessed. If you do not know, you are cursed and a transgressor of the law ' " (Luke 6:5, in the manuscript D) . If the man concerned works only

---

[5] See Karl Ludwig Schmidt, *Der Rahmen der Geschichte Jesu*, 1919.

out of indifference to the Sabbath, that is, if he considers that which Jesus has elsewhere said concerning the Sabbath to be simply a "general" law, then he is accursed in his working on the Sabbath, no matter how much he may appeal even to those other words of Jesus. Only if he knows what he is doing, that is, if he can support it from the concrete situation, is he blessed in his working on the Sabbath.

Precisely this is also the position of Paul concerning the ethical question. Here too there are no general ethical demands, but concrete applications in the light of the indicative which redemptive history presents. The sixth chapter of Romans shows in a particularly clear way how for Paul the imperative proceeds from the indicative of the dying and rising with Christ. The Holy Spirit must lead to the walking in the Spirit. This walk, however, Paul nowhere defines in the form of new commandments. Rather, the working of the Holy Spirit shows itself chiefly in the "testing" ($\delta o\kappa\iota\mu\acute{a}\zeta\epsilon\iota\nu$), that is, in the *capacity of forming the correct Christian ethical judgment at each given moment,* and specifically of forming it in connection with the knowledge of the redemptive process, in which, indeed, the Holy Spirit is a decisive figure.

This "testing" is the key of all New Testament ethics. Thus Paul writes in Rom. 12:2: "Be ye transformed by the renewing of your mind, in order that you may attain the $\delta o\kappa\iota\mu\acute{a}\zeta\epsilon\iota\nu$, the capacity to distinguish what God's will is." Likewise Phil. 1:9 f.: "This I pray, that your love may grow more and more in knowledge and in all sensitiveness for the $\delta o\kappa\iota\mu\acute{a}\zeta\epsilon\iota\nu$, the testing and determining, of that which is necessary." The same idea is present also in Phil. 2:13, when it is said that "God works in us the willing," that is, he causes our willing to agree with his. Certainty of moral judgment in the concrete case is in the last analysis the one great fruit that the Holy Spirit, this factor in redemptive history, produces in the individual man.

This "testing" rests upon the connection of judicial thought with spontaneous inspiration: "Quench not the spirit.

Despise not prophesyings, but test all things, and hold fast that which is good " (I Thess. 5:19 f.) .

It is characteristic that Paul does not reach his conclusion by using sayings of Jesus, but must add to them his own instructions (I Cor., ch. 7) . This too shows that New Testament ethics is always concrete, and that all instructions are intended to be only paradigms, signposts, and that the decision must be made ever anew.

No area of human existence is excluded from the moral judgment. Because the Lordship of Christ includes all things, because the indicative is related to everything that is in heaven and upon earth, the imperative too takes in all things. But nowhere does Paul give general rules; rather, he always gives concrete instructions for concrete cases. Precisely as in that word of Jesus concerning the Sabbath, it is said also in Paul: When such and such a condition is fulfilled, then act in such a way, but when it is not, then act otherwise, and do so even in the same matter. We need think only of the chapter concerning marriage, I Cor., ch. 7. It is impossible to derive general rules from it. He who does not possess in the Spirit the gift of " testing " will scarcely become wise by reading this chapter. The same thing is to be said concerning the attitude of the apostle in the question of meat offered to idols.

To be sure, from the indicative of redemptive history, which is the foundation of all ethics, there does result a *principle of application,* which is indicated by Jesus in the Synoptic Gospels as well as by Paul and the Johannine writings. This is the principle of *love,* love of God, which can express itself only in love of neighbor. In it the whole law is fulfilled; so say both Jesus (Matt. 22:40) and Paul (Gal. 5:14; Rom. 13:8 ff.) . The Johannine epistles take as their dominant motif that the imperative of love of neighbor grows out of redemptive history's indicative of the love of God for us: " Herein consists the love, not that we have loved God, but that he has loved us and sent his Son as an expiation for our sins. Beloved, if God has so loved us, we are obligated to love one another. No one has ever seen God. If we love one another, God abides in us, and his love is perfected in us." This is the catechism of the ethic of the New Testament; in no other place does it receive more classic expression. We here find it confirmed that this is the characteristic and new thing in the Christian ethic, that it is not conceivable without the Christian theology, and specifically the theology of redemptive history.

What is here said we find confirmed in all those concrete cases that are treated by Paul in their ethical aspects. Whether it is the question of the eating of meat offered to idols, the question of the strong and the weak, or of speaking with tongues, the principle of application is always that of love, just as also in the sayings of Jesus in the Sermon on the Mount the Old Testament law is radically fulfilled on the basis of love.

With the thus indicated anchoring of the imperative in the indicative is connected the fact that the New Testament sets up no actual catechisms, no general ethical rules. This will be done for the first time by the Apostolic Fathers, in whom in a characteristic way the indicative of redemptive history, and above all the atoning work of Christ, recedes quite into the background, when it does not completely vanish. In the New Testament, on the contrary, there are only rules of faith, but no catechisms. From these rules of faith, which briefly summarize the work of Christ, results the divine demand which is directed to the believer.

3

THE INDIVIDUAL MAN AND THE FUTURE STAGE OF REDEMPTIVE HISTORY (RESURRECTION FAITH AND RESURRECTION HOPE)

IN THE PRIMITIVE CHRISTIAN EXPECTATION, the future of the individual man is completely dependent upon the future of the entire redemptive history. Hence not only the Greek faith in the immortality of the soul, but also the opinion that the bodily resurrection of each man occurs immediately after his death, is foreign to this expectation. Both conceptions tear the individual resurrection out of the redemptive process as we have presented it. Moreover, in this way the Biblical proclamation is also robbed of one of its "offenses," and is made harmless; indeed, on such a basis the entire Christian hope of resurrection could be derived solely from the egocentric striving of man for blessedness. In reality, however, it is not at all the ego that stands in the foreground of this Christian hope, but rather the completion of the entire redemptive history.

By this we do not mean to say that with reference to the future there is no validity in the statement *tua res agitur,* "this concerns you," a statement which in the two preceding chapters we have strongly emphasized to be true of the past and present of redemptive history. On the contrary, we shall see that the individual is affected by the completion that follows in the future, just as he is by all stages of salvation. But precisely here the other side must be especially stressed: the starting point of this hope, in so far as it refers to the individual, is not concern for his individual happiness. Otherwise this hope would be differently depicted in the New Testament.

The Christian hope has in common with the Old Testament
one the receding of this concern, however much it is distinguished, as we shall see, from that older hope. Since by human
sin the curse of death has come upon the entire creation, the
entire creation must be released from the power of death, and
only in the framework of this redemption, which has already
been accomplished in Christ and yet will be completed only at
the end, is there individual bodily resurrection. The reproach
of satisfying only the egocentric striving for happiness can
least of all be directed at the Primitive Christian hope.

As a result, indeed, of this connection with the general redemptive process, even the bodily resurrection of the individual is bound to the temporal course of this process, and therefore it cannot coincide with the time of the death of any given
individual. Here, as the saying goes, we may make the test by
an example. Where the starting point is a philosophical concept of time and eternity, faith in the bodily resurrection of
the individual can be understood to mean only that this change
occurs for each person at the time of his death, which is an
escape from time into the sphere of eternity. I feel that in this
point Karl Barth's conception of the New Testament statements concerning the resurrection is an unjustified reinterpretation,[1] and the deeper ground of this feeling is that in his
interpretation of the New Testament concept of time and eternity I see a pervasive philosophical influence.[2]

In reality we find it confirmed that we can apply to the
future destiny of the individual precisely that time reference
which we established above in the chapter concerning "the
future state of redemptive history and its relation to the
Christ-event at the mid-point."[3] We have seen that the escha-

---

[1] See, for example, *Die Auferstehung der Toten*, 1926, p. 126 (Eng.
tr., *The Resurrection of the Dead*, 1933, p. 219) , where, in discussing
I Cor. 15:52, " When the last trumpet shall sound," he makes the following demand: " Do not forget for a moment to put this ' shall ' in quota-
tion marks; it refers to this quite particular *futurum resurrectionis* or
futurum aeternum! "

[2] See pp. 62 f., 66.

[3] See Part II, Chapter 3.

tological drama is no longer the center of the line of salvation, and we shall see that this very situation holds true also of the salvation of the individual. For him too the resurrection has already occurred, that is, in the resurrection of Christ. But, on the other hand, we are reminded that the future stage of redemptive history nevertheless has its own significance, inasmuch as only then is matter mastered by the Holy Spirit. Thus to the resurrection of Jesus Christ, which is even now decisive also for the individual, since he has already risen with Christ, there is added this fact, that his body will arise only at the end in the new creation, and that accordingly the resurrection of the body continues to be reserved for the future stage of redemptive history.

Connected with the anchoring of the individual resurrection in the general redemptive process in time is the fact that we nevertheless cannot speak of resurrection without also speaking of the past and the present. We shall show in what follows that those who have died in Christ, even as dead, do not yet belong in the future stage of redemptive history, but in the present stage; but they belong in the present stage of *redemptive history,* whose characteristic is the Holy Spirit as "earnest" (II Cor. 1:22; 5:5) and as "firstfruits" (Rom. 8:23).

Everything that relates to the resurrection has to do with the redemptive history. Thus death itself, in the New Testament, is viewed entirely from the standpoint of that redemptive history, and precisely for this reason it is taken seriously, in all its horror, as the thing radically opposed to God, as the "last enemy" (I Cor. 15:26). This is the Biblical conception of death, from the Genesis story, where the way to the tree of life is barred for the first men after they have let themselves be misled into disobedience by the serpent — death is the "wages of sin" (Rom. 5:12; 6:23) — on to the last book of the Bible, the Apocalypse of John, where death is cast into the "lake of fire" (Rev. 20:14). Thus death inspires even Jesus with "trembling and horror" in Gethsemane (Mark 14:33). It is thus not at all conceived as a "friend" and liberator from prison, nor as the "natural" transfer into another form of existence, as the Greek philosopher regards it. From the Greek concept of death one could come only to the doctrine of the "immortality of the soul." Resurrection faith, on the contrary, is only possible on Biblical ground, where all death, decay, and withering is a process that is opposed to God and is set in motion only by the sin of men. In this Biblical view, death and continued life after death do not constitute an organic natural process; rather, mighty powers stand here in conflict. When in the Bible life comes out of death, a miracle is necessary. Therefore Jesus says to the Sadducees, the deniers of resurrection among the Jews, that they are ignorant not only of the Scripture but also of the "power of God" (Mark 12:24; cf. also Eph. 1:19 f.). A miracle of God was necessary if there was to be resurrection; a miracle of creation by the omnipotent, life-giving God. The resurrection hope presupposes the faith in creation. Because God is the creator also of the body, therefore in the Bible "resurrection," in opposition to Hellenism, must be resurrection of the body.

Thus even in the Old Testament, on the basis of the faith in creation and of the already mentioned conception of death, the resurrection hope had been reached, and at least by the time of Jesus this hope was an integral part of the Jewish eschatological expectation, even if it was rejected by the Sadducees. But in Judaism, at the time of the New Testament, it was *only* "hope" and had no relation to the faith in the past and the present. In the New Testament, on the contrary, the resurrection hope is no longer merely *added* to faith, but resurrection hope and resurrection faith are now closely associated.

Resurrection ceases to be only an object of hope; it is faith, and in particular faith in a fact, the resurrection of Christ, which has already occurred at the mid-point of time. It is no longer possible to say, " We shall arise," without saying at the same time, " Christ has risen! " This is the new thing in the resurrection in the New Testament. The resurrection is no longer spoken of merely in the future tense, but also in the past: the resurrection of the body has already occurred! One has really risen from the dead, and indeed finally, not merely in the preliminary way in which arose the daughter of Jairus, the young man at Nain, or Lazarus, who must all die again. But this means that death is already conquered (Acts 2:24). If it was not able to hold in its power the one man, then its power over men is broken. Even if the others must still die, yet the omnipotence of death over men is once for all ended, since there is *one* man who " has taken from death its power " (II Tim. 1:10).[4] Through this " man " has come the general " resurrection of the dead " (I Cor. 15:21). The way is free for the resurrection of each one; through the fact that Christ is risen, he is the " firstfruits of them that slept." Therefore Paul calls Christ " the beginning, the firstborn from the dead " (Col. 1:18; cf. also Acts 26:23). Resurrection is no longer a vague apocalyptic theme of discussion between Pharisees and Sadducees. From now on it is not only the Sadducee rejection of the resurrection that is to be denied, but also the Pharisaic affirmation of the resurrection, if it does not proceed from the already occurred resurrection of Christ. All hope of individual resurrection now receives a concrete foundation in this fact of the past (Acts 17:31).

Since this fact of the past stands in the center of the redemptive process, it works out for the believer also in the present. With regard also to our resurrection a different present situation has come into being through the fact that there is now one body whose substance no longer is flesh but spirit. It means something for the present that at least *one* resurrection body, that of Christ, already exists now. Thereby the resurrection power, the Holy Spirit, has already entered into the realm of

---

4 Concerning the verb καταργεῖν, which is used here, see p. 153.

the physical. That which will happen only at the end, namely, the resurrection of bodies, is already reality in Christ. The Holy Spirit, indeed, is conceived everywhere in the New Testament as a part of the future, as a partial anticipation of the end. With the same expression, " firstfruits," that Paul applies to the risen Christ (I Cor. 15:23), he designates also the Holy Spirit (Rom. 8:23). This points to the fact that *the resurrection of Christ and the Holy Spirit are most closely related.* Not only Paul (Rom. 1:4), but also I Peter (ch. 3:18), regards the Holy Spirit as the power through which God has effected the resurrection of Christ. Thus the Holy Spirit, according to the Gospel of John, has entered into the world only since the glorification of Christ (John 7:39; 16:7).

The Holy Spirit is operative in the present as the power of the resurrection. Thus baptism, which mediates the Spirit, is conceived as a " rising with Christ " (Rom. 6:3–5). To be sure, all our human rising before the end of the days is only partial; the transformation of our fleshly body into the spiritual body is reserved for the future. But this does not mean that prior to that future date the resurrection power of the Holy Spirit can be operative only in our " inner life." Rather, according to the New Testament, the Holy Spirit operates even now upon the physical; even now he restrains, at least for a moment, the power of death, which in spite of the defeat which it has already met still continues to exercise its claim upon men; this temporary restraining of death through the resurrection power of the Holy Spirit constitutes the deeper meaning of all the New Testament healings of the sick and raisings of the dead. Miracles of healing and of raising the dead belong together. Even the resurrection miracles effected by Jesus in the Gospels do not represent the final transformation of the physical body, inasmuch as what is raised is only a physical body which again is corruptible; but these raisings of the dead, like the healings of the sick, do indicate that since Christ and in Christ the resurrection power is already at work. It is the Messianic time in which the New Testament places us: "The blind receive their sight, and the lame walk, the lepers are cleansed, and the deaf hear, the dead are raised up" (Matt. 11:5). The apostles also, by the power of the Spirit, drive back the still constantly active power of conquered death (Acts 9:40). But none except the "firstfruits" has as yet really and finally been raised, that is, been clothed with the new spiritual body. Even the "bodies of the saints," of which Matt. 27:52 says that they rose on Good Friday, are not thought of as spiritual bodies.

In so far as the transformation is possible only at the end of the days, resurrection remains in the New Testament the object of hope for the future.

The resurrection hope is intelligible only on the basis of the close connection that the New Testament establishes between faith in the already realized resurrection of Christ and faith in the present working of the resurrection power. Because we on the basis of the resurrection of Christ and by faith in this redemptive fact are able in the present to gain possession of the Holy Spirit, we know that we may hope for the resurrection of the body, which is effected *through the same Spirit* who already dwells in us: "But if the Spirit of him that raised up Jesus from the dead dwell in you, he that raised up Christ from the dead shall also quicken your mortal bodies by his Spirit that dwelleth in you" (Rom. 8:11).

This is the uniquely new thing that the future will bring for the individual. This will happen only at the end of the days. On this point all books of the New Testament agree. The New Testament knows nothing of an immediate resurrection of the body that will occur for each one immediately after his death.[5] The very gospel that most strongly emphasizes the present reality of the salvation attained in Christ, the Gospel of John, in which Christ designates himself as "the resurrection," does not permit the future to be separated from the present in such a way that no room remains any longer for a

[5] Otherwise the entire discussion in I Thess. 4:13 ff. would have no meaning.

special eschatological event. To be sure, the believer already *has* eternal life, but here too the raising of the body takes place only at the last day, and it will not do simply to discard all the Johannine passages that speak of the resurrection at the end (John 6:39, 40, 44, 54; see also ch. 5:29).[6] It belongs to the time tension in which we now live between the resurrection and the return of Christ that, as Paul says, "God *has* delivered us from death and *will* deliver us" (II Cor. 1:10).

Does this mean that according to the New Testament those who have died before the last day are excluded for the time being from the resurrection power? Is the resurrection for them alone to be *only* a future thing, while we, the living, even now share partially in the resurrection of Christ through the resurrection power of the Holy Spirit? Is there now to be a category of men, the great host of all who have already died and of all who will yet die before Christ's return, for whom no longer exists the tension between present and future that resulted from Christ's resurrection? *If that were so, then indeed all these dead would be in precisely the same situation as were the Jews before the resurrection of Christ.* If that were so, resurrection for them would again be only a remote apocalyptic event, without connection with Easter and the presence of the Holy Spirit. If that were so, we, the living, would certainly now have a tremendously great "advantage" over the dead (I Thess. 4:15).

In the New Testament, however, we hear in more than one passage that those who die in Christ are with Christ immediately after their death. One may recall the word of Jesus to the robber: "Today shalt thou be with me in paradise" (Luke 23:43).[7] There is further the word of Paul in Philippians: "I have a desire to depart, and to be with Christ" (ch. 1:23), and his discussion in II Cor. 5:1–10, where he is full of con-

[6] The most recent recurrence of this attempt is that of R. Bultmann in *Das Evangelium des Johannes*, 1941.

[7] The explanation according to which "today" is to be connected with "truly I say to you" is grammatically possible, but it is not the most likely interpretation.

fidence precisely with reference to the intermediate state of those who die before the return of Christ. Some have barred their way to the understanding of these passages, inasmuch as they have conceived that this " being with Christ," and also the being " in Abraham's bosom " (Luke 16:22), means that the dead have already received the spiritual body. Such an interpretation of the " being with Christ " of those who have died in him is not suggested, however, by any of these passages, and it is permissible to think that these dead are kept with Christ even before their body is raised, even before they receive the spiritual body. Now precisely this seems to me to be the meaning of the much discussed passage II Cor. 5:1–10. It is, to be sure, a fact that the apostle is oppressed by the idea that we are " stripped of the body " if we die before the return of Christ. This condition of " nakedness," created by death, which is hostile to God, remains an imperfect condition. But Paul overcomes his horror as he faces this condition, and he does so on the basis of the certainty that we have already " received the Spirit as an earnest." Precisely in this passage, with regard to the intermediate state of the Christians who have died and may yet die before the last day, the apostle repeats the designation of the Holy Spirit as an " earnest " of the end (v. 5), and by this word can only be meant here the earnest or guarantee of the resurrection of the body at the last day. This same idea also finds clear expression in the already mentioned passage Rom. 8:11.

This, however, means that the possession of the resurrection power of the Spirit is decisive not only for us who are living, but particularly for the dead. *This possession cannot be lost,* and it is not the case that for the believers who have died, and may yet die before the end, everything remains provisionally in the old state, as though Christ had not yet risen, and as though the Holy Spirit had not yet entered into the realm of human life.[8] The connection with Christ, which is estab-

---

[8] I first pointed to this role which the Holy Spirit exercises with reference to the dead in *Grundriss*, 1942, pp. 66 ff. This article, which is here

lished through the Holy Spirit and is already effective even while we are still in our physical body, becomes — not yet complete, to be sure — but nevertheless more intimate as soon as we put off this physical body. Only so can we explain the fact that the apostle, even before the return of Christ, has " a desire to depart and to be with Christ " (Phil. 1:23 and II Cor. 5:8), although even this intermediate state of being "unclothed" does not yet signify completion, and even the dead who by the power of the Spirit are kept with Christ still wait to be "clothed upon" with the spiritual body. In the Apocalypse of John also (ch. 6:9 f.), the souls of those who "were slain for the word of God" are already found "under the altar," and therefore, to speak literally, are especially near to God. What is here said concerning the martyrs holds true in Paul for all who have died in Christ.

We now see how important it was to emphasize the relation of the Easter fact to the present working of the Holy Spirit. The alleged contradiction between the passages that speak of the resurrection of the body at the end and those that reckon with a " being with Christ " immediately after the individual death of each Christian is resolved [9] as soon as one has recognized that the " being with Christ " does not yet signify resurrection of the body, but does signify a closer connection with Christ which is already effected through the resurrection power of the Holy Spirit. Hence *the dead likewise live in a condition in which the tension between present and future still exists.* For them also the question arises, " How long yet? " (Rev. 6:10). Indeed, it is perhaps even more in place for them, in

---

reproduced with few changes, was entitled " Auferstehungsglaube und Auferstehungshoffnung im Neuen Testament." As I now learn, Ph. H. Menoud, in his recently published work on *Le sort des trépassés,* 1945, agrees with this thesis of mine.

[9] Moreover, the assumption of Albert Schweitzer, in *Die Mystik des Apostels Paulus,* 1930, p. 137 (Eng. tr., *The Mysticism of Paul the Apostle,* 1931, p. 137), according to which Paul expected that he personally as an apostle would experience an immediate rapture as a special privilege reserved for a few men of God, is not satisfying, especially since it finds no sufficient support in Paul's letters.

view of the fact that they are out of the body. In company with the living, they all belong in the present whose limits are marked by the resurrection and Parousia of Christ. Therefore neither the one group nor the other has any advantage (I Thess. 4:13 ff.) .

As to just how this intermediate state is to be conceived the New Testament nowhere speculates. Where the fact of the resurrection, anticipated upon the basis of the already occurred resurrection of Christ and the present possession of the Spirit, is an object of such powerful faith and hope as is the case in the New Testament, there no longer remains any room for speculations concerning the " How." When anyone says something more definite concerning this intermediate state and actually makes mention of purgatory, not only are these statements arbitrary assumptions which have no foundation in the New Testament, but such an interest in the " How " is above all things a proof of little faith. It is a sure sign that faith in the already occurred resurrection of Christ has begun to waver and that the resurrection power of the Holy Spirit is no longer effective. For the New Testament resurrection faith it is sufficient to have concerning this intermediate state of the dead the one certainty on which alone everything depends, that he who believes in Christ, who is the Resurrection, " will live, even though he dies " (John 11:25) .

The same thing must also be said, however, concerning the " How " of the resurrection body which we shall receive at the end of the days. Concerning the nature of this body we learn only one thing, that it will be a *spiritual body,* that is, that the Spirit will be not only its principle but also its material (I Cor. 15:35 ff.) . When Paul says in Philippians that this our resurrection body will be " fashioned like unto " the body of the Risen Christ (Phil. 3:21) , this means precisely the same thing. Christ also, " by the resurrection," has been installed as Son of God " with power, according to the Holy Spirit " (Rom. 1:4; cf. also I Peter 3:18) .

Thus once again we are reminded that in the New Testament all resurrection hope is founded upon faith in a fact of the past; it is the fact at the mid-point of the redemptive line to which the apostles bear witness: that Christ is risen. This hope is founded also upon a fact of the present which follows from that former fact: that in those who believe on the Risen One the resurrection power of the Holy Spirit is already at work, and cannot be lost even to the end of the days. It is in that end time, for the individual believer also, that the redemptive history finds its specifically future completion, when " he that raised up Christ from the dead shall also quicken your mortal *bodies* by the Spirit " (Rom. 8:11) .

INDEXES

INDEX OF SCRIPTURE REFERENCES

INDEX OF AUTHORS